SEXUAL MORALITY

Sexual Morality

A NATURAL LAW APPROACH TO INTIMATE RELATIONSHIPS

John J. Piderit, S. J.

OXFORD
UNIVERSITY PRESS

Nihil Obstat : Rev. David S. Ciancimino, S.J., Provincial
New York Province, Society of Jesus

OXFORD
UNIVERSITY PRESS

Oxford University Press, Inc., publishes works that further
Oxford University's objective of excellence
in research, scholarship, and education.

Oxford   New York
Auckland   Cape Town   Dar es Salaam   Hong Kong   Karachi
Kuala Lumpur   Madrid   Melbourne   Mexico City   Nairobi
New Delhi   Shanghai   Taipei   Toronto

With offices in
Argentina   Austria   Brazil   Chile   Czech Republic   France   Greece
Guatemala   Hungary   Italy   Japan   Poland   Portugal   Singapore
South Korea   Switzerland   Thailand   Turkey   Ukraine   Vietnam

Copyright © 2012 by Oxford University Press, Inc.

Published by Oxford University Press, Inc.
198 Madison Avenue, New York, New York 10016

www.oup.com

Library of Congress Cataloging-in-Publication Data
Piderit, John J.
Sexual morality : a natural law approach to intimate relationships / John Piderit.
    p.   cm.
Includes bibliographical references (p.) and index.
ISBN 978-0-19-979327-3 (hardcover : alk. paper)—ISBN 978-0-19-979328-0 (pbk. : alk. paper)
1. Catholic youth—Religious life.   2. Sexual ethics for youth.   3. Sex—Religious aspects—Catholic
Church.   4. Natural law—Religious aspects—Catholic Church.   I. Title.
BX2355.P48 2011
241'.6765088282—dc22
2011003543

1   3   5   7   9   8   6   4   2

Printed in the United States of America
on acid-free paper

To my brother Jesuits

Contents

Preface

MODERN AMERICAN SOCIETY has greatly expanded effective freedom in many areas of the lives of young adults. Young people play a much stronger role in deciding what they do after high school and, in particular, which college or university they attend or what type of job they seek out if they choose not to go to college. Finding a job after college is rarely easy, but they choose the areas in which they seek a job or additional training or education. From high school on, their favorite music is delivered right to their ears, and they can see an enormous variety of movies, videos, and other images in theaters, on their computer, handheld devices, or with their friends in other venues. Opportunities for regional and international travel have increased immensely, and with increased travel young people develop a greater sensitivity to cultural differences. Even in print media, students have better textbooks than ever before, a greater variety of resources available via the Web, and areas friendly to young inquiring minds.

In a developed society, freedom, though definitely good for adults, brings mixed blessings for young people on their way to or in the initial stage of adulthood. Freedom with few public bounds, which is the prevailing context in Western society, means corporations, groups, and individuals are permitted to produce and disseminate materials and images, many of which are not deemed wholesome for young people. Given this reality, freedom also means young people are exposed to unhelpful practices and images at much younger ages; sadly, such images and approaches rival the roles and influence parents and family members have traditionally had.

Even as the amount and modes of freedom change and expand, some issues continue to be challenging. Meeting and making friends with members of the opposite sex remains an intricate process now, as it has been for thousands of years. The context of meeting people has changed, but increased information and images, the variety of chat rooms, or places where young people gather have not eased the process. Finding someone to whom one might commit for life and with whom one hopes to have children, and then together care for and nurture them and eventually enjoy the rewards of grown children—this task is still problematic.

Meeting and sharing with those selected members of the opposite sex with one of whom one might like to share one's life in an intimate manner will always be tricky. Indeed, it is unclear whether any organizational or technological innovation can simplify in any substantial way the challenge of meeting the "right one." The primary difficulty is most young people don't really have any specific idea about how the "right one" might appear to them. Part of the magic, mystery, and romance of meeting a person of the opposite sex is that one expects a mini revelation. One expects that, whoever the "right one" is, that person will be luminous in his or her person. The person will certainly be beautiful or handsome, but in addition one expects a level of goodness and excitement that should appear after the seeker and the sought get to know one another.

What is being sketched here is not some modified version of "love at first sight." The point is rather that the person searching for a companion is on the lookout for some known qualities, but the person also expects to be illuminated by him or her about even more important qualities once the seeker becomes interested in the other person. If the "right one" is to be right for a lifetime, the person should both correspond to deep yearnings in the person looking and also awake new deep yearnings or high aspirations in the seeker. There has to be a glimpse of lifelong learning and satisfaction. The person who potentially wants to commit to another person has to feel sure he could devote himself to her (or herself to him) for his entire life and that he would find satisfaction in making her happy by helping her to flourish as a person, wife, friend, collaborator, and mom.

In short, increased freedom has not made the dating scene smoother or made it easier for young people with similar deep interests and yearnings to make initial contact with one another. Furthermore, what is true now and will likely be true until the end of time is that the "right person" has to be encountered in the appropriate venue and subsequent meetings have to gently awake in the seeker or observer a glimpse of an exciting life with the potential partner. In order for this to occur, the process by which two people get to know one another should be persuasive. At the very least, the process of becoming acquainted should not dissuade the other person.

SEQUENCE COUNTS

Consider a schematic and simplistic representation of events that eventually leads Mr. A to get to know to Ms. B fairly well. As an extreme simplification, suppose a young man is on the path to good personal knowledge of a young woman. Somewhat arbitrarily, let's focus on the first fifteen meetings or events in which A and B participate. Suppose that at each of these fifteen meetings he reveals one important aspect of himself and he in turn learns one important aspect about the young woman of interest. Of course it is totally unrealistic to think there would be just one single important aspect that each person reveals to the other in each encounter, but the reader's indulgence is requested. Suppose each mutually revealing event is designated by E1, E2, E3,..., E15. By the end of event 15, the young man would have some knowledge and a certain perspective about the young woman.

Now suppose we simplistically and arbitrarily rearrange the order of these meetings, but leave each event identical in content. This means that the second sequence might be E13, E9, E1, E6, E15, and so forth, or some variation on this, where E13 or E9 refers to the exact same meeting and "revelatory exchange" as earlier. The only thing that will have changed is the sequence of the encounters.

First, any couple knows rearranging these events would dramatically change everything. What happens in one meeting organically influences what happens in the next meeting; this means that in the real world any event, E8 for example, could not possibly remain the same and be independent of the sequence prior to when it occurred. But even if it were theoretically possible to rearrange the mutually revealing interactions while maintaining the revelations the same, what the young man would know about the young woman at the end of the second sequence would be dramatically different than what would be known at the end of the first sequence. The reason is that the order in which a person chooses to reveal things about him- or herself is enormously important to the way the two persons envision one another and how highly they come to esteem one another.

Young adults understand that sequence makes an enormous difference. They know the order and structure of events are crucial in the business world and in family relations. They certainly realize sequence counts when getting to know another young man or woman. It is why young women think so carefully and discuss so thoroughly with one another how they should meet and conduct themselves with young men, and why a young man who has done crazy things with a variety of young women does not usually share that information in any early encounter with the young woman who he eventually suspects will be the "right one."

Since sequence counts, it certainly follows that how and when one becomes sexually intimate with another person reveals much about the person. Yes, it also makes a difference when it happens a second time and when it starts to occur regularly. Also informative to the couple is whether it was a "mistake" in the sense that one had made good plans to avoid it, whether it was only partly intended, or whether it was definitely not yet the right time for one of the partners.

Sexual intimacy is just one of the activities married couples engage in. Since sex involves the possibility of children, who bring enormous changes into the life of any couple, sexual intimacy is an activity with potentially powerful implications. Sex is central to commitment in marriage. However, the activity most likely to keep a couple committed to one another for a lifetime is not sexual intimacy. Over time, sex will remain a valued activity in marriage, but for most couples sex subsides in importance as the marriage ages. What continues to bring great satisfaction (and occasional regrets or turmoil) is the couple sharing information about themselves to each other.

Sharing information may sound rather boring to some, but, once they meet the right person, most young people understand that sharing is exciting, rewarding, and at times quite complicated. It is the way a relationship begins and it is the path along which a lasting relationship continues to deepen and flourish. Any enthusiastic engaged couple tells one another the thing they most enjoy doing is simply being with one another. They just like sharing. Engaged and young married couples are experts at sharing everything. And indeed, throughout married life information remains extremely important.

Couples sometimes get annoyed if a partner does not share even trivial information, and one partner can be (but need not be) insulted if important information is not shared. But still, part of the fun of life is not having all things revealed all at once. A husband or wife may want to prepare quietly for a surprise birthday party or trip for the spouse, perhaps to celebrate some special event. Or the mother and the children may decide to make something nice for Dad. They keep the information from him because they are confident he will like both the surprise and the gift. So, for months on end they work on Dad's gift in secret. Or a husband worries about his wife and hesitates for months to raise some issue with her. He does this not out of annoyance, but because he loves her and doesn't know whether this is the right time or because he is not sure how best to raise the issue. A wife may realize her husband is greatly concerned about a parent or a sibling who is in danger or ill health. The husband only talks about it occasionally because he gets so upset about it. The wife has to think how, absent a complete discussion of the issue with her husband, she can best help him.

Happily married husbands and wives discuss most things, but not everything. Ideally out of love, but sometimes to spite one's partner, not all information is shared. Curtailing information applies also to incipient love. Prior to engagement, a couple strongly interested in one another shares many things, but not everything. They understand information should be sequenced. Each one plans events, sometimes with a strategic advantage in mind, because he or she knows that certain common activities or experiences have a big impact. One claim made in this book (and, yes, good reasons will eventually have to be given to support the claim) is that, were couples not yielding to strong messages coming from modern secular culture, all couples would be more concerned about the long-term consequences of their intimate actions with one another. Absent such pressure, couples would try to "keep on message" and not inject sexual intimacy near the beginning of the relationship. This book seeks to support young adults in developing reasonable relationships that are likely to endure until death parts the partners. This is marriage as it is understood by a variety of Christian churches, including the Catholic Church, and by other religious groups as well.

MORALITY AND CULTURE

This book is primarily an exploration of how young adults can participate in a culture that supports the development of long-lasting personal relationships. Beginning with an explanation and justification for the basic building blocks, the book develops a systematic approach to sexual morality that does not rely explicitly on religious beliefs for knowing what is morally good or bad.

Any morality develops within a culture. In this account of morality we identify the ways in which morality, for good and ill, is embedded in culture, particularly American culture. The basis for a reasonable culture leading to human flourishing is the pursuit of certain expansive values. These broad values, it will be shown, are common to all human beings, no matter the individual culture in which people put them into practice. Critical reflection on the pursuit of those values enables us to recognize thousands of activities that promote human well-being and satisfaction. Through critical reflection we also come to see that pursuing these central human values means that we have to place constraints on our activities. In particular, via reason we come to see that some activities undermine our pursuit of the fundamental human values. That is, they are "forbidden," not by some external authority, but by people who want consistently to pursue certain values.

Although this book includes important discussions of both theology and philosophy, its main focus is culture and practice. Philosophy and theology appear here as critical reflections on the pursuit of good living. They offer a way to explore how rational a particular culture is. While the book draws on insights from these disciplines, its goal is to present and justify practical ways to find lasting satisfaction in relationships.

The framework in which reasons for acting one way or another are made plausible is called the natural law approach. Natural law offers a general way to conceive what all human beings are called to do in the various spheres of their lives. Embedded within this general framework is the central human value of friendship, which entails sharing one's hopes, fears, and expectations with others. Friendship has various degrees of intensity. It certainly includes particularly deep forms such as marriage and family life. However, like the other fundamental values, friendship is broadly conceived and therefore includes the extended family, friends from work or school, members of clubs, firms, or other organizations, and even people living in the same city or country. There is a great variety of ways in which people share common experiences or backgrounds.

Friendship, I claim in this book, is esteemed in all societies. Different practical ways to realize friendship are evident around the world, but the value of friendship itself is universally acknowledged. Marriage is a particularly profound form of friendship, and the sexual act engages the human person in various ways. Sex should promote friendship at its deepest level, not undermine it. To determine whether friendship is being promoted or weakened via sex, the most important components of the sexual act have to be identified. Then one is in a position to determine in what context sexual intimacy at its deepest level promotes friendship. (In certain circumstances, which I describe later in the book, one can substitute the word *love* for *friendship*.)

This book endorses the natural law approach to all human activities and desired goods and benefits. This means that many activities are considered natural, good, and conducive to human flourishing while others, because they undermine the very pursuit of the value, are always wrong. Expressed more carefully, a wide variety of activities are shown to be good and natural, while a limited group of activities are shown to be always wrong. One virtue of this approach is that the reader can personally judge what things are always good, no matter what the culture, and what things are always bad, no matter what the culture or the circumstances. It is the voice of reason that persuades us. A person may deceive himself (and so too may a culture) into thinking something is acceptable when it is in fact seriously wrong. Despite such self-deception, people do not lose their critical faculties. Sooner or later, alert people in any culture note the deception and call for change. Reason itself exists within a culture, but it has the capacity to rise above the culture and exercise a partial but important critique of the culture.

In subsequent chapters a number of norms or guidelines are presented to assist young people who are seeking a deep friendship with a member of the opposite sex, a friendship possibly resulting in marriage. These norms can be described as conservative. Nonetheless, if a statistical analysis were done, the vast majority of people around the world would say they believe the norms presented here are good and helpful. These are norms, it will be claimed, which are acknowledged as fundamental to human well-being. Furthermore, these norms are endorsed by the Catholic Church, a great variety of Christian denominations, and some branches of Judaism, Islam, and other religious traditions that affirm the existence of God or a Supreme Being.

RIGHT REASON IS THE OVERALL NORM

Because the goal is to present the most convincing arguments to support a modern approach to personal relationships, the philosophical arguments rely only on reason. Various objections to what modern young people might perceive as constraints on their freedom are candidly considered. Whether the responses to these objections are persuasive depends on the reader's reactions to the arguments presented. In the end the reader chooses what path he or she will follow. In the book, however, consistent answers to the various issues raised with respect to loving relationships are laid out. That is, we adopt a general perspective, provide arguments for it, and then use this natural law perspective consistently as we address various issues relating to friendships and sexual intimacy.

Unlike many modern texts, this book does not offer arguments for a variety of different ethical approaches and then leave it unclear which ethical approach is more persuasive. The book is written from a natural law perspective that reserves sexual intimacy to marriage. As noted earlier, this perspective requires rational justification. Using reasoning, examples, and invoking cultural practices, we attempt to convince the reader that such an approach is genuinely human and fulfilling. The emphasis in the first two-thirds of the book is on reason alone. Religious issues are occasionally raised, but the goal is to provide a rational justification for the individual norms and guidelines we propose.

Most people are able to give a reason for their actions. However, good reasons for actions have to be consistent with a wide variety of human activities. Also, good reasons should give proper weight to physical, historical, cultural, and psychological considerations. The code words for respecting these realities, without overemphasizing one reality, are *right reason*. Everyone thinks his reasons are good. But *right reason* refers to an argument or a position that fully accounts for the complicated context in which human beings exist. That is, human beings have consciousness, live in society, have biological needs and appetites, have memory and imagination, and interact to protect themselves and advance their interests in a vast, beautiful, abundant, but sometimes threatening universe. When all these factors are properly accounted for in developing an argument or justifying a moral position, we say a person has used right reason.

Without invoking religious traditions, right reason and a culture take us pretty far. This is true as long as culture itself (which consists of the accustomed ways of doing things by some group of people) is in approximate conformity with right reason. Proceeding in this manner allows us to present a positive view of moral norms that, if adhered to, lead to a deeply human and satisfying life. The benefit of this approach is that friendship at its highest level is linked to other basic human values. Rather than picking and choosing which norms suit a person's fancy, the general approach offers reasons why all people seek some values (such as the fundamental value of life, which is an easy one to acknowledge) as good and reject some actions that undermine the desirable values (murder is wrong because it destroys life).

Although right reason and culture alone are the code words for parts I and II of the book, in most chapters personal practices are also examined carefully. Furthermore, chapters on moral theory are interspersed with chapters offering accounts of a developing relationship between Dave and Maria. They are young people in their twenties who like one another, want more or less to do things correctly, and are sensitive to religious issues. They sometimes discuss big moral issues, but not in a theoretical way. Rather, their focus is on particular practices.

In the end, the reader will decide whether he or she finds the arguments justified by right reason and culture alone sufficiently persuasive to influence future behavior. However, right reason and general secular culture do not offer a complete picture. Religious culture also makes contributions to moral norms and moral behavior. As in a photo or a painting, religious culture adds definition, perspective, beauty, and feeling.

The "right reason alone" approach taken here is not historically the manner in which right reason first developed. Religion played a central role in the development of reason. Indeed, unlike philosophers and theologians, most people in the world do not separate religion from reason. Moral norms are closely linked to religious practice and often also to religious belief. In general, the hopes, desires, and expectations of most people are developed both by right reason and religious belief. The last third of the book explores the connection between the norms based on right reason alone that are developed earlier in the book with the same norms set in a context of religious believe and practice. The discussion in this section draws upon the Christian experience, but it strives to show how religious practice enables people to enhance their moral skills and also become better human beings.

AN EXPANSIVE TREATMENT OF NATURAL LAW

By consistently following a natural law approach, the book indirectly offers a way for students and professors to critically evaluate the natural law approach as applied to sexual intimacy. In classes on ethics, a natural law approach is often outlined in a lecture or two or in a chapter of a book. But students do not get a feel for how it is developed and, in particular, how one justifies that some actions are forbidden while others are permitted or encouraged. In a style accessible to students, this book can be used as a supplementary text in a course in general ethics or moral theology. At least in the area of relationships, students can quickly identify the areas in which natural law differs from, for example, a utilitarian or Kantian approach.

One strength of natural law is that it predicts that various societal convictions with respect to sex and sexuality will be broadly accepted. Absent a general societal conviction about the existence of natural law, the only way to explain such practices (for example, that married people can't have sex with other people) in a utilitarian or Kantian framework is as quaint remnants from earlier, but now outdated, systems of morality.

A standard objection to the natural law approach is its prescriptive results do not convince everyone. That is, if natural law theory is based on human nature and right reason, and if human nature and reason are the same for everyone, why do more people not subscribe to the natural law approach? This important issue is addressed directly, and a persuasive response, though perhaps not sufficiently compelling for every reader, is provided.

In order to clarify issues and make them easier for people to focus on the main factors in an argument or an approach, some simple diagrams are used. One diagram in particular is used a number of times in the early chapters. Although the basic diagram remains the same, it is modified in different ways in various chapters in order to illustrate how people make good or poor moral decisions.

As was noted above, the "Dave and Maria" chapters address whatever moral issue is currently being explored theoretically in more personal and practical terms. These chapters enable the reader to understand better the importance of the theory chapters. They also allow a professor to ask the students to address the specific issues raised by Bill and Maria and indicate what an ethical approach other than natural law would prescribe.

PERSONAL CONTEXT

For over forty years as a priest, the author has regularly interacted with young people, most often in educational settings. As a professor of economics who lived in residence halls for fourteen years, as a parish priest for nine years, as an administrator at two universities for over ten years, and as a teacher of religious education to children in the higher grades of Catholic grade school for three years, he has been in many pastoral settings with young people. Presented in this book are the author's strongest, broadest, and most persuasive arguments for human flourishing. The book combines the theoretical approach of the natural law with specific practices that help young people mature morally in a liberated, but also challenging and confusing, culture. The book is written especially for young adults who want to improve the likelihood of a long-lasting marriage relationship and who are disturbed, challenged, or unpersuaded by the casual attitudes some of their peers have toward sexual intimacy.

The positive goals articulated here are likely to be very attractive to a wide swath of young adults. Nonetheless, many from the same cohort of young adults will likely claim that the approach taken is heroic but totally unrealistic. For the latter group, the context in which certain sexual activities are to be avoided is vanishingly small. Even for young people in this latter group, however, good reasons should make them pause and cause them to wonder about whether they are headed in the correct direction. It is true: right reason alone is rarely powerful enough to change significant behavioral patterns. Absent religious conviction, avoiding sex prior to marriage probably is unrealistic. But the last part of the book highlights the enormous contribution made by regular religious practice to human flourishing and attaining good moral skills.

This book would not have come to be without the support, advice, cultural insights, candid criticism, and close, critical reading of my colleague, Melanie Morey. Various parts have been read by Dr. Mary Byrne and Thomas Rogan, Rev. Peter J. Byrne, Rev. William Grogan, Marie McCarrick, Rev. John Michael McDermott, S.J., Prof. John Cavadini, Msgr. Michael J. Curran, Prof. James F. Keating, Dr. Marian and Joseph Liberatore, Donald Moglia, Joie de Marie and Chris Morrison, Rev. Joseph Kelly, Msgr. Thomas Derivan, Msgr. Pau Sanchez, Rev. Paulinus Odozor, Prof. Montague Brown, Prof. Thomas Cavanaugh, and Rev. William Pape. The aforementioned have provided comments that have helped me sort out and refine my views, and also identify useful practices that assist young people in their relationships. Whatever errors or less-than-convincing arguments remain are my responsibility.

SEXUAL MORALITY

1

An Aptitude for Excellence

GETTING A LIFE

YOUNG ADULTS ARE about the business of "getting a life." They imagine lives for themselves that are defined almost entirely by the good things they seek. Most would like to make a reasonable living, to have good friends, to meet someone they love and who loves them deeply, to marry and remain faithful all their days, and to have a family. They want to lead good and decent lives and somehow make a difference in the world, and they want to have some fun along the way. Of course, whether they reach their goals will depend not just on their abilities, aspirations, and circumstances, but also on the decisions they make. Some decisions young people make will help them to realize their goals. Others will work against their ever achieving what they most fundamentally desire.

"Getting a life" takes work and prudence. It requires that over time we come to know ourselves, to understand other people, to develop a life plan, and to figure out how to make good decisions that ultimately will get us where we want to go. We form our plans and make our decisions not all on our own, but within a cultural context that shapes not only what we value but also how we actually behave.

Hook-up culture—the practice of being sexually intimate even though the partners are not even committed to one another as special friends—is the social reality in which most young people in the United States find themselves today. It is hyped by media and marketers, it holds sway in high schools and on college campuses, and there is little meaningful pushback against it from parents, educators, or even religious leaders. Many young people accept hook-up culture as a given and many conform to its norms and practice its rituals even though doing so is often personally troubling and deeply unsatisfying. Many of these young adults would never think to look to the traditions of their religious faith when figuring out what to think and do in terms of friendship, romance, and sex, and they suffer because of it.

In her recent book *Sex and the Soul* (2008), Donna Freitas pulls back the curtain on hook-up culture, revealing what students today actually experience as they try to negotiate friendship, sex, and romance on college campuses. The culture described in their stories is its own moral universe. It is defined by norms, narratives, and apparent benefits, and is reinforced by countless rituals that indicate what is valuable and what is not, what is permissible and what is off limits. Students accept this cultural reality as "the way things are done" even though participating in it often makes them feel disappointed, ashamed, and confused. Their stories are both revealing and deeply disturbing, as this brief selection about one student makes clear:

> On the surface, Amy is a star: the student everybody knows or at least knows about, the girl everyone either wishes to be or dreams of dating, the daughter that would make a parent proud, the student a professor would bend over backward to admit into an already crowded class, the ideal spokesperson for a college, the one promising prospective students, "this could be you!" (p. 4)

But there's another side to Amy. Part of her strategy to find a boyfriend is to party hard, which means drinking a lot. "You would never just walk up to someone and just start making out with them if you weren't intoxicated. It makes your inhibitions go" (p. 5). Despite hooking up and friends with benefits, Amy is still looking, since so far she only has heartache.

Narratives like Amy's abound in Freitas' book, and reading them makes you think there simply has to be a better way for young adults to operate. The norms, narratives, and values of hook-up culture are destructive and its accompanying rituals dehumanizing. Young people need a more supportive cultural milieu for satisfying relationships. They also need a moral framework that enables choices that actually lead to realizing their deepest desires and fondest dreams.

This book is about a better way toward lasting intimacy. Most young people realize that current practices are unlikely to lead to deep satisfaction. Many young people experience that sinking feeling right now in their lives. Even worse, they suffer the nagging doubt that the hook-up path can possibly lead to any lifelong satisfaction in a relationship. Deep down, most young women and young men realize that hook-up culture cannot possibly provide a foundation for a whole lifetime of growth in commitment, intimacy, and love. In fact, the type of intimacy that now passes for most desirable among the college-age crowd would bore most young adults once they reach thirty. There just has to be more to life than sixty or eighty years of hook-ups. This is true especially if one is unlucky and a particular hook-up connection lasts four or five years.

PROMISES, PROMISES, PROMISES

For many years I taught economics at the university level. Any economist is particularly aware that promises have value. In the business world, people in forward and futures markets pay good money for a promise. In order to avoid uncertainly about future prices, a farmer may promise now to sell one thousand bushels of wheat ninety days from now. Or, a U.S. importer may choose to sign a promise to buy one million yuan thirty days from now. Such promises are then traded in markets; that is, they have value.

Consider now promises involving relationships. Setting aside the issue of money, let's estimate the comparative value and attractiveness of three promises. The first one is "I love you now and I will love you through the night." The second is "I love you now and I will love you until we agree to part amicably." The third is "I love you now and I will love you until death parts us." Without thinking of money or financial instruments, how would one value these promises? Which has more worth than the other two?

In order to focus on the primary issue, let us suppose the person making the promise is credible. That is, he or she can be relied upon to fulfill the promise. Similarly, assume the person hearing the promise is also reliable. She has the ability to make a similar promise at the same level and keep it. These, of course, are big assumptions, but they enable us to focus on content rather than on the person making the promise. Each promise has some value to the person to whom the promise is made. Even in the first promise, the guy is not leaving right now. He stays until the morning and then leaves. An extended hook-up!

The second promise is not crazy, but it focuses on benefits—friends with benefits. It's a nice, pragmatic relationship. As long as the benefits are clear, tangible, and sufficiently high, the relationship goes on. But, of course, *sufficiently high* is a relative term. For some guy, sufficiently high may be determined by some other sweet young thing or, for the young women, some handsome hulk who happens to appear on the horizon. What this promise really says is, "I really like you, but I have not yet seen the whole field of players. I would like to keep my options open." So, you live together, do things together, maybe even have babies together, but you would be crazy to think the relationship will last forever. As in business, there is always competition, and this second type of promise acknowledges how destructive competition can be to relationships without lasting commitments. After all, a current friend with benefits may not be able to measure up in the future. Today he or she is one's absolutely, all-time, most wonderful friend, until, of course, a genuine competitor appears, perhaps tomorrow, next month, or next year.

The third promise is interesting because the promise closes off options, even though the person making the promise does not know how the future will unfold. The person making the promise must have great confidence in his partner—that she is engaging, fun to be with, a help in time of troubles, and a joy most of the time. He does not know what will occur in the future—for better, for worse, for richer, for poorer, in sickness and in health—but he knows that he wants to love her and serve her and in this way develop his own life, passions, and interests with her.

This book is written for the person who considers the third promise the most valuable or at least suspects that it is the one a person would like most to hear from another person. The third promise implies an excellence in living which far exceeds the quality of life implied by the other two promises. If a person only suspects that the third promise is the best, this book is written to highlight why the third promissory option is the most valuable, the most excellent, the most sophisticated, and also, in the long run, the most realistic.

THE HUMAN APTITUDE FOR EXCELLENCE

Human beings have a natural inclination to identify the normal shape or form something takes. When a "thing" is alive, it changes. But even in the case of living things human beings are good at recognizing the purpose or goal of the plant or animal.

Consider three items: a pebble, a rose, and a tiger. A pebble is inert; it doesn't do anything. It is just there. It can be used by someone, it can be polished in a stream, it can be washed up on a beach, but it does not move of its own accord. It does not strive to be anything. It is just hard, sometimes smooth, easy to hold in one's hand. Children love to throw pebbles and, when thrown into a lake or puddle, they make beautiful, expanding concentric circles. They are what they are and they can be used by humans for both good and ill. But they do not strive to be anything.

Living things, on the other hand, are characterized by striving. At the very least, they strive to do things enabling them to survive and grow.

A rose grows on a vine. In order to grow, it needs water and nutrients, which it gets from the vine and the environment. It also protects and projects itself by responding to the ambient temperature. In addition to struggling to "fulfill itself," the rose is pretty. Whatever color it comes in, it usually has a form that is beautiful. Its beauty, however, can be modified and perhaps enhanced by a horticulturist. The horticulturist can breed roses in different ways to produce different colors or a greater number of petals, or more flowers on the rose vine, or flowers that last a longer period of time. As far as we know the rose does not suffer. If one cuts a rose off the vine, the rose does not experience pain, though we will undoubtedly learn more about "plant pain" in decades to come.

A rose may be malformed in some way, but the rose does not thereby suffer embarrassment. Indeed, the misshapen or mal-colored rose may have an attraction all its own. Some roses are more beautiful than others, some last longer than others, some smell more enticing than others. The rose does not make decisions; everything is determined by its genes. Even without knowing the genes, however, human beings can appreciate the goodness or excellence of being a rose.

The tiger is a beautiful animal. Cute when small, fearsome when of age, elegant in its movements, wonderfully fast when pursuing its prey, but lethargic and seemingly content after a meal of fresh wildebeest. This is a complicated and fascinating animal. The tiger has a type of "family life" and even shares its prey with others, after taking the best part for himself. A tiger with a deformed and unusable leg from birth probably does not live long, because it cannot secure enough food for itself. Such a tiger is still a tiger and still shares in a degree of excellence. We may even be moved with compassion for the tiger because we understand that because it cannot compete, it will likely die at an early age.

It is important to notice also that excellence in animals can include things that are abhorrent to humans. Healthy tigers compete, in part by killing or beating competitors to the prey. The tiger is not evil for killing its prey. Killing another animal is consistent with its goal of striving to live and also generate other little tigers. Some tigers are stronger and bigger than others, some are faster, some have more beautiful skin or eyes, some are more agile than others. But we understand that tigers have an excellence that is a wonder all its own. These descriptions as well as the observations of deformities mean that "tiger excellence" includes a range of capacities and performance, and this is also true for other animals. In some areas, one tiger has more talent or ability than another. Thus, another way to refer to excellence is as a pattern of distinction. One tiger's speed might be below average, another's average, and another's superlative. Furthermore, one tiger may perform one action (chasing prey) better than most, yet lag behind in another activity (mating). Various patterns of distinction exist within a single animal.

Humans—even young children—are able to recognize excellences in rocks, flowers, and animals. The DNA of human beings is such that even young children at least partially understand what makes for a good stone or a good flower or a good tiger. Admittedly, children are helped along in this realization by parents, who themselves emerge from a particular culture. Nonetheless, whatever parental interpretation of the facts is offered, this interpretation has to be at least partially confirmed by the child's experience. In addition, when the child understands the excellence or good in a flower or animal, this does not imply moral good. Depending on the age of the child, he might not catch this distinction because he himself has not yet reached the age where he not only understands right from wrong but also controls his actions so that he can chose right and avoid wrong. But the child understands a good amount of this and understands also that "good" implies a certain type of excellence.

An aptitude for excellence includes a respect for excellence. Humans want to promote it, or at least not destroy it. One of the attractive moral features of modern society is that most people very strongly want to protect the lives of animals and protect nature. They acknowledge an excellence there that is not of their own making. Despite the fact that the source is from elsewhere, the human aptitude for excellence includes protecting and even promoting excellence in nature and the world of animals.

In addition to having an aptitude to recognize forms of excellence in inanimate things, in plants, and in animals and to protect and promote this excellence, human beings also recognize human excellences that attract them in their own lives. This recognition is linked to the gift of consciousness or self-awareness, since human beings are aware that their very identity is linked to the way in which they decide to strive for different types of excellence.

These human excellences might be quite rudimentary when the child is young. For example, young children realize there is an excellence involved in learning how to ride a bike. It requires balance, coordination, and the courage to experience and overcome initial failure. Children properly understand riding a bike as something wonderful. They not only take great delight in learning how to ride a two-wheeler, but they then seek greater control and mastery by being able to ride fast or with no hands. The pursuit of excellence is somewhere in our human genes.

SHORING UP THE CULTURE OF LASTING INTIMACY

The author of this book has an abiding interest in culture and a particular interest in moral and religious culture. He has explored how a dominant culture interacts with sub- or countercultures. He also explores what things are necessary for a culture to survive. His main area of interest is how personal moral norms and skills are fostered or undermined by prevailing cultures. What moral views people have and what moral skills they develop in adolescence and beyond are profoundly influenced by the culture in which they live. Furthermore, even the ability to think clearly about morals is influenced by cultural norms and perspectives. Culture, after all, is generated by people, some of whom are far more influential than others. Most cultural norms and understandings develop slowly over time. They gain in influence as more people become persuaded that their stature as human beings is enhanced by adhering to one culture rather than another. Thus, even dominant cultures have to strive, since they confront competing cultures.

Within every dominant culture, there exist sub- or countercultures. Some subcultures have the ability to flourish among a certain type of individuals, even when very powerful and dominant cultures surround them and hedge them in. Religious colleges and universities, for example, exist within the very strong culture of nonsectarian private and public colleges and universities. In the United States the dominant culture in which subcultures exist is largely defined by business, entertainment, education, style/fashion, and relationships. To a great extent, the dominant secular culture in the United States is suffused with sexual content, action, and innuendo and has a bias toward radical independence and unfettered opportunity.

Part of American wealth is that the United States has many vibrant subcultures. If one isolates attention on personal relationships, some subcultures run decidedly counter to this dominant culture. Some subcultures, for example, strongly support friendship that lasts a lifetime. Such subcultures may grow in influence over time if they attract followers who glimpse in them a type of human satisfaction not likely to be reached through the dominant culture. The central human issue for young adults is whether a strong encouraging subculture in support of lifelong friendship can continue to flourish in our time and whether they are inclined to promote such a subculture.

This book seeks to highlight those aspects of a particular subculture that supports excellence in personal relationships. One goal is to show how young women and men can be active players in the dominant secular culture, even while enjoying the benefits of an active subculture that promotes very high human commitment and satisfaction. The book also helps young adults take good advantage of both current secular culture and religious culture. No one can create a culture themselves. However, a person can praise important components of a supportive subculture that tend to be either mocked or pushed to the background by the dominant culture.

THE PLAN OF THE BOOK

This book is organized into three distinct parts. The first part explains what we mean by an aptitude for excellence among those things that human beings strive to realize in their lives. Even though we use "aptitude for excellence," technically it should be rendered as "aptitude for excellences," the reason being that human beings have a natural aptitude to recognize and pursue excellence in a number of different areas. We identify seven basic spheres of excellence and call them fundamental values. This is the heart of the natural law approach as it is presented in this book. Part II looks at a series of issues related to the fundamental value of friendship, which for many people involves at some point romance and sex. Young, maturing friendships are explored in separate chapters that juxtapose an ideal, a path to reach that ideal, and normal obstacles encountered along the way.

Part III discusses practical moral skills that can help young adults develop lives and loves that are ethical, meaningful, and deeply fulfilling. It also looks at religious rituals, practices, norms, and narratives that provide greater motivation and strength to pursue human flourishing at its highest levels. In this final part, we focus on the ways religion, particularly as expressed in various Christian denominations, supports young people in their efforts to lead good and descent and ethical lives.

The book presumes the reader has or is open to belief in God and has a desire to fulfill whatever plan God has for each person. In Part III, we highlight the benefits the regular practice of religion offer to young people in specifying and achieving their goals. However, we downplay these religious aspects in Parts I and II. The reason for treading lightly on the religious component for over half the book is to highlight the universality of natural law. The natural law approach relies on basic types of human excellence and appeals in principle to all people who believe in a Supreme Being who made the world. Without belief in God or a Supreme Being, men and women might have moral qualms but they have no justification for treating moral "obligations" as binding. They may choose to do things because it will advance their goals or the goals of others. But a moral obligation means that I do it because something inside me—my conscience—tells me I should do it and I am convinced that, if I want to be a good person, I have to listen to this voice and abide by the direction it provides. If God does not stand behind my conscience and it is only me, I can decide to act against my conscience by simply redefining myself.

People have natural aspirations to achieve important values. The natural law approach says that these important human values apply to all human beings, no matter the culture or society in which they were raised. The particular ways in which people strive to reach these values differ enormously and often legitimately according to the ambient culture, subcultures, and personal taste. But the claim of natural law is that certain big values are common to all human beings. The commonality of the human calling and the general characteristics of that calling are emphasized in Parts I and II. The wonderful additions that religion offers to explaining, specifying, and realizing these basic human goals are then addressed in Part III. Only at this point do we draw upon the wealth contained in the Old and New Testaments of the Bible.

PART ONE

The Framework

AS THEY MATURE, all human beings think about which actions are really excellent ones, which ones are reasonable or at least acceptable, and which ones should be avoided. But long before young people reach this stage of reflection, they have very naturally undertaken thousands of actions. Many of these are at the prompting of or in imitation of their parents. As they reach adolescence, school and neighborhood friends become much more important as influences on their actions. As young people move through their teen years, media also increasingly impact what young people think is appropriate or excellent.

This first section looks at general values about which most everyone agrees. The claim is not that everyone agrees which actions are right or which are wrong, but rather that there is a fair amount of convergence of views with respect to the goals human beings seek. The agreement is understandably greater among people who live in the United States, and we would have to be more nuanced if we simultaneously considered all countries or cultures. Nonetheless, in this section we note the very wide agreement that exists with respect to the larger human goals, which we call fundamental values, as well as with respect to actions that lead toward those goals and actions that undermine those goals.

Note that we are not claiming that everyone agrees on everything, which would be a foolish assertion. Rather we are pointing out that, with respect to the big goals in life, there is a remarkable amount of agreement. Additional concurrence prevails over many actions that are considered wrong. Such harmony among goals and against certain actions requires an explanation. If every person did whatever he or she liked and was not guided by any natural inclination or "law," agreement about goals that result in humans flourishing as human beings and consensus that some actions are just wrong suggest that in their clear moments human beings are not guided by whim, fancy, or pleasure, but rather by some natural inclinations they have somehow embedded within them. This set of inclinations, experienced by an individual living in society, is what is referred to as the natural law.

Technically, of course, the natural law is not a law of politics or science. Natural law has certainly not been formally passed as a law by any political body, though the concept of the natural law is embedded in the Declaration of Independence. Nor is it strictly speaking a law of nature, discovered centuries ago by perceptive scientists or philosophers. The first articulation of the natural law goes back to the Stoics in Roman times, but no empirical proof of it was offered. More precisely expressed, the natural law indicates that practically all human beings, by the way they are constituted, are oriented by their nature, which is in turn nurtured in society, to pursue certain important values, called fundamental values. The orientation and inclination toward these values are part of nature and common to all people. However, the specific ways in which people pursue the values are influenced by family, country, culture, and religion. By nurturing the pursuit of the fundamental values, these groups excite young people to seek them in ever more exemplary ways. Family, country, culture, and religion affirm the universality of the fundamental values, even as they suggest a very broad range of possible actions by which people can participate in the values.

In chapter 5 Maria and Dave make their first appearance. These are young adults who have started going out with one another. Throughout the book, they act, interact, and discuss topics similar to the ones presented in the more theoretical or expository chapters. Their role is to make the general points more specific and to suggest practical ways to implement the natural law.

2

Self-Evident Human Aspirations

THE HUMAN APTITUDE for excellence has been around for a long period of time. Practically every religious and political group promotes different forms of excellence. Many of them emphasize how universal different types of excellences are.

A very basic human excellence is thinking clearly and logically about everything we experience. In order even to speak about human excellence, a person has to be convinced that truth, including clear and consistent reasoning, constitutes a very important type of human excellence. Furthermore, most people in the world have some experience of God. For believers God is real, infinite, and interested in human beings. Responding to what God wants of us constitutes a type of human excellence.

AN AMERICAN FOUNDATION FOR EXCELLENCE

An aptitude for excellence is strongly associated with the Christian churches and the Jewish faith, but it is hardly confined to one category of religious faith. Four basic principles undergird all appeals to pre-eminent qualities or desires of human beings.

1. Human beings possess the ability to reason, which ability they develop by participating in one or more communities or institutions.

15

2. Through reason we can understand reality or what is true.

3. The truth that we are made by God can also be discovered through our reason, and this realization requires that we conform to God's will by doing some things and abstaining from others.

4. Because reality and truth can be understood through human reason, there can be consensus in society about what is right and wrong.

Every 4th of July, Americans are reminded of these basic principles when we recall the words from our Declaration of Independence, "We hold these truths to be self-evident, that all men are created equal..."

A person may have an attraction to human excellence, but why should she act on it? An adult is free to do or not do something. Certainly someone should not be compelled by others to pursue a particular human excellence. Within the confines a particular society, a person can choose which excellence she wants to pursue. But it is almost inconceivable that a person not pursue some excellence in her own way. Being a couch potato has some benefits; otherwise, people of all ages would not be so inclined to head for the couch. However, even the person who enjoys watching TV on the couch knows that being a couch potato is not a human excellence. One realizes one should be engaged in activities that are more fulfilling, though undoubtedly more demanding.

One good reason to pursue true human excellence is the conviction that an all-knowing God created human beings and is the source of our reason. For several good reasons, many people believe in God. In large measure, this belief is still present in American society as it was at its inception. The rest of the phrase from the Declaration of Independence witnesses to a general conviction of the American Founders: "... and that they are endowed by their Creator with certain unalienable Rights, that among these are Life, Liberty and the pursuit of Happiness."

The aptitude for excellence is deep within each individual. However, the way interactive and social human beings conceive of these excellences and actually pursue them is mediated by institutions, which can be viewed as mini-cultures. The institutions may be large—such as the U.S. government, the UN, or any particular religious denomination—or small—such as a local soccer club, a high school, or the family itself. These institutions embody various ways to realize the excellences or values we cherish most deeply. Those excellences that humans value most deeply we refer to throughout this book as fundamental human values, or simply fundamental values. Institutions usually allow plenty of room for individual choice, but they also generate firm expectations about what is a right and wrong in pursuit of an excellence and what are acceptable or inappropriate ways to seek excellence.

Consider a high school. Every high school—be it public or private, religious or nonsectarian—has clear views with respect to various behavioral issues: matters of lateness, cheating, fighting, dress code, language, physical contact, respect for teachers and administrators, homework, course requirements, tests, honors, failing a course, qualifications for graduation, good standing, or participating in sports or club activities, etc. Whatever the student handbook may state, the actual, prevailing policy is communicated by which actions are praised and how the school reacts when rules are violated or conditions are not met. Silence and failure to react are every bit as powerful in communicating norms as strong statements and swift action. In any normal high school, doing homework is important. But not in every high school. In a particular high school, the student handbook may say nothing about homework. Even if it does, it may be that most teachers in that school do not require students to hand it in. Regardless of the deleterious effects on college preparation and despite strong encouragement to the contrary, such a school is communicating a crystal clear message to students: homework is optional.

Any particular institution is an imperfect reflection of those patterns of distinction we value most deeply. For example, in various American states and at the federal level capital punishment is condoned, even though many citizens find capital punishment no longer a necessary deterrent to crime. Some municipalities may neglect their poor and homeless. A culture may condone taking the life of another human being as long as the human being is still within the uterus of the mother. Not everything in a municipality, country, or institution, no matter how well established, will be good. However, for good or ill, by their recommended or required actions institutions embody what many people consider important values. In many instances, these values are partial realizations of the full complement of human excellences, which we enumerate in subsequent chapters.

Institutions play a pervasive role in the life of every person. When younger, we are formed by institutions we did not choose. As we approach adulthood, we choose the institutions with which we are affiliated. Different institutions influence different people in particular ways, shaping the ways we perceive and formulate issues. By regularly participating in these institutions, we repeat some actions hundreds of times. The repetition can inure us to some important ethical concerns but it can alert us to others. Institutions can and often do keep us on the right path and away from those things that are harmful.

Seeking to improve ourselves and our country is ingrained in us as American citizens. However, most people have a concern for justice that is global in its reach. Discussions about human rights, including the rights of immigrants and prisoners, the denunciation of genocide, slavery, and apartheid, arguments against the death penalty and in favor of free trade, critiques of torture and the sex trade, defense of religious liberty and the rights of women and the unborn, and calls for ecological and environmental stewardship all seek to free people everywhere, now and in the future, so that unhindered by unnecessary restraints they may pursue actions leading to greater human excellence.

Although most Americans don't usually invoke the word excellence when talking about morals, most of us are familiar with the approach to morality and ethics characterized by an aptitude and respect for excellence. This is especially so in the arenas of politics, economics, social justice, and the common good. What we are less familiar with is its connection to personal morality and the decisions we make about how we behave in relation to each other on a day-to-day basis. In other words, it is our actions that move us closer or further away from the goals or types of excellence that we seek. Our goals with respect to friendship, sex, and romance can only be realized by specific actions that move us closer to our goals. The relationship between our desire for intimate human friendship and the actions we undertake to develop that type of friendship is the focus of this book. But before turning to a fuller description of fundamental human excellences or patterns of distinction it is useful to spend a little time describing what we mean by morality.

MORALITY AND MORAL WORLDS

When referring to *morality* we are talking about living our lives in a way that maximizes genuine human flourishing. Morality involves figuring out who we should be and choosing actions or practices that help us get there, while refraining from actions that move us in a different direction. The drive and energy in morality is positive. It comes from our aspirations and desires, from whom we most truly want to be and the good we want to accomplish. Of course there is also a negative component in morality – things that we simply should not do. But what defines things as morally off-limits is their potential to upset our "apple cart," which bears our long-term aspirations as well as our immediate concerns. Things that interfere with our becoming more authentically human are bad for us and must be avoided.

A *moral world* acknowledges a person's call to become more fully human by undertaking actions that correspond to and do not undermine central, core values that all human beings are called to realize. Any moral world requires a particular view of human flourishing. This appealing vision of what people are expected to become also dictates those activities that are off-limits because they impede our flourishing. Whether it comes through institutions such as American culture, religion, or the family, the vision of human fulfillment provides an appealing goal that motivates action. For Christians, Christ is the ultimate model and the goal of a life well-lived and Christian morality is the path that leads to that goal. Nonetheless, with respect to fundamental human values, Christians claim that all human beings, whatever their religious beliefs, can perceive the binding power of these values.

Figure 2.1 represents the field of human action and activity. Notice that the set of actions and behaviors that are morally off-limits is fairly small. Even though good and exemplary actions and behaviors drive our deliberations according to the approach in this book, in fact most discussions about morality and ethics focus on what is off-limits. Of course these "thou shalt nots" are part of human experience and to omit dealing with them would be dishonest. However, it is the vision or goal of what is good and excellent and what we want to accomplish that spurs us on in life. It is that same vision of true human fulfillment that defines what we cannot do. Any actions that disorient and therefore impede and frustrate our natural movement toward human fulfillment are simply off-limits.

PURSUING FORMS OF EXCELLENCE

All admirable and exemplary activity is in service of some particular value and involves some expenditure of time and effort directed toward promoting that value, which is a formulation of an excellence at its highest level. Consider for instance the value of knowledge. To promote the value of knowledge in one's own life requires more than just talking about its importance or simply singing the praises of smart people. It requires time and effort in doing such things as reading a book, puzzling over something, speaking with a wise and informed person, helping a child learn, giving directions to a stranger on the street, looking a word up in the dictionary, or consulting a website. These are the kinds of things that actually promote knowledge.

Human beings are naturally inclined to think of good ways to pursue important values, but some ways to pursue them are anything but good. Within the framework of knowledge as a category of human excellence, think about cheating on exams, stealing books, hacking a corporate website, or reading someone's personal correspondence without their permission. These are certainly ways to get information and knowledge, but they are hardly good ways of going about it.

Some ways to pursue knowledge are destructive and therefore forbidden and off-limits. Many, many more are admirable or exemplary. We are all tempted from time to time to take shortcuts or take advantage of other people. Nevertheless, both individually and in community we can be imaginative and resourceful in finding lots of different ways to pursue good things.

MAKING CHOICES

The way people go about maximizing human flourishing is by pursuing values or particular forms of human excellence. The way we pursue values is through specific actions and activities that promote those values. In order for any of this to happen, we have to make choices. Choices channel a person's activities in a particular direction.

Over time our choices become more informed and lead to strategies and patterns of action. Oftentimes the decisions are not earth-shaking. For example, one person might come to understand that reading is preferable to watching TV as a pre-sleep ritual and will decide to move the TV from the bedroom to the living room. Another might say, "I do not need to drink as much, so I'll go to the gym, not the pub, after work on Fridays." In both of these examples, individuals make a choice that situates them at some place in Figure 2.1. In some instances, there is a specific decision to steer clear of off-limits activities on the left edge of the diagram. In other cases, the decision is a more general attempt to figure out approximately where to be in the broad center of the behavioral playing field. And is some cases, strategies are developed that will help situate individuals in the milieu of noble, admirable actions on the right-hand side of the diagram. In each case, people, realizing that past actions can influence future ones, make decisions about what they aspire to do and what they hope to avoid in relation to some particular value.

This pattern is generally true regardless of whether people are Christian or non-Christian, agnostic or even atheist. But are religious beliefs *necessary* to determine what is right or wrong? If specifically religious issues (such as the obligation Catholics have to attend church on Sundays or confess their sins) are excluded, the answer is no. The Christian approach claims that most people are pretty much in the same moral situation with respect to what they should aim for and avoid. Whether or not they are religious, all people know that there are some distinct ways (by seeking excellence through knowledge, beauty, and life) in which human beings flourish. They also are aware that there are some particular actions (such as killing, lying, and adultery) that are always wrong and should be avoided. That is true whether or not they believe that Jesus is the Son of God. People can differ greatly about the circumstances in which killing, for example, is permitted. But whatever their religious background, most people know that one should avoid

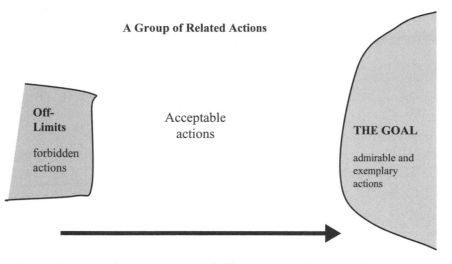

A Group of Related Actions

Off-Limits

forbidden actions

Acceptable actions

THE GOAL

admirable and exemplary actions

FIGURE 2.1 Three general types of actions: forbidden ones, acceptable ones, and admirable ones.

killing people. There are some exceptions to the claim that most people know what things are wrong, and these often involve people doing things objectively bad, although the people performing the acts are unaware the actions are wrong. These cases will be addressed in subsequent chapters. Most Christian denominations claim that all people who are raised in a reasonable community with appropriate institutions should have at least a general idea of which values all human beings should strive for and which actions are wrong because they undermine or go directly contrary to those values.

If everyone knows pretty much what in general they are expected to strive for and what particular actions they are to avoid, it seems reasonable to wonder whether revelation by God is necessary or even advisable. In fact, both the Old and New Testaments contain many positive and negative prescriptions. If they are already known to us via human excellences which we admire and respect, why do they have to be "revealed" in the Old or New Testament? What is the role of revelation, Christ, and the Bible with respect to the moral life?

One should note that, from earliest Christian times, Christians acknowledged two "books," or sources, of revelation. One book humans "read" is the world, that is, what God created. Just studying creation tells us a lot of about God and about what our role in the world should be. In fact, it is in this first book that we find the natural law, a law that binds all human beings. It is from creation that we first learn about human excellences.

The second book is the Bible (both Old and New Testaments). Certainly one role of biblical revelation is to portray how God dealt with his people, the Jews, and how He sent His Son for our salvation. A second role of Biblical revelation is to confirm and affirm what we know through the natural aptitude and respect for excellence which God has put in us through evolution and His personal stamp, the human soul tightly linked to our body. For this reason, theologians have often thought of the main tenets of the Ten Commandments as confirmations of particular approaches to human excellence. That is, even prior to God giving the commandments to Moses on Mount Sinai, human beings knew the nonreligious commandments were binding on them.

Of course, the first few of the Ten Commandments are specific and, as formulated in the Bible, are not generally applicable to all people. For example, the regulation to "Keep holy the Sabbath" (Deuteronomy 5: 12) is a specific command to the Jewish people. Like some other commandments, this formulation applies specifically to the Jews. This may be an instance of God teaching His people how to conduct themselves in religious matters. It may be that God's plan was to instruct other religious groups through the religious practices of the Jews how the other groups could render proper worship to God, once they take their own history and cultural development into consideration.

Adhering to the Ten Commandments and other rules promoting human excellence occurs within a community, and every community is partially defined by the many institutions upon which it relies. As noted earlier, these institutions do not always promote various types of human excellence. Consider one neuralgic example: abortion in the United States. Certainly it is important that individuals be free to pursue basic human values in the way they consider most appropriate. So, personal freedom is important. On the other hand, we all know we should avoid taking human life. American political institutions may have evolved in such a way that personal freedom is mistakenly granted greater prominence than the protection of human life. As a result, people raised and formed by these institutions may have the sincere conviction that, as long as human life exists within the womb of a mother, she alone has the right to determine whether that life will continue or be ended. As we shall argue, this view, even though sincere, is erroneous. The point here is simply that for a large number of people in the United States personal freedom is so institutionally enshrined within our legal and political system that some people do not consider taking life within the womb as wrong.

Christian revelation is lived by a religious community with its own imperfect religious institutions and also in a larger society, with its own institutions. Just as modern secular institutions can call Christian institutions to task for neglecting certain important human values, so revelation, as embodied within Christian institutions, can exercise essential critiques of secular institutions. Thus, one is justified in saying that "Christian revelation embodied in institutions" provides a correction to secular mores and institutions.

Christ, the Bible, and the community interpreting the Bible also have an impact on the personal goals of people of faith. For nonbelievers, Christ can be a question, perhaps a challenge, or maybe even an obstacle. For a variety of reasons, some who are familiar with Christianity may reject what they think Christ stands for. For true Christian believers, however, Christ is central in their lives and is also at the center of the life of the Christian community to which they belong. For believers, Jesus is the ideal who helps them gain self-knowledge, and gives them strength to become holy in God's eyes.

Jesus is the new Adam, the human ideal revealed in the New Testament and experienced in Christian community. Christians would not be believers unless they were attracted to the excellence visible in Jesus' words and deeds. Belief in Christ and the practice of the faith should encourage us to aim for what is admirable and exemplary and act accordingly. So, a Christian collection of activities that promote fundamental excellences will differ from a non-Christian system in terms both of the exemplary things for which we aim and also of our path for getting there. That is, the actions Christians select as acceptable or exemplary as well as those from which Christians generally abstain are likely to be markedly different from those who are not believers. In chapter 4 and again in part III we return to this issue to explore more precisely what the "Christian difference" is in terms of one's life plan.

3

Constraints, Discipline, and Happiness

YOUNG PEOPLE ARE fairly happy and carefree. By and large, every day offers them lots of potential fun. When they are still in college, graduate school, or training programs, life is not fabulous because they still have papers to write, exams to prepare for, and evaluations to undergo. But papers, labs, and exams are at worst a type of intermittent agony, and well worth the freedom that academic life or life on one's own brings with it.

Even once they are in the workplace, most young people enjoy themselves immensely, at least for a few years. At some point, a few dark clouds appear on the horizon—slow-moving ones. These clouds may loom on the relationship front. Depending on gender, geography, and aspirations, by their late 20s a good number of young people get apprehensive if they are not in a relationship. Young men begin to see their friends pairing off and young women who hope one day to have children become more acutely aware of their ticking biological clocks.

Let's optimistically designate the situation of young adults as "edgy exhilaration." Now, it would not be surprising if the exhilarated twenty-somethings reading this book might be getting a bid edgier than usual as a result of reading the last chapter. Talk about forbidden or off-limits actions surely gives them pause. Yes, the emphasis was on positive goals and the broad array of acceptable actions, and, yes, it was pointed out that the area of off-limit actions was small compared to the overall field of acceptable and exemplary actions. Still, a good number of young people would be fearful that the off-limits area is eventually going to get bigger and have some real bite. At some point in a fast approaching tomorrow, they fear that shaded area is going to "cramp their style."

FUN CONSTRAINTS

Let's take a look at freedom and constraints, especially among young adults. An image of perfect freedom is a bird flying high and far, to wherever wind and whim should lead. The image implies seeing and learning about new things or seeing old things from a dramatically different perspective. Because the bird represents the freedom of a man or woman, the bird is implicitly endowed with intelligence, even as it assumes the wings that will get it aloft.

Although the bird does not in fact have intelligence on a level remotely similar to that of a human and wings big enough to enable us to fly would probably be an encumbrance, the image works. Indeed, the combination of wings and intelligence is a powerful one. The possibility of humans flying like birds suggests a breaking of boundaries, a release from all constraints, even constraints of nature.

In fact, however, we live in a world of constraints, and we freely choose restraints to enhance our lives. Many young people love music and some enjoy either reading or writing poetry. Both music and poetry entail considerable constraints. What makes music fun is that it adheres to a beat, it has rhythm. In most songs, the beat remains the same throughout the song. The lyrics are short, evocative, a mixture of unusual images and perhaps some rhymes as well. The lyrics of a song are much more constrained than ordinary conversation. But the constraint also yields a pleasure in hearing lyrics tightly connected to one another and to one's experiences in life.

Poetry has meter, a cadence that gets established early in the poem. It may also have rhymes. Like lyrics in a song, a line of poetry is short, curtailed. Poets think hard to create connections between words and use images that evoke beauty, horror, satisfaction, or some other emotion. Poetry does not come easily. A poet has to struggle to create something compelling, but hard work alone will prove insufficient without inspiration. Poetry has to have something new, not expressed in a predictable way and that relates to current experience. Poets may write primarily for themselves, but most poets write for others, and good poetry has a strong impact on other people. Three or four stanzas of poetry are as nothing compared with a novel, but because it is so concise, the impact and insight can often be more arresting. Poets are constrained by the literary form they embrace. And in the end it is those very constraints that unleash a poet's power and potential.

Young adults accept the constraints of rhythm, beat, meter, or rhyme that come with the turf in music and poetry. They also accept the constraints common to athletes. Almost daily practice, attention to eating properly, preparing mentally for a contest, helping team members both during a game and afterward, carrying out the directions of the coach or team captain—all these properly belong to fun participation in sports. And all of the activities—including arduous practices—are deemed to be satisfying and necessary for peak performance.

Young people have already voluntarily assumed significant constraints on their activity. After all, no one has to go to college. High school students may feel parental pressure when it comes to whether they will go, but there are alternatives. Those who do choose college also choose the constraints of college, of which there are plenty. Sure, undergraduates have a lot of new freedoms, especially if they don't live at home. But new restrictions and constraints also abound. It all comes together in this package called "college." Many young people never think twice about accepting the whole thing. And later in life, many recall their college years as among the happiest and carefree of their lives. And this, despite all the constraints!

CONSTRAINTS IN A RELATIONSHIP

Young people have close friends, and, at least with their friends, they are used to dealing with constraints. If Betsy's close friend Tiffany has a birthday coming up, Betsy will arrange some event to celebrate, no matter how busy she is. If Tiffany's mom, dad, or sister dies, Betsy will drop practically everything to be at Tiffany's side. This is what friends do, willingly. They bind themselves to another person, and in so doing they freely assume constraints.

Marriage is a very high—perhaps the highest—form of friendship. A wife and husband share their lives, their hopes, their bodies, and the children that God grants them. Because newly marrieds are establishing a new level of friendship, the early months of any marriage represent an adjustment.

The newly married husband may be accustomed to going out with his buddies. Now that Alex is married, of course he realizes he will be spending much more time with his wife Betsy. Nonetheless, other adjustments are also necessary. Alex may decide that he has not gone out with his friends for several months. So, he calls them up and arranges a day when they go out. When he goes home and for the first time reveals to Betsy his plan, she might be rather annoyed. Initially Alex interprets this as jealousy by Betsy that Alex still has other friends with whom he remains close. Betsy probably believes, he muses, the friends are butting in on the marriage relationship.

In fact, Betsy's objection has nothing to do with Alex going out with his friends. She is probably delighted to have an evening at home alone to get things done. Betsy's objection is not to what Alex is going to do, but to how he arranged it. She tells Alex that, before she agrees to anything, she always calls him or speaks with him in person to make sure it is fine with him. It's not hard for Alex to say to friends, "Okay, let's agree tentatively that we will meet at Joe's Bar next Tuesday. But let me get back to you; I just want to check with Betsy that she doesn't have something else planned for that night." Some statement to this effect to his friends is important because it accords Betsy her rightful position as wife and, therefore, most important friend. Also, it reminds Alex that he always wants to be on the same page with Betsy. Practically all newlyweds get used to these constraints, which emerge from the new relationship of committing to being best friends for life.

UNNATURAL CONSTRAINTS IN A NON-RELATIONSHIP

It is interesting how sexual hook-ups can also involve constraints, even though they are designed to involve none. Hook-ups, which involve sexual intimacy, but perhaps not sexual intercourse, are supposed to be commitments lasting minutes or at most a few hours. Nothing more than a fun time for a while is implied in hook-up culture. It may lead to a more sustained relationship of friendship, but no one should have expectations that it will. The hook-up is just supposed to be fun for both people involved.

In *Sex and the Soul*, Donna Freitas describes her conversation with one young college student who looks forward to hook-ups. From the context of the conversation, it appears he engages in hook-ups with some frequency, say, a few times a month. When Freitas asked him how he felt about the hook-ups, he said he liked them, but he hated it when the girl called him the following day. He found this annoying and presumptuous on the part of the girl!

The young woman he finds so irritating clearly does not get it when it comes to hook-ups. Imagine the nerve: a young woman thinking that being sexually intimate with someone implies some type of friendship! In her innate human desire for heterosexual friendship, i.e., sharing thoughts, emotions, and aspirations with a guy, the young woman gives him a call to see whether he wanted anything more than something free, fun, and purely physical.

What we have here is a basic human desire in the young woman saying, "Sharing my body with someone must mean I am allowed to share my thoughts and reflections with him, too." She's right! In fact, an important issue for the young woman to address and for us to consider is if sex comes first, are deep thoughts, emotions, and aspirations ever likely to be a priority in the relationship?

NATURAL CONSTRAINTS

Many constraints in human interactions and undertakings are natural; they clearly contribute to a particular type of excellence. They emerge from friendships, writing poetry, being a member of a sports team, the desire for a particular type of education, etc. Most of these are good and valuable constraints that enhance participation in various activities. Other constraints—such as those in a hook-up culture—are unnatural in the sense that most people understand something is really wrong with a guy being satisfied with a series of sexual acts and not wanting any sharing that is less physical but just as personal. Unnatural in this case means that something damaging is involved, definitely not an excellence. It is also unnatural in the sense that it does not contribute to our flourishing as human beings.

The pursuit of excellence constrains human beings. However, good constraints should conform to the deepest parts of our nature. Reasonable people can come to see they are creative constraints, constraints that help us to be more fully human, more deeply satisfied, and flourishing more fully in all our relationships.

4

The Illusion of Morality Free Zones

You think it is wrong to have premarital sex. I don't. It's a free country.
You make your choice and I'll make mine.

THIS STATEMENT CAPTURES how many young people begin their moral reflections when deciding what they will and will not do concerning physical intimacy. It is certainly true that we live in a free country. Because a person decides what to do in life, the basis for the decision is personal conviction. The person may have to take legal consequences into consideration; the person may calculate family-related consequences; and the person may be influenced by institutions such as a school, local church, family, or peer group. Whatever the process of decision making or the influencing factors, in the end, the person, provided he or she is of age, decides.

As long as we Americans avoid breaking the law, we are pretty much free to choose to do whatever we want. We always exercise this freedom, however, within some kind of a moral framework, which results from the conglomeration of institutions influencing us. Even when we decide to adopt a new moral framework, we are exchanging it for an existing one. Simply put, we act morally long before we ever think about choosing a moral framework.

Parents hand onto their children the most important things they possess, including their own ethical system. Although it cannot be handed on like a prized necklace that is passed from one generation to the next, still it is possible to introduce children to an appealing ethical system. Patiently, carefully, and with good modeling and explanations, parents first insist on certain behaviors and then, as their children grow older, they build on that foundation by advocating and justifying a variety of activities their children should pursue.

Moral action begins at a young age. At some vague point (in our society around seven years of age) children gain enough knowledge to anticipate consequences, achieve enough self-control to make a choice based on something other than their emotions, and obtain enough insight to know that certain things are wrong, and some things are seriously wrong. When children can do all these things, we say they have reached the age of reason. Clearly the age of reason entails much more than just the ability to reason. It includes some control over emotions and the ability to understand that something is not merely naughty ("Mommy doesn't want me to do it, but she'll let me do it") but wrong for me to do, not simply because Mommy tells me not to do it.

Reaching the age of reason does not mean that seven-year-olds are capable of choosing from among a set of moral principles the ones most suitable for a given situation. It merely means that they can personally commit to the set of *dos and don'ts* of their parents. They understand that certain things are good and other things are bad and that the two are somehow related. Most seven-year-olds know they are not supposed to steal. They might think it is okay sometimes to hit their siblings, but they know it would be very bad to do something that would really hurt them. They know not to harm animals or make people suffer. And they have gotten the message that they should share, help other people in need, be nice to older people, obey their parents and teachers, et cetera. Somehow all of this makes sense to most seven-year-olds who have endorsed the moral standards set for them by their families and the communities in which they live. Children at this stage acknowledge these standards even though they have not chosen them from an array of alternatives. They also have the general sense that if they agree to abide by them, they will become better people.

As children grow older and interact with their peers and adults, they gradually go through a second stage of moral development. With increased exposure to the world outside both home and village, youngsters come to understand two important moral facts. First, some people do not follow the moral laws they have learned. So, even though most students know that cheating is wrong, many actually cheat, and it poses a big problem in most schools. The second fact they come to understand is that not everyone agrees about what things are wrong. For example, some people think it is okay to avoid paying taxes. In fact, many people get some or all of their pay "under the table" in cash. That way they can fudge on the income they declare to the IRS.

CHOOSING A MORAL WORLD

By the time young people get to high school and beyond they realize that there are different moral systems to which people more or less adhere. One easy way to highlight the differences in moral worlds is to return to the diagram from chapter 2. In the new version of this diagram, Moral World B differs from Moral World A in only one class of actions. In figure 4.1 there are now two different "off-limits" areas on the left-hand side. In addition to the shaded "off-limits" area A, there is another area B (indicated by the striped area) that represents an alternate moral world. In this particular moral world, all actions outside area B are permitted. Included among these could be stealing and cheating, actions belonging to area A.

In this new moral world, some things that were permitted in the previous moral world are now forbidden. For example, in the moral world represented by area A it may be that telling a lie is always wrong, whereas in the moral world of area B, telling the truth is forbidden in certain situations. One situation in which truth might be forbidden for this group could be when it results in a friend being tapped for cheating or stealing. Using these examples, area A could be thought of as a traditional moral world and area B the moral world of a thief.

Being aware that there is more than one moral world requires a certain level of maturity and an understanding that moral activities fit a pattern. In any moral world, some logic relates off-limits actions among themselves and provides reasons for separating them from what is good, decent, and acceptable. Even a thief's moral world has a certain consistency or, loosely speaking, logic to it.

We cannot choose a moral world without first being in one. Every person begins life in a community and every community, with its related institutions, has some type of moral world. Whatever that moral world is, it has an impact on parents and children. The formative community may be predominantly religious, secular, or ethnic. Whatever it is, the community contributes to the moral mindset of children who grow up within it.

It is also true that we cannot choose a moral world entirely from the outside. Because a moral system consists in accustomed ways of acting and because accustomed ways of acting are transmitted through institutions, we have to "try on" a community and its institutions in order to evaluate it. Communities embody certain ethical systems, but because a community has various cycles, "trying it on" entails living in it for a number of years. During this trial period we would strive to attain the community's ideals and avoid its forbidden or off-limits activities. After having done that for a time, we would then have to make a judgment. We have to see whether living in the system leads to human fulfillment as defined by that system, whether this type of fulfillment corresponds to our own deep human desires, and whether the system's experts and most authentic adherents can also effectively defend it in the face of either sympathetic or aggressive criticism. No ethical system is perfectly consistent, but some are better than others in

A Group of Related Actions

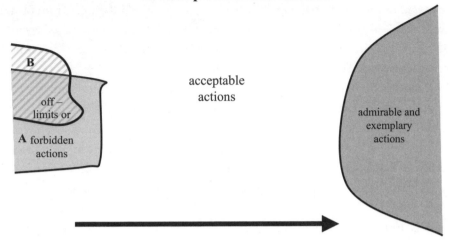

FIGURE 4.1 Moral world A differs from moral world B in its forbidden actions.

responding to various challenges that emerge in society via science, medicine, technology, or new trends in the way people interact.

Trying out a moral system takes time measured in years. It requires understanding how individuals are formed by the system in a great variety of circumstances. That not only means experiencing the system personally, but also assessing it in terms of other people's experience within that system. In this way it is possible to gauge whether a moral system is helpful to people with a variety of talents, aspirations, beliefs, and circumstances. Since life is short, the number of moral systems any one person can try out is limited to perhaps two or three. For this reason, people rely on tradition and on those known for their wisdom. They look to communities that have adhered to a moral system for a long period of time and have an appealing way of life, and they pay close attention to evaluations provided by people with a reputation for wisdom.

DEFINING MORAL SYSTEMS

Identifying what constitutes authentic human flourishing and values helps define a moral system. These different values help determine which actions are off-limits in that system. They also help identify which actions are acceptable, admirable, or exemplary. Since Christ is the goal of Christian belief and living, it is not surprising that belief in Christ helps determine which actions Christians select in their pursuit of essential human values. For Christians, the coming of Christ is the turning point in history that reverses the sin of Adam. Jesus is the new Adam, the new creation. He is the Son who shows us the way to the Father. Jesus demonstrates a self-emptying love for us by being obedient to the will of the Father. He reverses the disobedience of Adam by his own self-sacrificing obedience. The gospels and other writings of the New Testament capture much of what Jesus said and did and how people reacted to Him.

A committed Christian takes Jesus as the model of true human flourishing and, after prayer both in private and in the Christian community, formulates a plan to follow in the footsteps of Christ. A very partial representation of that plan is given in figure 4.2. The dotted area of the diagram indicates the types of activities one person who wants to imitate Christ would like to undertake. This dotted area represents one person's aspirational plan for where she would like to be at a given point in her life. She might live up to it and then again, she might fail. She strives to do some outstanding things and she has no plans to go off-limits and dabble in what is forbidden. For the most part, however, she foresees that many, if not most, of her actions and activities will be ordinary, good, and decent. Figure 4.2 presents the plan for one single Christian. No one size fits all. Each Christian gets to choose a personal plan, and plans can differ. Therefore, in figure 4.2 it is possible to imagine a whole array of odd-shaped areas (not necessarily connected), corresponding to various plans of individual Christians.

Not everyone has a Christian motivation. But Christians claim that all people acknowledge or can be brought to a position where they acknowledge the essential human values. People's actions as children and young adults demonstrate that they have some motivation to pursue these values and they have some notion of what it means to succeed morally as human beings. Based on their moral experience prior to reaching maturity and based on their convictions, everyone formulates action and activity plans. In order to clarify what differentiates the Christian vision of human fulfillment, it will be helpful to outline a modern, secular view of human fulfillment and then explore how the desired actions and activities within that secular plan or framework differ from those in a particularly Christian, or even more specifically, Catholic framework.

A SECULAR MODEL

From the many possible secular views of human fulfillment, we choose one that emphasizes personal satisfaction and recognition by others. Suppose a good percentage of people adhere to this simplistically formulated model of human fulfillment that emphasizes achieving certain goals resulting in social honors and recognition for genuine contributions to human society. In this secular model,

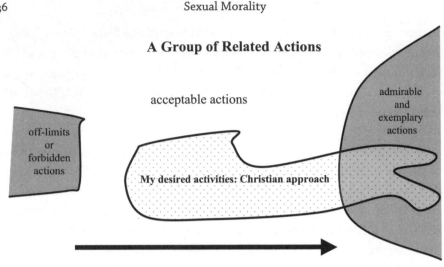

FIGURE 4.2 The area with the dotted points specifies a group of actions that a Christian person chooses because she judges them to promote the activities suggested or modeled by Christ through his preaching, death, and resurrection.

a second important value (we assume) is enjoying exciting opportunities to explore the world. We call this is an "achievement and satisfaction approach" to human flourishing.

In this secular worldview, God plays little or no role. A person subscribing to it seeks acknowledgement for the genuinely good deeds (as defined by this moral world) he performs in society and for society. In order to perform these good deeds, the person wants to be financially well-off and in a position of some authority, since authority brings with it some recognition. The more you can move up the ladder, the greater financial resources you will have available and the greater the good you will achieve. "Good" consists in promoting education and the arts, being politically engaged, and making sure some resources are provided to the poor and less fortunate. But, first and foremost, in this framework is a responsibility to family. Children should receive a good secular education, whatever the cost. Furthermore, this education should be enhanced by family trips, which offer an opportunity for the family to be together and enjoy the good life, but they also provide wonderful educational experiences for the children.

People who subscribe to this view of human fulfillment use whatever goods available to advance their position. Certain groups of "forbidden actions" that a Christian would try to steer clear of are not a concern to people espousing this secular approach. The secularists readily admit some things are wrong. But other actions that Christians might judge to be off-limits fall within the acceptable range of this secular model. People adhering to this model want to help society but they also want to amass resources and spend them prudently.

This account is a brief outline of a secular ideal of human fulfillment based on achievement, knowledge, recognition, and expenditure of resources on family and those who are less fortunate in society. This view of human fulfillment has admirable qualities, yet it is distinctly different from the Christian outline previously developed.

Figure 4.3 offers one possible comparison between these two moral universes. Since the secular approach has a different view of human fulfillment, the array of admirable and exemplary activities changes, even though there is some overlap. There is also a shift in what is off-limits or forbidden. Some things that are forbidden in a Christian framework would be acceptable in a secular one and vice versa.

Another point to highlight in what is depicted is that we assume good intentions on the part of the secular person, just as we did for the person with the Christian view. For both the Christian and the secular person, desired activities include only two groups: those considered acceptable and those considered admirable and outstanding. (The secular approach in figure 4.3 does include a small segment of forbidden actions; the actions, however, are forbidden according to the generic natural law approach, not according to the secular approach.) However, people can give some goals prominence over others. In the secular model of this chapter two values received heavy emphasis: achievement and satisfaction. The natural law approach does not reject those values. However, it claims there are certain human values that are more fundamental than achievement and satisfaction.

This book explores natural law morality. Ultimately, our goal is to understand natural law within a Christian framework. At the outset, however, it is important

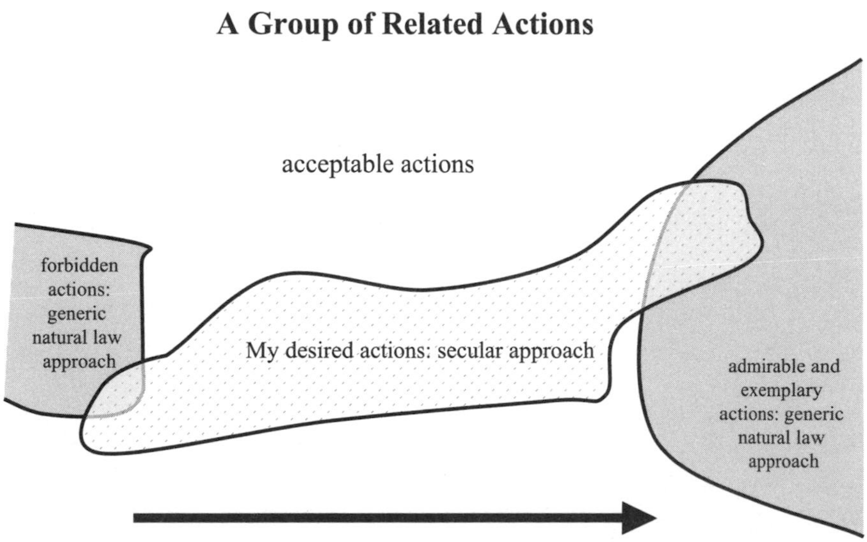

A Group of Related Actions

acceptable actions

forbidden actions: generic natural law approach

My desired actions: secular approach

admirable and exemplary actions: generic natural law approach

FIGURE 4.3 The area with the pattern of dots illustrates the preferred activities for a typical person with a particular secular approach to human flourishing.

to get a sense how two distinct moralities differentiate themselves from one another. Christians have their ideal of human fulfillment and secularists have theirs. Christians maintain their approach is valid while secularists argue for the soundness of their approach. It is totally appropriate to assume that the secular person has good will, intends to do the correct thing, and has a reasonable justification for acting in a particular way. It is similarly appropriate for a nonbeliever to assume a Christian is of good will, wants to do the right thing, and also has a plausible reason for acting in a particular way. The traditional Christian approach to morality is through natural law. According to natural law, one has to offer a plausible reason for undertaking various actions. So, before turning to things Christian (including Catholic), it will take several chapters to get the natural law approach down.

The natural law approach emphasizes deep desires for human fulfillment within each person, without respect to any particular religion. For that reason, we will leave most Christian considerations off to the side for the remainder of parts I and II of this book. Instead, we will focus on what moral norms can be derived from thinking clearly about human fulfillment, without recourse to the Bible or Christian teaching. In part III we highlight the moral benefits that Christian commitment and practice confer on our goals and our ability to attain those goals.

5

Theory and Practice

SOME YOUNG PEOPLE are drawn toward ethical discussions. Others are bored by a careful review of assumptions and meticulous arguments demonstrating why some conclusion is justified. Those in the latter group are far more interested in doing the right thing than in being able to explain persuasively why it is the right thing to do.

COLLEGE CASES

Without getting too theoretical, consider a few practical issues that young adults have to face in their latter teens and in their twenties. Let's return to hooking-up. There are two basic options – go with the flow or resist. Reactions can be ginger or robust, but resistance or acquiescence are the alternatives.

Think of Dave as a typical young decision maker. He may say hooking-up depends on his mood, but even Dave knows enough never to say that to anyone but his best friend. It makes him sound like a complete jerk. Most young women and men would like to offer some reason why they do what they do. It could simply be: "Everyone does it"—that perennial lame favorite that sends every parent in the world over the edge. But, as lame as it is, at least it is a reason. And at this point we are content to emphasize the need for a reason or two for action—regardless of how persuasive it might be. We'll get to strong reasons for resisting actions a bit later.

Consider another college issue: cheating on exams. Is it okay to cheat on an exam? Does the answer depend on a person's mood, or is there some reason why cheating on an exam is always wrong? If for our friend Dave, once again, mood is a prime determinant, there is a pretty good likelihood there will be times in his life when Dave is in the mood, not only to cheat on exams, but also to cheat on his girlfriend or wife or taxes or his firm, et cetera.

The claim made in this book is that things such as cheating—on an exam or on your spouse—are always wrong. They are wrong because these activities are not in accord with our nature, and therefore do not lead to human satisfaction. They may produce some transitory happiness or gratification because they advance immediate personal goals. After all, as a result of cheating on an exam it might be possible to avoid the cost and hassle of summer school or having to repeat a course. But those short-term gains, we claim, are not truly fulfilling, and the actions actually diminish people in their own eyes, as well as in the eyes of God. We realize we have to justify the previous statements with arguments. But our basic approach will be to emphasize that forbidden actions are forbidden precisely because they go directly contrary to what we are as human beings. What is directly contrary to our natures cannot result in human fulfillment. Eventually we will have to show how cheating, hooking-up, killing, and lying all undermine that fulfillment.

CUTTING CORNERS AND THOUGHTS ABOUT MARRIAGE

Let's move from the academic to the annoying. Suppose Maria, who is perhaps a year or two younger than Dave, has started going out with Dave. Now let's also suppose that at a fairly early stage in their being with one another this seems to be a very promising relationship. We also presume that they have not yet been sexually intimate with one another. This may not seem so ideal to some readers, but even though it is unusual in our society, it is ideal, so the argument will be made, because it corresponds to deeply human standards. So, just think of Dave and Maria as getting off to a great start, albeit with one small flaw from Maria's point of view.

Dave and Maria live in a fairly congested urban area and they have driven numerous times together during rush hour. When Dave is driving and traffic gets heavy, he pulls a maneuver Maria simply hates. He gets in the break-down lane and drives ahead of the patient people waiting in the other lane of traffic. She wants to crawl under the dashboard every time he does it. Maria has complained to Dave about it, but he always responds with some half-baked justification. "He has to know," Maria says to herself, "he's cheating on others. You can't be human and not realize that this is unfair to all the other drivers."

Maria truly likes Dave, but this driving maneuver really distresses her. Maria knows that women who resolve to marry saints, don't marry. She also knows she is not a saint. But still, this pattern seems to be more than an irritating, but minor, traffic violation. Maria is beginning to wonder if Dave's automotive one-upmanship is a deal breaker when it comes to a lasting relationship. True friends can have different political views, they can root for different sports teams, they can work for competing firms, they can like starkly different types of movies, and they can come from different countries. But there are some activities that either prevent friendships from occurring or gradually destroy them.

The triviality of riding in the break-down lane should be at most a minor annoyance, or so it would seem. But what if Dave's boorish driving is part of a broader and far more serious pattern? A wife must be able to trust her husband. She can't be worrying about what rules he has decided don't apply to him.

Take the extreme case, a "Dave" who cuts both big and small corners with abandon. A young man who thinks it is okay, even after marriage, to have a sexual liaison with some new or old acquaintance is not suitable for marriage. Whether or not the young man has plausible reasons for his open approach to sex, no woman in her right mind would marry him. He clearly is not commitment material, not even in the short run. To his way of thinking a little fling with an attractive woman is not a big deal. But in a marriage it is always a huge deal.

Back to Dave's expedient driving maneuvers. What Dave is doing is unlawful, but it is unlikely he will ever get cited for it. He might get a warning, or a police officer might stop him and detain him for a while to teach him a lesson. But does that really matter? In Maria's judgment, Dave is being unlawful in only a minor way, but he is being uncivil in a major way.

Should any of this cause Maria serious concern? Probably not, but it depends. On the one hand, it is a rather harmless little quirk. Dave likely picked up the habit somewhere and thinks it is smart. He is probably dismissive of people who object to it. Maria has objected, but not strongly. Dave responded to her objection, but not carefully. He just keeps on doing it, and Maria has taken to fuming quietly.

Think now of Maria in the mode of: Dave-could-be-the-one. Maria is thinking of marriage, even though it might still be a way off. Maria may already know Dave fairly well and know that he is loving and considerate of both her and others. In that case, Maria may correctly judge the driving performance as a behavioral outlier she should learn to grin and bear.

A number of on-the-other-hand arguments come to mind, however. If Dave's practice really makes Maria uncomfortable, she should say so. Annoying practices should not derail a relationship that is developing, nor destroy a marriage over time. However, marriage involves sharing, and Maria should share her frustration or anxiety. She might also point out that she enjoys being with Dave, whether in the car or otherwise. If Maria is the most important thing to Dave, her company in the car should help defuse his impatience. He should be able to sit back and enjoy the ride—even if it is stop and go.

Dave's driving foible may simply derive from a blind spot and/or quirk. But it may be something more. Cutting corners (though not sexual ones) may be a big part of how Dave operates and Maria just does not know that yet. He may do so at work, with his family, or even among his friends. Annoying habits are bothersome, but no reason to rethink a relationship. Annoying behaviors that are part of a larger, troubling pattern could affect the heart of their relationship. These rightfully cause concern and Maria's apprehension may grow over time. In that case, she should revisit the issue with Dave. It may be merely an annoying practice, but it also might reveal a difference in fundamental goals and/or strategies.

Marriage is a very high form of friendship. In order for a marriage to work, spouses need to share the same basic goals and trust each other. If Maria suspects one or more of the major goals are different, in a nice way she has to probe Dave's moral world to make sure they are both headed in the same direction, and can trust each other.

MORAL WORLDS AMONG FRIENDS

Every one of us has our own set of off-limit activities, things we think are unacceptable and determined not to do. We also have goals that are very important to us. Not every friend has to agree with our goals or have the same list of off-limit activities. But if we plan to spend a lifetime with that person, we better agree on the big goals as well as the activities that are way off the reservation.

It is not possible to figure out what people really think about what constitutes right and wrong just by asking, "Do you adhere to the natural law approach to morality?" This is the kind of question that can turn a promising date into a final date. It is simply too in-your-face. And besides, it really does not get to the heart of the matter. Yes, people have to be able to explain why they do some things and fail to do others. But none of us can offer perfectly coherent explanations. Generally we just try to do our best. But even if we get the theory right or the explanation is persuasive, it is not enough.

Moral rationales may be important, but what is even more important is what people actually do. Dave may assert the primacy of truth in one's life but fairly regularly lie to family and friends. In this case there is a big gap between words and deeds. Dave may wax eloquent about the beauty of nature, while defacing the highways and byways with litter. He might talk about the importance of the cultured life and yet always find a reason he can't join Maria at the opera or a concert or on a visit to a museum.

Love can be clear-eyed and still committed, or it can be a blind love that does not mind being fooled. Love in marriage should definitely not be blind to important moral convictions or the correspondence between convictions and practice. The moral world a person inhabits counts, for good and ill.

6

Moral Guidance in Human Nature

THIS BOOK EXPLORES an understanding of morality consistent with the Christian tradition of morality. Yet the premise of the book is that this approach to morality can help all young adults, no matter what religious group they indentify with, figure out how to lead the kinds of lives they want and truly deserve. How is that possible? How can a moral framework be both broadly appealing to all who believe in God and at the same time consistent with the revelation of Jesus Christ as the center of all history?

Natural law does assume a person believes in God, but it does not rely on belief in the divinity of Christ. God is the creator and God places us in the world in a framework by which we can know what God wants us to do. However, the natural law conviction is that by our human nature, we know what it is that we are supposed to strive for and what we are supposed to avoid.

The moral standards in a natural law approach are built on human nature (which is part of the larger "book of nature" referred to earlier). But human nature includes the world in which a man or woman exists. So, for any person, "human nature" includes not just the person, but the community in which he is raised and in which he now lives. It also consists of his relationship to the physical world and includes whatever knowledge he has of himself, society, and science.

Natural law uses as its norm the "plain man" or the "plain woman." The person need not be particularly well educated. She just has to be raised in a community and do the normal things that people do when they are young.

The plain woman or man exists in a larger framework. One reason Western society is so well off is that for hundreds of years people in this culture have been inquisitive about why things are the way they are. The various sciences, which include the physical, biological, and social sciences, seek to understand and explain how nature works, and moral philosophy builds on that understanding. Evolution is a scientific explanation that provides a good, but limited foundation for understanding our present situation. In the opinion of most young adults, including many who believe in God as the creator of the universe, evolution provides a reasonable way to understand at least partially the development of earth and the universe.

Because natural law only requires a belief in God who communicates his will for us through creation and the use of reason, natural law can be convincing to any group of people who value reason and also believe in God the creator. Christians certainly fall in this category. Christians understand that nature and science reveal something about God, and because this conviction is expressed repeatedly in the Old Testament, from earliest times Christians have been attracted to natural law. Understanding ourselves and our deep desires is an important source for learning how God wants us to act. The God of Scripture and the Creator God are the same. Furthermore, God cannot contradict Himself. Christians who do not see evolution necessarily in conflict with the Bible believe that as we come to understand evolution more fully we also perceive better how God made us in His own image and likeness.

NATURE

Figure 6.1 presents a schematic of what "nature" includes. Better, it presents a modern account of how a human person experiences his nature in our modern world. The background represents the physical context in which human beings find themselves "embedded." It includes not only the biosphere all around us, but also the world—such as the solar system and the Milky Way—that extends far beyond earth. Nature also includes all that we are and experience as human beings: our human DNA, the natural appetites that motivate many of our choices and actions, as well as the social context in which we were born and from which we have emerged. The full array of relationships in figure 6.1 will be explored later in the chapter.

Nature Includes DNA

As human beings, our physical organs are determined by DNA. But we now know that over 98 percent of the DNA of human beings is shared with nonhuman primates who are our ancestors, whose own organs are slight variations on those found in other mammals. That means that many of the most important of our biological systems link back millions of years and have been "improved" and made more reliable through evolution. In other words, our breathing, eating, thinking, digesting, procreating, et cetera, are well-honed systems.

One of the most important of these well-honed systems is our emotional system. Linked to our emotions are various human appetites. All of these have a physical basis, but the yearnings produced by the appetites may extend beyond physical satisfaction. The desire to eat and drink, to be physically close to another human being, to have children, to hear and smell pleasant things, to be consoled by beauty, to be afraid of danger, to avoid disease and injury, to be accepted, to be acknowledged, to care for someone in need—these are some of our physical appetites. Because our physical appetites are stimulated in part by connections with the brain, the appetites express themselves partly in the way a human being assimilates culture and her surroundings.

Human beings have complex ways of reacting to various situations, but the quickest and most elemental reactions are emotional or appetitive. For the most part, emotions and appetites are involuntary physical reactions triggered by some chemical change. But because emotions are also linked to the brain via chemical reactions, the brain can review these emotions or even anticipate them. That is, human beings can evoke feelings by specific actions they undertake. For example, watching a movie with a tragic ending can make a person sad. Similarly, sharing a candlelight dinner can make a person feel romantic. Or, looking at a delicious ice cream sundae can make a child hungry.

At various times, our emotions and appetites convey significant information about the most important things in our lives. As important as they are for human beings, however, emotions and appetites are not unto themselves sufficient ground for action but they emit important signals about what we are inclined to do in a given situation. Sometimes they should be followed and sometimes they should not. What makes us specifically human and different from other animals is our ability to employ intellect and conscience and weigh our emotions and appetites when considering what we ought to do. In other words, human beings operate within a moral framework.

Communities

Human beings are unique individuals, to be sure, the pinnacle of nature's hierarchical ladder. (Many scientists do not judge humans to be higher than other types of animals because this is judgment of worth or value, about which scientists *qua* scientists do not offer judgments. Nonetheless, most of us readily consider humans to be more important and have more value than other animals, even if practically all human beings want to avoid hurting animals.) But we are our distinctive selves only within a larger human cavalcade of other unique individuals. We actually come to be in the intimate communion of two individuals. Our prenatal development occurs literally within another human being, our mother. And from the moment of our birth onward we spend all our days living in community.

In figure 6.1 we have identified schematically four human communities, all of which are placed along a fuzzy timeline that indicates past, present, and future. The placement of the communities on the timeline is merely illustrative, and the timeline does not represent an accurate measure of how much earlier one community appeared before another. The timeline merely points out that our present era has been preceded by communities in the past, and, God willing and humans cooperating, there will be other distinct communities in the future. Also, it is likely that one or more communities, such as community A, has an impact on another community centuries later, even though people from community A died

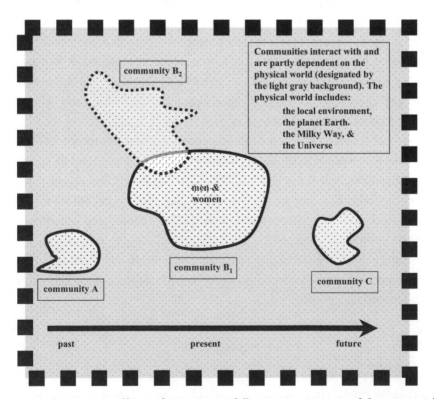

FIGURE 6.1 Communities of human beings exist at different points in time, and they are partially dependent on the physical world surrounding them.

out long ago. For example, within the context of Western civilization, Greek and Roman society still impact the way people in Western society think. In the diagram, community A could refer to Greek and Roman society, while general modern Western communities are designated by B_1 and B_2. In the future, community C will likely be partially influenced by A, B_1 and B_2.

B_1 and B_2 refer to two communities existing at the present time. These two communities overlap both in the sense that some people are members of both communities and that the communities exist at the same point in time, though we suggest by its positioning that B_2 came into existence prior to B_1 and will pass from the scene prior to B_1.

Competition and Cooperation among Communities

Part of the story of evolution is that, in relation to food, fuel, water, materials, technology, the arts, and other resources, various groups of people collaborate and/or (depending on which resources) compete with one another. As was noted above, many of the organic workings of humans are similar to those that exist in other animals. Many things that are instinctual for nonhumans are reflected in human reactions, emotions, and outlooks. Certainly, both competition and cooperation existed among primates. Earlier forms of man—hominids—existed for a few million years before the emergence of the man and woman we call Homo sapiens. It is estimated that Homo sapiens first appeared on the scene approximately two hundred thousand years ago. Thus, men and women with roughly the same biological make-up as our own have been used to a pattern of some competition and some collaboration for a long period of time. Somehow this has become integrated into our emotions and our way of thinking.

By representing communities B_1 and B_2, we highlight the realization by human beings that all societies have two fundamental orientations – competition and cooperation – and both dynamics have been around for more than two hundred thousand years.

People feel and understand that communities are worthwhile and, provided they are nonthreatening, should be protected and enhanced. How much of this feeling and understanding is in our DNA is unclear, but some of it is. People also understand that, if communities are to survive or if there is to be a future community of some description (community C), there are at least two requirements. First, people have to have babies and care for them. Second, people have to contribute to their communities in some way so that they can secure sufficient resources and compete effectively with other groups or communities. There has to be some system of government, customary ways of dealing, or financial understandings whereby resources are made available to provide for the needs of the community. People may differ strenuously about how many resources any particular community needs in order to prosper and how the community should be organized to secure these resources, but all people would agree that some resources are necessary.

VALUES ARE EXPRESSED IN COMMUNITY

In most cases, we do not freely decide to join a community without first spending some time gathering information about the community. Furthermore, the community in which we were raised, with its many institutions, establishes the initial framework in which we make sense of our experience, formulate the pros and cons of our decisions, and articulate expectations for the future. In the previous chapter, we pointed out that long before people consciously think about and decide what they ought to do, they have already assimilated an ethical or moral framework and operated within it. Here we are making a similar point. We are always in community. We may eventually decide to distance ourselves from family, city, country, or even Western civilization. Even then, however, we will look around for another community—no matter how small or distant—in which we anticipate we might better prosper.

Nature broadly conceived to include our experience in community is the norm for the natural law approach. Human beings, living together in community, are able to discern patterns in nature and they make judgments about which actions are good. When people from one culture interact with people from another culture with which there has been almost no contact, confusion is likely to arise initially. After all, the institutions existing in one culture, since they rely on common understandings, may appear not only foreign but odd to the people in the other culture. Despite the initial confusion, human beings in one culture use their own cultural bearings as a way to navigate the new cultural reality. First they try to relate the new culture's institutions, as best they can discern them, to those of their native culture. Then they seek to identify which values the new, unfamiliar institutions promote. After extensive interaction with the new culture, people in another culture, relying on reasoning and conscience, may judge that some aspects of the new culture offer the possibility for greater human flourishing. Other practices of the new culture may be viewed more skeptically or even be harshly rejected by the other culture.

In summary and schematic form figure 6.1 is supposed to capture all the significant relationships with the natural environment and other human beings that a person living in society can have. The only fundamental relationship not directly treated is the very important one with God.

Although the human orientation to and relationship with God is not highlighted in figure 6.1, the diagram allows for God's regular interaction with the world and for man's interaction with God. The interaction with God is visualized by a band of separated blocks on the border of figure 6.1. This stylistic border represents a porous "world below" through which "God above" communicates with us and through which we can communicate with God. God is simply not on the same plane with creation, however. God is infinite, far beyond our comprehension or imagining. Since we are made by God, we know that God must desire the fullness of all things truly human and that God put some of his own traits in us. But God is infinite and we cannot imagine infinite beauty, truth, playfulness, goodness, et cetera. Yet, as we shall see when we provide content to the natural law approach, qualities such as truth, beauty, and playfulness are goals for human beings. Hence, the Creator God must at least affirm those qualities in us, even as he possesses them infinitely Himself.

We live in a culture that questions everything, and in this environment, any-body, even a committed Christian, may have doubts about the existence of God. In order to be inclusive and not make value judgments about the beliefs of others, some people might be inclined to bracket out a relationship with God. However, in order for the natural law approach to be binding in any way on an individual and in order for the natural law approach to conform to our natural orientation to God, one vital component of this approach is that it includes a conviction that a superior, all-knowing and powerful authority exists. For most believers, this superior authority is called God. As we develop the natural law approach in subsequent chapters, we reason that all people who acknowledge that the demands of conscience come from God and who are of good will can (but not necessarily will) also acknowledge the binding power of the natural law.

For two millennia Christian morality has taught both that God has given us natural law as part of our natures and that our conscience tells us we must abide by natural law. We know that many of our intellectual, emotional, appetitive, and religious longings and behaviors depend on our physical nature and are linked to the brain. We also know the brain is necessary for consciousness, though we do not yet know what physical part or parts of the brain plays this supportive role.

In this sense, our higher spiritual powers, such as participating in God's life through grace, must build on very physical things within us. Even our higher spiritual powers, however, presuppose our ability to read nature, to read God's desires for us through the world He created. This is what natural law is. In some sense, therefore, it must be that the natural law is "physically within us," at least in the sense that our most important inclinations are validated as worthwhile by our intellect. The intellect is undoubtedly influenced by community values, but the natural law approach claims the intellect and emotions are "hardwired" toward goods that promote genuine human fulfillment.

We know gene sequences in DNA control most of our physical development. We also realize that to some extent emotions and appetites can be directed and channeled by the intellect. We may be angry, afraid, or amorous, but we can take actions that direct those feelings one way rather than another. Sill, our initial emotions result from our DNA and our personal history, which evolves from our experience in community. It is through these emotions and dispositions that we are attracted to certain things we judge to be good. We like life, knowledge, beauty, friendship, and fun; we have a longing to praise our Creator and we desire to be reasonable in our actions. We are hardwired to seek these things. Both individually and as a society, we affirm that they are good desires. The desires are in our nature and based in our genes.

We also have a conscience. No one has located some physical part of the brain that can be identified as the conscience. However, it is likely that there are physical parts of us (including the brain but not limited to it) that support the activity of the conscience. Of course, the physical substratum is not the same as conscience itself, though it plays an essential supporting role. Similarly, the brain plays an essential role in considering what we will do and what we will not. However, the brain is not the same as free will. The claim of free will is based on our experience. Whether scientists one day will be able to locate free will in a part of the brain is unlikely, since free will is a comprehensive quality the mind recognizes in itself.

In short, whether or not free will can be found physically in us, it is part of human nature. The graces we receive through our Christian community enable us to use our free will to develop ourselves in God's image and likeness, as revealed by the Son, in the choices we make. It is in this way that grace builds on nature. For the next several chapters, however, our focus will be nature, not grace, and what corresponds to our deepest aspirations as human beings.

7

Experiencing the Natural Law

MARIA GREW UP in a small town in the Midwest. She loved the years of her youth as well as the people and community who nurtured her. She enjoyed the regular change of seasons, the activities and joys of harvest, followed by the dark of winter, and then by the scent and colors of spring. She received a fine education in her town and was accepted at a large university on the West Coast. But the change in communities was difficult for her. As welcome and exciting as it was for Maria to live on campus on the West Coast, the switch in communities introduced confusion into her life about basic values. Only now, some years after her college experience, is she in the process of gaining reasonable clarity about her future direction.

As much as she appreciated her upbringing, the secure standards she inherited from her Midwestern rural community were fundamentally challenged by the moral universe of so many students at the university she attended. Only recently has she found a way to combine or sufficiently integrate the thrill of university life with its diverse moral standards, on the one hand, with the security, strong clear morals, and depth of human fulfillment she experienced and, she is convinced, still resides in her community of upbringing.

JUDGING COMMUNITIES

Part of the natural law approach means that we are capable of "judging" communities. The term *judge*, as we use it, does not imply judging individuals in the community to be good or bad, helpful or hurtful, smart or ordinary. Rather, the claim is that, no matter the community in which we are raised, once we have matured through experience, we are capable of discerning activities we participated in which developed us as human beings and therefore yielded true human satisfaction.

Maria enthusiastically embraced the definitely more exciting university community in which she spent four happy years of her life. Her happiness was not unalloyed, since she did encounter difficulties. Nonetheless, she found many activities in the life of that community very compelling and satisfying.

Now she is a young adult and looking to get married. She feels she has to make a fundamental personal judgment about which community or which types of community correspond to what she understands to be genuine human fulfillment.

Maria knows she carries within her the lessons of the two communities. She is not trying to make believe that she has not been molded or formed by those communities. She also realizes the tension that exists between her regular activities in the two communities. Maria knows some things that brought her great satisfaction at both times of her life. She is sure of certain things and doubtful about others. Despite uncertainty about activities in a number of areas, Maria knows she is not wrong about some of these activities or realities. Her confidence stems partly from her greater maturity, her living now in the third community of the business world, and partly from her reflection and prayer.

The natural law approach affirms Maria's conviction that she has the wherewithal to judge correctly. Her judgment will not be primarily a logical one, though she will try to think clearly about the issues.

As a biology major, Maria loved learning about DNA and how it is the code for the full development of the human body. As is true for any person, Maria also knows she is a bundle of emotions, hopes, regrets, aspirations, and longings. She realizes all these feelings or sentiments within her have a bodily foundation. That is, they are supported and made possible by physical organs and processes. Despite the necessary functioning of her bodily organs in order for her to experience these aspirations and sentiments, Maria also knows she partially controls many of these sentiments. Maria values her emotions, aspirations, and even her fears, and she knows they play a role as she forms a judgment about what she considers the most central activities of her young life.

Maria is also experienced in making judgments; unfortunately she has to acknowledge that a good number of her judgments have been faulty. Sill, with the benefit of hindsight, even the faulty ones have alerted her to the dangers of judging in haste or not considering carefully unsavory realities. When she made bad judgments, it was often because she had deceived herself. At the time of the decision she often did not realize her self-deception. Now, with the passage of time, she understands that sometimes she almost knowingly fooled herself. She now has enough experience to know that, if she proceeds carefully, consults with others, and does not shy away from looking at unpleasant realities, she can make good judgments.

Maria's confidence in judging whether some activities are more fully human than others stems not only from her experience but also from a little thought experiment she has used many times since the end of one disastrous college relationship.

This "disastrous relationship" caused Maria to think about and reflect on the patterns of promises and commitments, both within her university community and in her home town. Conflating her observations and reflecting on the bad experience she had in the relationship with a young man, she concocted three marriage scenarios and then pondered them over a period of three or four months. One scenario was that she married a guy whom she liked and with whom she had had sex occasionally before marriage. The second scenario was she married a guy with whom she had lived for two or three years prior to marriage. The third scenario was she married a guy whom she loved but with whom she had not had sex. She assumed he did not expect it before marriage and she could easily wait. These were theoretical scenarios. Of course, she wanted to get married. She tried to treat these scenarios as if they were "value free." That is, she just wanted to explore what she would like best. She focused on what she thought would be most fulfilling for her as a person and an eventual mother. Also, she kept a little journal for several months and on most days she wrote down some reflections of how her feelings changed with respect to the scenarios.

From the beginning she did not like scenario two. Even though it sounded romantic, it seemed to her as if the guy would almost have to be a wimp. They would be living together because he (or, even worse, she!) could not make up his mind. She wanted a husband who was more ready to clearly endorse her. So, scenario two was not something she wanted, if she could avoid it. For the first two months, she was undecided between scenario one (occasional sex) and scenario three (no sex prior to marriage). Both had their appeal. She wanted someone who desired both her and her body; hence the attraction of occasional sexual intimacy. But as the weeks passed by, she became more convinced that scenario three was the most desirable. She reasoned that, just by dating and being with him so often, she could easily tell whether the guy really desired her completely, spirit and body. Also, when they dated and got serious, they would certainly talk about children. She wanted them right away and she would easily be able to read what he wanted. And she liked the fact that the guy could wait for marriage. Very important for Maria, also, was not to put herself in a situation where she could get pregnant. She wanted to get pregnant, but only when she was married, when she was in a position to rejoice in the pregnancy and care properly for her baby. So, by the fourth month, her conviction settled on scenario three and it remained there. This would be her ideal path to her ideal husband and a satisfying marriage.

Maria's deliberation on the three scenarios also clarified for her the type of community she finds fulfilling. She knows there is more to life than just finding the right man, but, at least for her, the central issues revolve around marriage. For her, many decisions related to marriage are influenced by communities.

Part of the process of "judging" communities involves making a determination about where to live, how to live, and with what group of people to live. Maria knows she does not want to live on a farm as in her youth. However, she does want to live with people who support many of the values she learned in her farming community. For instance, although Maria likes city life, she doesn't always like what she thinks of as city ways. Divorce is pretty common among the people Maria has met in the city and at the university. It was rare among the people she knew at home. Maria wants to enjoy the great things about cosmopolitan living but she also wants to live in a community that values faithful lifelong marriage. She knows that people with the best of intentions and good preparation may fail in carrying out their promises. She does not condemn them. However, all things considered, she would like to have a circle of friends that includes many couples who are faithful to one another. She knows this group will help her and that the friendships of her children with their children will be healthier with good role models of biological parents living together.

SCIENTIFICALLY DETERMINED OR SELF-DETERMINED IN COMMUNITY

Although she did not excel academically, Maria did do well in her biology studies, which she enjoyed, in part because she learned so much about the complexity of the human body. However, she also gradually became aware of how narrow biologists could be. For Maria, biologists get some things right and other things they get wrong, mainly because they are too narrow in their deliberations.

In her view, biologists rightly emphasize the importance of replicating results, either in the lab or in the clinic. If strict replication is impossible, comparing similar cases is very important. It is not enough to see a phenomenon once. In order to understand it, one has to understand the conditions under which it arises. This is a reasonable way to study the human body.

But she noted that a good number of the faculty members she admired took very strong stances on things that were influenced by more than just biology. For example, she knows many biologists are strongly pro-choice, pro-human cloning, pro-sexual experimentation in relationships, et cetera. Maria acknowledged their right to have convictions on these issues, but she thought it ridiculous they justified their positions mainly by appealing to biological research. Many things other than biology influence a person's position on these issues. She began to think of biologists as imperialistic and pushing the boundaries of biology into areas not permitted by the science's foundations. Many biologists she knew thought biology itself was sufficient to determine basic political and ethical issues. She was quite sure they were wrong in taking this approach.

As far as Maria is concerned, these biologists were rather narrow empiricists. They emphasized certain kinds of data, but dismissed her personal experience. Because they implicitly looked at her experience as "personal," somehow they interpreted that to mean unreliable and no basis for action. Maria acknowledged that the personal nature of her experience meant it was not open to someone else. But it was nonetheless her experience. She likes science, but she knows many things can be verified by her as true. Others have to look to their own experience to determine whether Maria's conclusions correspond to their own experience.

Maria is confident she can make valid judgments about right and wrong. She now has enough experience to know whether certain activities lead to human fulfillment. She knows her confidence in making such decisions depends in part on the communities in which she has lived. Although people who live in different communities emerge with different views of human satisfaction, what she experienced in her three (home, university, and business) communities has provided her with genuine insight into what belongs at the core of human fulfillment.

Biologists and other scientists live in a community, and they make their judgments based in part on their experiences in those communities. Their moral and political judgments frequently do not fit her experience. Furthermore, she is not going to let these individuals determine her experience. They can make their own judgments about their own experience. However, she is the only person capable of evaluating her own experience and she will evaluate it based in part on the communities in which she has lived. In doing so, she will pursue activities that in her judgment correspond to deep human fulfillment.

8

Sin

MORAL MISTAKES

HUMAN BEINGS MIGHT be hardwired to pursue their own self-interest and do what they perceive is best for themselves, but both history and our own experience tell us human beings are equally adept at doing things that undermine their goals and hopes. In other words, humans seem very adroit at blowing it. What accounts for this apparent contradiction? In a word, sin. Sin is actually a religious word that means an offense against God. Here we expand its meaning, as is often done in common parlance, to signify any action that is against what we know we should or should not do.

THE CONTORTIONS OF SIN

Doing wrong does not promote human flourishing. This chapter explains why that is true. Nonetheless, it is true that people can think doing wrong will benefit them. It may indeed be the case that it benefits them in the short run, but it does not help them become more deeply human. People know this at some level since practically everyone agrees that doing something morally wrong diminishes them as a person. Because we are rational beings and because we understand this, we have to deceive ourselves in some fashion in order to do something that diminishes us. The deception allows us to convince ourselves that certain actions that will actually undermine our well-being are somehow going to help us.

When one contemplates doing something wrong, two general possibilities for deception exist. The first path of deceit is for the person to focus primarily on good intentions or motives, while the second path creates a smoke screen so that a person mentally moves what he knows to be a forbidden action into the area of acceptable actions. In both cases, self-deception takes place.

Any action involves the object of the act, the intention of the act, and the circumstances associated with the act. In this book, the main focus is the object of the act, that is, what happens as a result of the act. Most of this chapter and subsequent chapters in parts I and II focus on the object of the act. Before examining the object of the act, let us briefly consider the issue of proper intentions.

People can deceive themselves fairly easily via good intentions. Along this path of pretense, one chooses to focus on reasonable intentions and distracts oneself from the act itself or the object of the act. Consider the following rationales that people concoct for themselves: Sex before marriage is good because it will lead to marriage and will enable me to have a baby (or enable me to have a loving wife). Lying in this instance is good because I am only trying to protect the other person. Revealing information given to me in confidence by my friend is good because people should know what type of person this is. For me to have an affair with someone is permissible because it will teach my cheating spouse a lesson. Having the abortion is not great, but it is okay, because otherwise the baby would be born into a situation I cannot handle.

In all the above cases, the focus is on the intention; the person does not look carefully at the object of the act but emphasizes instead the good intention that is foremost in the person's mind. But for an act to be morally good, it must naturally lead to participation in one of the fundamental human values without undermining a value. If the object of the act naturally undermines the pursuit of one of the fundamental values, no good intention can elevate the moral value of the act to "good."

It is true that a bad intention can make a naturally good act (i.e., one that does not undermine a fundamental value) bad. If a person gives money to a poor person primarily because he wants to be seen and admired as compassionate by others, the natural object of the act remains good, but because the person is motivated by vainglory, morally speaking the act is bad.

Natural law recognizes the importance of a person's intentions in any action. It also realizes that oftentimes people do not even admit to themselves their true intentions for undertaking some action. While all this is true, the challenge in our age is that people do not examine carefully the object of the act, what the natural result or impact of the act is, and whether the act undermines the pursuit of any fundamental value. For this reason, the focus in this book is on the object of the act, and although deception via good intentions is indeed a regular path of personal moral fraud, we do not dwell on it in this book.

In figure 8.1 our standard figure now includes a buffer zone between the acceptable actions area and the area of forbidden or off-limits actions. The lined area is intended to suggest a smoke screen. Actions in the vertically lined area are in fact off-limits actions. But, a person uses some kind of personal smoke screen in order to deceive himself. To the right of the smoke screen are actions and activities that are acceptable, good, or decent. These may include actions that are fairly far to the right in the diagram. However, when sin occurs, the closeness of acceptable actions is being used, along with the personal smoke or hazy thinking, to justify actions that in fact are in the zone of forbidden actions (which consists of both the dark area and the area with the vertical lines). The smoke screen allows us to distort our perception and in so doing we slide into actions that, were we not so intent on deceiving ourselves, are clearly off-limits.

It is easy to sin, but it requires either at least a few seconds of tricky duplicity or inexcusable blindness. These are the two basic ways to create the blurry or smoky area which, in the diagram, includes forbidden actions. Either we have to be blinded by some sort of selfishness or rage or, alternatively, perform some mental gymnastics that allow us to see good, at least in the short run, in what is actually bad for us as persons, and we are persons for the long run.

A mental blindness is inexcusable if someone is familiar with the relevant facts and patterns but refuses to interpret them in a way that takes the data seriously. Consider Erica, who is in high school with Kimberly. Kimberly is a young woman well-liked by a group of students in school. A nice teenager who is reasonably kind, Kimberly does not say bad things about other students. Nonetheless, Erica chooses to be mean to Kimberly. She does this primarily because Kimberly is popular. The mean girl never sees the good in Kimberly because she is blinded by Kimberly's popularity. Envy blinds Erica and she speaks badly of Kimberly.

For tricky mental gymnastics, think of someone cheating on an exam. The test-taker knows that cheating is wrong, but focuses on some other things, perhaps including intentions. He creates reasons that seem compelling to him. For example, he says the following things to himself: I've been sick and have not had time to prepare for the test. The exam score will determine whether I am accepted to graduate school. My grades have been good and I know he will do well in graduate school when I get in. The exam is a stupid hurdle, he says to himself, and many people think it should be done away with.

In terms of our diagram, at the moment he consults his crib notes or copies from a fellow student, we claim the test-taker perceives the forbidden act to be somewhere in the region of "acceptable" actions. In reality, via a personal smoke screen he is deceiving himself and almost realizes it, but not quite. If he really thought that cheating would diminish his humanity and not be in his self-interest as a person, he would not cheat. In order to cheat, the test-taker needs some cover that allows him to see cheating as good for him. Thus, he commits the bad act "under the guise of the good." The "guise of the good" is actually a phrase used by Thomas Aquinas in the thirteenth century in his book *Summa Contra Gentiles* (2:27). So "the guise of the good" is a traditional explanation for how good and well-disposed people can sin.

The smoke screen enables us to make forbidden actions cloudy and hazy, so that they appear at least fleetingly reasonable to us. It is as if the person is standing in the area of acceptable actions and looking back at a forbidden action. He looks quickly at some good actions, then peers through the smoke at the forbidden action while he is still thinking of the acceptable actions. He deceives himself, at least at the moment of decision. Without completely acknowledging what he is doing, the sinner undertakes an act that definitely belongs in the out-of-bounds area and, despite generally being aware of this, convinces himself that it fits comfortably within the acceptable area. The smoke allows him to see forbidden actions with a nice, comforting haze of acceptability around them. Unless a person can convince himself that certain off-limits, forbidden actions are in some way acceptable or beneficial, he will not go ahead with them.

Any moral act is partly determined by the act itself and partly by the intention of the person committing it. In the case of sin, the intention is to do something the conscience clearly indicates is forbidden. However, through a series of mental

**Actions in Pursuit of a
Single Fundamental Value**

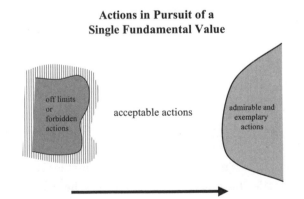

FIGURE 8.1 The smoky or blurry "sin area" is the "lined" buffer zone at the border between acceptable actions and actions that are off-limits. All actions in the shaded and lined zones on the left are off-limits or forbidden actions. However, when committing a sin, a person is able to persuade himself that the sinful action he is contemplating, which falls in the area defined by the vertical lines, actually belongs to the area of "acceptable actions" and not to "off-limits and forbidden actions."

gymnastics sinners deceive themselves about the action or their intentions and in this manufactured state of mind they go ahead and do something wrong. Over time, however, the insight that enabled the person to do something wrong can be perceived as culpable deception.

Consider the example of telling a lie to a trusted friend. A person may convince herself at the moment of the lie that this is really for the best, and that she is only telling the lie to spare her friend hurt and pain. Some weeks, months, or years later, however, she might be on the receiving end of a lie in similar circumstances. At this point, she realizes that her previous rationalization for lying was merely a self-serving ruse. Now she is contrite and realizes that what she did much earlier was more than merely unfair to her friend. Telling the lie, she now realizes, also had corrosive repercussions for her, the one who lied. In her contrition she resolves never to do the same thing again. Even though she might falter and tell another lie, even a big lie, her disposition and intention at the moment of realization and sorrow is a firm resolve to avoid lying in the future.

The reverse of this type of deception is also possible. That is, it is possible to perform an objectively good act—such as working in a soup kitchen—but to do it primarily for self-aggrandizing purposes, such as impressing your boss or polishing your resume. While the intention is wrong in this case, the service-giver might not attend much to the intention. Either by carelessness or by willingly neglecting her motives, she does something that is indeed good and helps others. Nonetheless the act detracts from her human integrity because she did it for an unworthy reason.

EMOTIONS, APPETITES, INTELLECT, IMAGINATION, MEMORY, AND WILL

Profound self-deception is not commonplace. However, in some way, we all live in a world of our own creation that tends to be somewhat more flattering than might be warranted. Self-deception that leads to sin does not have to be profound. Rather, self-serving self-deception is a very human process that can easily come into play whenever we make decisions with some moral import. Human beings have appetites, desires, emotions, imagination, memory, and intellect or reason. All of these play some role in any decision we might make. Whenever we decide to do something – no matter what it is – our practical reason has determined that in some sense it is "good" to do.

This kind of self-delusion seems to be second nature to most of us, and for this reason it is good to ponder whether this type of self-deception can be avoided. Human appetites, desires, emotions, and intellect (which includes practical reason, memory, and imagination) often compete with each other in making claims on the will. In particular, our memory and imagination present us with graphic, alluring images from the past and possibilities for the future if we are willing to commit to certain actions. With greater or less immediacy and accuracy, we perceive what benefits we get by performing certain actions. The decision to go ahead and undertake these actions occurs through the will. But it is a will that is subject to different tugs by practical reason, emotions, appetites, and especially the memory and imagination, which together offer an improved picture of the fine things (or not so great things) that will occur if we actually do what we are contemplating.

Virtuous people accomplish moral good. They do so because they control their appetites and emotions and align their wills with the intellectual judgment of their consciences. They also manage their memory and imagination so that they create realistic images. When people consider something, their emotions may push for a "yes." A realistic imagination, combined with a good memory, may perceive difficulties and disadvantages with moving ahead. If, as a result of these various tugs, their conscience says something is wrong, virtuous people get the signal and avoid the contemplated action. When their conscience says something must be done, such as feeding a starving person, virtuous people act accordingly. Virtuous people are not perfect people, however, and they also sometimes freely act in ways contrary to what their consciences direct. On occasion they too, like all the rest of us, sin.

Ideally, a person should take notice of his appetites, desires, and emotions, and then pay careful attention to judging which actions are acceptable and which actions are morally off limits. To simplify terminology, we combine three things – emotions, elemental desires, and appetites – and refer to them simply as "sentiment." In this book, the words *reason* and *intellect* are often used interchangeably. Judgment is an action of reason or the intellect. Practical reason is the part of the intellect that deals with what we are planning to do. It is contrasted with speculative or theoretical reason, which sorts out arguments in literature, mathematics, science, political science, philosophy, or a host of other academic disciplines. Speculative reason focuses on causes and effects and also whether various generalizations are good guides for thinking.

The will resolves any conflicts between the intellect, on the one hand, and sentiment, on the other. Sentiments arise within us. For the most part we do not control when they arise, though once they appear we do determine the extent to which we attend to them. Mature adults, for instance, can choose to distract themselves from their emotions and redirect their focus, thereby paying little attention to what their sentiments suggest.

Sentiments are effective elements that operate within all of us and, often unbidden, get our attention and motivate us. Powerful and pushy, they are difficult to manage, as they constantly compete for the will's acquiescence, looming large one moment and fading the next. Because these elements are so unruly, taken alone, they do not serve us well as a guide to behavior. Memory and imagination, if properly managed, should enable us to envision fairly accurate outcomes of contemplated actions. In the end, practical reason is the balancing faculty that allows us to evaluate and interpret what we experience affectively and anticipate imaginatively.

COMPLEX DESIRES

In terms of sentiment, we distinguish between emotions and appetites, on the one hand, and desires on the other. Desires are definitely a part of us, but they are more complicated than emotions and appetites. Furthermore, desires often arise at the same time we are experiencing various emotions and appetites. Desires may be elemental, in the sense they proceed from or are directly linked to an emotion or appetite. However, they can also be complex rather than simple. Complex desires are linked to plans of action, which should always be subject to review by reason.

Consider specific examples of simple and complex desires. At any give time people may desire ice cream, comfort, or sexual activity, each of which, as an elemental desire, is neither good nor bad. However, if those desires motivate a particular plan to maybe steal ice cream, get drunk, or have sex with another's spouse, the desire is bad because it is linked with a plan to do something wrong. Each complex desire we have has to be interpreted and evaluated by practical reason because it involves a plan of action. Consequently, for the purposes of this book, we consider complex desires as engaged in reasoning. When we refer to simple desires apart from any plan, we will be pointing to an undeveloped wish or yearning proceeding directly from an emotion or appetite.

Sentiment is akin to desire. However, as we noted earlier, sentiment alone is an insufficient basis for action. Our actions have to be imagined and then balanced and reviewed by practical reason that makes an evaluation whether the desires arising from sentiment are at least reasonable. If practical reason judges that actions are not in this category and are among the forbidden actions, the will should turn away from them and they should avoided. Practical reason considers whether actions are good or bad. If, on the other hand, actions are deemed acceptable, the will is under no moral constraint and can choose how to proceed. In this latter case, the will can either favor sentiment or practical reason. Favoring sentiment that sometimes merely reflects a passing whim may result in actions that, while morally acceptable, do not further a person's own best interests.

One typical way for sin to occur is that a person's sentiment tugs strongly on the will for attention and action. Combined with memory and imagination, it presents demands to the will and wants action. The demands of sentiment are analogous to a child in a store insisting his mother buy him a toy he fancies. The toy is there, in his hands, and he wants it, now! No practical reason, all sentiment. He can easily imagine the fun he will have with the toy as soon as he gets home. Clearly, for a child, the insistent demand for the toy is not sinful, just childish. For an adult, whose intellect and conscience are developed, it can be sinful to yield to the demands of sentiment alone.

In an earlier example, a person tells a lie to a friend who trusts her. By doing so, she avoids some painful acknowledgement to herself or her friend. In another example, a guy cheats on an exam. He passes and is guaranteed entrance to graduate school. In both cases, against better judgment, sentiment was allowed to overrule intellect. Sometimes it is better to do the more difficult thing, precisely because it keeps one's heart and mind clear and pure in the pursuit of the fundamental values.

SERIOUS AND LESS SERIOUS SIN

Understanding what counts as serious sin, as opposed to less serious or venial sin, is not difficult. However, applying the general principles to particular cases requires careful distinctions. Because space does not permit that type of analysis in a book of this size, we restrict ourselves to what is fairly straightforward.

A seriously bad action severely undermines the pursuit of one or more fundamental values. "Undermines" means that it either frustrates pursuit of the value in the present moment, because it moves away from participation in the fundamental value, and/or it impairs the ability to pursue the same fundamental values in the future. Notice that the use of the phrases "my pursuit" and "my ability" have been avoided. The reason is that, in addition to constraining the person's pursuit of the fundamental value, a major impact of a person's action may be that it impairs the ability of someone else to pursue one or more fundamental values.

A full presentation of the fundamental values is offered in chapters 10, 11, and 12. The claim will be made that an action that is directly contrary to pursuit of one of those fundamental values is corrosive. In order to be able to illustrate what constitutes actions that are seriously corrosive in this section, the reader will have to take it for granted that some fundamental values are, indeed, fundamental. In particular, the examples used in this section assume that friendship is a fundamental value. As is the case for each fundamental value, friendship should be broadly construed. Not only does it include relationships among friends as normally understood, but it also includes the close bonds among family members as well as the loose bonds among people working in the same firm, belonging to a particular city or country, or members of a club or fraternity.

Consider a simple example: Someone steals $5,000 from a middle-income family. This act certainly impedes the family's ability to pursue the fundamental values, and this act is seriously wrong. So, even though the deed is the thief's action, the adverse impact is not just on him. "Winning" or being granted a $5,000 salary increase, on the other hand, may impede my competitor on the job whom I beat out for the raise, but in that instance my actions were not directed against the competitor; rather, they were presumably ethical actions undertaken to benefit the firm for which I am working. Using the same reasoning, stealing $10 from a friend or relative is corrosive, but whether it is seriously so depends on circumstances. The action may not impair the friend's or relative's ability to pursue the fundamental values to any serious extent, but it may indeed seriously jeopardize the friendship or the trust which is essential for family life.

In general, the seriousness of a moral wrong in the natural law tradition depends on how much the act impairs the pursuit of the fundamental values. A child who tells an ordinary lie to his parents does wrong, but he does not usually prevent himself or his parents from pursuing the fundamental values in any serious way. However, a young man who lies to his parents regularly because he does not want them to find out he has a girlfriend, which his parents have explicitly forbidden, puts himself in some jeopardy (see below about near occasions of sin), but even more importantly prevents his parents from acting in ways that will assist his development as a moral person. It is seriously wrong to deceive his parents in this way.

Solemn promises—such as marriage and vows made by a religious sister, priest, or brother—are important activities. The person who makes such a promise calls upon the community to bear witness to her public affirmation that she will abide by her promise and not undertake actions that directly jeopardize fulfilling the promise. Furthermore, by making the promise public, a person invites the assistance of one's family and friends in keeping the promise. In the case of marriage and religious life, one is committing to a very high realization of the fundamental value of friendship and/or religion. For this reason, an act that goes directly contrary to the intended goal—friendship for life in the case of marriage, for example—is very corrosive, not only of one's own pursuit of the value of friendship and that of one's spouse, but it also weakens a social commitment to keeping one's promises. Consequently, adultery is seriously wrong, or, using a traditional

Catholic term, a mortal sin. Similarly, a religious sister who vows not to own anything of her own but maintains a large bank account for her own purposes commits a mortal sin or does something seriously wrong.

Yet another factor influencing the degree of corrosiveness of an act is its potential to trap a person in repeated actions of the same kind. Absent a good medical reason, taking addictive drugs only a few times can change a person's life for the worse. For this reason, taking addictive drugs or engaging in addictive actions is seriously wrong and corrosive. Impermissible sexual contact usually has a bewitching and disruptive effect on oneself and at least one other person; for this reason it is usually seriously wrong even for unmarried persons.

Finally, how wrong or corrosive an action is also depends partially on awareness and freedom. In order to do something seriously wrong, one has to know that the act is wrong and still freely intend to perform it. One might deceive oneself, as was described above, but after the deed, the person may still acknowledge he knew the action was seriously wrong. The person also has to freely choose to commit the deed, if the deed is to be judged seriously wrong. He cannot be compelled to do it or commit it by happenstance without realizing what he was doing. In the same way, in order for a person to do a good act, he has to intend that the act be in accordance with the fundamental values.

NEAR OCCASIONS OF SIN

By experience and/or by attending to others, we all know some circumstances are more morally dangerous that others. In some situations sentiment or passion very forcefully present imperious demands to the intellect and will. Some of these situations are common to practically everybody, while others tend to be unique to a given individual. We all experience sin's danger zones, or what are often termed near occasions of sin, be they commonplace or peculiarly our own. It is important for each of us to know our personal near occasions of sin. That is especially true if we hope to lead virtuous and ethical lives.

A young single man walking along a crowded street holding hands with a young single woman to whom he is physically attracted is not in a near occasion of sin. However, the same young man is probably wallowing in a near occasion of sin if he is slightly buzzed, sitting with that same young woman at 3 A.M. in her bedroom, and with no one else in the room. And so is she. Reason, prudence, and religious traditions teach that we should avoid near occasions of sin. In these circumstances sentiment presses so strongly upon us that it is very difficult for the will to choose in favor of reason. A sensible person who wants to lead a good moral life avoids near occasions of sin. A fair amount of parenting involves parents first of all making clear to their children what constitutes a near occasion of sin for any person of the child's age and what constitutes a near occasion of sin for this particular child. Both are important insights for a child to attain moral maturity. Equally important is for parents to help the child acquire the moral skills necessary to avoid near occasions of sin. More will be said about near occasions of sin when moral skills are addressed in part III.

9

Bitter Human Failings

SIN OCCURS RATHER easily and not infrequently. Most of us can be sympathetic when listening to stories about sin because we have all been there. Despite its superficial appeal, however, sin undermines our humanity. Sin involves willful blindness, as is illustrated in the separate experiences of Dave and Maria.

YOUNG ADULT BLINDNESS

Dave was a senior in a private urban high school. For some time, he had been annoyed at his mother; especially during his senior year, she had restricted his activities with his friends. On weekdays when he had school, she insisted he had to be home by 7 P.M. and to stay home and do his homework. On the weekend, he was allowed to go out with his friends, but his mother required him to be home by 1 A.M. This meant he had to leave his friends at midnight and then take the bus home. Dave had complained often to his mother about this, but she said that his priority in his senior year still had to be academics and she wanted him to get into a good college.

Because money was tight, Dave's mother was always careful with it. She was a single mother raising three children and it was always a stretch to pay the bills. His mom always enjoyed the time she spent with her children at home, but the demands of two jobs often kept her away in the evenings. One evening, Dave found a single $50 bill just outside his mother's bedroom. He was delighted with the unexpected windfall and pocketed it to use when going out with his friends. Later that night when his mom came home she began looking frantically for the $50 that she intended to use for a special purpose. She asked both Dave and his two younger sisters whether they had seen any money in her room, where she was sure it must have been. They all said no and that was the end of the matter. Because he had not technically lied to his mother, Dave felt he was off the hook and then happily spent the money with his friends. It wasn't until years later that he thought of the matter again.

College was a great experience for Dave. He gained wonderful new friends at college and in the waning months of his senior year he was pleased to have landed a job at a very good firm. Commencement was wonderful. He had such a sense of achievement, and his mother was so pleased for him. He did not like saying good-bye to his friends, but he knew he would see them again. His mother arranged a graduation party for him about three weeks after commencement and many of his friends came. Dave's family never had much money, but somehow his mother had saved enough for a really nice celebration. At the party, his only well-to-do relative, Aunt Tully, gave him a card and said there was something in it for him.

When Dave opened the envelope from Aunt Tully the following day, it had a nice note and it contained two crisp $50 bills. When Dave saw the money he suddenly remembered the event of four years earlier. It dawned on him how hard his mother had been working for him, only wanting him to succeed in high school and college so that he could have a good life. He was in tears, thinking about how cruel and thoughtless he had been. He could hardly believe that he had taken $50 that he knew she needed for the family and spent it on himself.

Dave was upset with himself the whole day and he did not know what he would do. He did not really want to tell his mother what he had done, especially when she was feeling so pleased and proud of him. But he knew he had to do something, and he came up with an alternate plan. Dave's mom loved to garden in her free time and over the years she had worked hard on the garden in their front yard; she particularly liked flowering shrubs. Dave was pretty clueless about plants and shrubs, but he could identify azaleas. So, he went to Home Depot and bought two azalea bushes and brought them home. He then presented them to his mother with a card, thanking her for all she had done for him in high school and college. On the card, he wrote that part of the gift was that he would work with her and help her plant the azalea bushes in the front of the house. Naturally, Dave's mother was thrilled, and she thanked God privately that her son had turned out all right.

FALSE COMFORT

Just before she graduated from the university on the West Coast, Maria did something that seemed compassionate at the time, but later caused her much regret.

Among Maria's suitemates, Amanda was without a doubt her favorite. Amanda's family lived in California, although they had originally come to the United States from Mexico. Unlike Maria, who had only one sibling, Amanda had many brothers and sisters and a large extended family. Maria and Amanda could not have been more different, and yet they had become very close over the course of their college years.

Shortly after Christmas vacation of their senior year, Amanda met a young man and soon began spending more and more time with him and less and less time in the dorm. Amanda had always said she wasn't interested in having sex before marriage, but since she spent most nights at her boyfriend's, Maria and the other girls in the suite assumed that "falling in love" had changed her mind.

One afternoon about three weeks before graduation, Maria and Amanda were in the suite by themselves. Amanda seemed a bit edgy and it was clear she really wanted to talk. At first she spoke a bit about the anxiety of graduating and getting a job. But then Amanda brought up the topic of abortion, which was a bit unusual. Abortion had only come up once before among the suitemates, and that had been a political discussion. This time was different. Amanda wanted to know whether Maria thought abortion was always wrong. One of the things Amanda liked about Maria was that she had such clear moral views and was always able to explain them so that they made sense to Amanda's way of thinking. Maria was a bit taken aback by the question. She didn't know how Amanda felt about the issue and she didn't want to come on too strong in her reply.

Maria gave the best short answer she could. Basically she said that, whatever the law was, she did not see how a potential mother could justify ending her own baby's life. If the mom was healthy and nothing else occurred, the young life, which was already human and alive, would become a real baby. Amanda pointed out that a mother needed to be ready to care for and raise her baby. Maria agreed, but she said that the possibility of becoming a mother is one reason she decided not to have sex until she got married. Maria didn't tell Amanda, but about two years earlier for a few tense weeks Maria thought she might be pregnant; this was during what she and her suitemates later commonly referred to as Maria's "disastrous relationship." It had scared Maria to death and she was determined to never allow herself to be in that situation again.

Amanda listened thoughtfully while Maria was giving her views and raised one or two objections. A little while later, however, one of the other suitemates came in with news of a job offer she had received. Naturally, the conversation shifted and the issue of abortion never came up again.

About a week before graduation, Maria and some of the other girls were sitting around discussing the activities of Senior Week, when Amanda came in and after a quick hello went directly to her room, shutting the door behind her. It was obvious to everyone Amanda had been crying. The girls urged Maria to see what was up. When she entered, Amanda was sobbing and just could not stop. Eventually she just blurted out, "I hate myself, I hate myself, I can't believe what a jerk I am. Now I will never be a good mother. How could this have happened?"

Pretty soon it became clear that Amanda had just returned from an abortion clinic where she had ended a pregnancy. Maria could see how distraught Amanda was. She seemed so desperate and Maria just wanted to comfort her and make her feel better. She rubbed Amanda's back and kept telling her, "Don't worry, you did what you thought was right. Things will be all right. It's not that bad. You'll have another chance to be a mother. You'll be a good mother." For her part, Amanda said a number of times, "Please don't tell anyone I had an abortion. I don't want them to know I am a bad person."

Amanda finally drifted off to sleep. Maria went back to the girls and explained that Amanda had broken up with her boyfriend and was taking it very hard. Not surprisingly, a week later they actually did break up.

In the ensuing days, Amanda would appear briefly in the apartment and then leave. She explained that her relatives were visiting and she was spending time with them. Maria invited Amanda out for coffee and they chatted for a bit, but Maria avoided any talk about the abortion. Then came graduation, and Maria and Amanda had no contact for months after that.

Maria's heart went out to Amanda, but Maria began to feel she herself had not handled the situation very well. Maria knew Amanda was a strong Catholic and that Amanda's tears and words were a clear sign she knew she had messed up in a big way. Maria had no moral qualms telling the girls that Amanda had broken up with the boyfriend. Personally, Maria felt that was going to happen anyway, even if it had not yet occurred. What did bother Maria was what she said to Amanda as she tried to comfort her. Maria kept saying, "You did what you thought was right.... It's not that bad." Maria just wanted to comfort Amanda, but she knew it was wrong to say this. Amanda was upset precisely because she did not believe this. Maria should not have minimized what happened by saying, "It really doesn't matter; after all, you can get pregnant again." Amanda did something she knew was terribly wrong and that's why she was so upset. Amanda was ashamed of herself. She absolutely did not want even her other suitemates to know what she had done.

When Maria thought about what had happened she realized she was wrong to minimize things. She had not really given Amanda any true comfort. Maria should have acknowledged what Maria knew, namely, that she had done something really wrong. She could have tried to help Amanda face things and then maybe take another step that would have been more comforting. Maria realized it would have been much better had she said something like, "Amanda, you were confused, you were upset. We'll find a way to get you back on track. Together we'll overcome this setback." Something along these lines would have avoided repeating the lie that abortion does not make much difference. Furthermore, in the days after the abortion, Maria should have spoken with Amanda about how she felt. She also could have volunteered to help her connect with the Project Rachel program, which helps young women who have had an abortion and would like to talk with someone honestly about it. This would have been something positive. At the same time that Maria's offer would have acknowledged Amanda did something wrong, Maria would be saying, "I will do whatever it takes to help you heal and get back on track."

THE MORAL

Acknowledging serious personal sin is sometimes quite difficult. We can be blind ourselves to it. We can also fool ourselves into thinking a comforting lie is better than honest compassion when dealing with others. Acknowledging our sinfulness can occur quickly after the sin. More frequently, when big issues are involved it takes a long time. Once people realize they have sinned, they genuinely want to do something to get things back in order, to get on the right track again. We all need honest and compassionate friends who will help us tell the truth about what we have done and stand by us as we try to move forward.

10

Fundamental Values

THE BASIC PRINCIPLES of natural law have remained consistent over centuries of ethical discussion and debate. But exactly how those principles are understood and explained has varied. This book relies on one explanation that is based on fundamental values. In this approach seven values—*life, knowledge, beauty, friendship, playfulness, religion,* and *practical reasonableness*—are deemed intrinsic to being human. The claim is that in the context of their own community all people can recognize how various good activities are oriented toward the pursuit of one or more of these fundamental human values.

CRITERIA FOR A FUNDAMENTAL VALUE

Obviously, to be truly "fundamental" or "fundamentally human," a value has to be centrally important for everyone. More carefully expressed, seeking the value through particular activities or practices should yield genuine satisfaction to each person. A fundamental value should be one we know by experience and reflection belongs to the heart of what it means to be human. Figuring out which values those are is a challenge. Polling every person in the world is not feasible, nor does it get to the heart of it. In the end, the values that humans call fundamental have to correspond to our being, the way we are made, the way we are constituted, in part by our DNA.

With that in mind, we can begin a process of ruling some values in and some values out of the "fundamental" category. In order to be "fundamental," values must satisfy three criteria. First, individuals must be committed to pursuing them through their actions and resistant to acting in ways that undermine them. This means that individuals not only think a value is significant, they also demonstrate respect for it in what they say and what they do. At least in most instances—in their good selves—people act in ways that allow them to participate in the value, and they avoid any activities that undermine the value. Second, values are fundamental when respect for them extends beyond individuals to the whole of human society. Fundamental values are those values deemed to be such an integral part of being human that it is inconceivable to imagine a decent human society in which they are not pursued and respected. The activities used to pursue the values may be particular to a community or society. One society may struggle to understand how another society pursues a fundamental value through the particular activities of that society. Nonetheless, if the value is truly fundamental, any member of one society coming in contact with another society wants to understand how the other society pursues each fundamental value. Finally, values are fundamental when they are perceived as precious gifts that are ultimately beyond our complete grasp. That means there has to be an infinite quality to fundamental values so that no action, no matter how elevated, can be the best or ultimate way to participate in them. For any fundamental value, there are always other deeper, more elevated, or more intense ways to participate in it than those we have experienced or imagined. In other words, even though we can only participate in them through particular, finite actions, fundamental values themselves are always forever beyond us.

A corollary of this third criterion is that fundamental values are gifts that keep on giving. No matter how many people participate in fundamental values, no matter the extent to which some individuals excel in pursuing them, the values themselves can never be exhausted. They can always be fulfilled in more ways and by more people. Furthermore, people are grateful to share in fundamental values, no matter how many others also share in a similar way.

Even though a fundamental value is experienced as a gift, people may have to work hard to participate in it. For example, whether in humans, nonhuman animals, or plants, the value of life is a wonder we do not entirely control and something that brings us great satisfaction. However, in order to maintain good health and thereby participate in the value of life, we may have to exercise regularly and avoid eating foods which are not good for us. That takes hard work.

As a way to clarify the criteria for fundamental values, it might be helpful to consider two prominent values: work, on the one hand, and freedom, on the other.

These two realities have value, but our claim is that they do not qualify as fundamental values.

Employing a slang term, one can distinguish two types of work: drudge work and creative work. Drudge work is onerous and repetitive and barely requires resourcefulness. Creative work may be repetitive, but the person involved in this work is at least occasionally looking for ways to conserve resources, enhance the quality or volume of output, persuade or instruct people, or discover new uses for existing products. The distinction is not really between intellectual and physical work, since some intellectual work is onerous and can be repetitive and boring. A teacher marking objective exams is a good example. Reading very similar responses and making notations based on these responses becomes very tedious if there are many exams to be marked. Nonetheless, marking the exams enables students to better participate in the fundamental value of knowledge. Farming is an ambiguous example. On the one hand, farming can be repetitive and at times onerous, but at least for some people it involves exploring new ways to conserve resources or enhance yields. But even farming enables people to participate more fully in the fundamental value of life. As we shall see in a subsequent chapter, creative work participates in the fundamental value of practical reasonableness and usually enables participation in other fundamental values. Thus, creative work, while not a value in itself, creates resources or ways to participate in a fundamental value.

Most work is creative in some way. But whether drudge or creative, work is valuable because it provides ways to participate in fundamental values. Work itself is not a fundamental value, but rather an action leading to participation in a fundamental value.

Drudge work, on the other hand, is something we would prefer not to do. Although we may be grateful we are healthy enough to do drudge work and even though drudge work may keep us in pretty good health, health is something that falls under the fundamental value of life. Drudge work is something necessary in every society known to man. Without it, goods necessary for society cannot be produced. That is, drudge work is necessary for the production of materials or goods that are helpful in pursuing the fundamental values. But work itself is not always experienced as a gift. Not only is drudge work a means to pursue the fundamental values, it is by our definition a burdensome means. Furthermore, if we encountered a society in which people did not have to do drudge work, we would be amazed, perhaps a bit skeptical, but probably also delighted, recognizing as we would that such people could still participate extensively in all seven fundamental values and thereby strive to be completely human.

In sum, creative work is a way to participate in the fundamental value of practical reasonableness and likely other fundamental values as well. Drudge work, on the other hand, is purely instrumental; it enables us to earn or make resources that can be used to pursue the fundamental values. Neither type of work is a fundamental value in itself, but both types enable participation in fundamental values.

Freedom is an important instrumental value that is necessary in a just society and allows individuals admirable flexibility in the pursuit of the fundamental values. However, freedom is not a fundamental value because it is not sought for itself. If we had as a goal freeing ourselves from all constraints, we would not be living truly human lives. For instance, a person who wanted complete freedom and made no commitments would have no friends.

One could make an argument that being completely free would prepare people to lead truly human lives since they could then decide how they wanted to participate in life, knowledge, friendship, beauty, playfulness, religion, and practical reasonableness. But until we actually choose to do things, we can't increase our participation in the fundamental values. Unless we enter into the constraints that particular commitments entail, we are not engaging in the human project. Therefore, freedom is a very important value and a necessary means toward more effective participation in the fundamental values, but it is not a fundamental value itself.

HIERARCHY WITHIN BUT NOT AMONG THE FUNDAMENTAL VALUES

There is no hierarchy among the fundamental values, but there is a hierarchy within each value. For some fundamental values the internal hierarchy is objective. In the others, individuals create an implicit one of their own.

Each fundamental value is recognized as worthwhile in itself, and among the seven no one is more valuable than another. The only priority that exists stems from the relative preeminence of life. Unless a person or other animal is alive, participation in other fundamental values is impossible. Human life is a *sine qua non* for participation in the other fundamental values and therefore life in its various forms should be sought and protected. If we eat poorly, fail to exercise, or lack medical care, we can die early, foreclosing the possibility of participating in the other fundamental values. We are called to protect and nurture the gift of life, not treat it as disposable.

But even the value of life does not enjoy an absolute priority among the other fundamental values. One can easily imagine situations where parents would freely and legitimately give up their lives to save the life of a child, or a person would freely and responsibly give up her life so as not to divulge knowledge personal to him or someone else, knowledge important for the safety of his country or other people, or refuse to lie about their religious commitment in order to save their life. As a value among the other fundamental values, life enjoys a general priority, but not an absolute one.

Within an individual fundamental value, a hierarchy exists. Some people, things, or activities participate in these values at a higher level than others simply by being or by what they do. For example, human life is higher than non-human life and knowledge of how the world works is higher than knowledge of sports scores. In general, people committed to the fundamental values try to realize each value at a high level and do not act directly contrary to any value.

One might think that killing an animal corrodes the fundamental value of life. However, if killing an animal enables a human to maintain his health and stamina, life at a higher level is being promoted. That is, life at one level is being not just disadvantaged but destroyed, while it is being sustained or advanced at a higher level. In this case, it is appropriate to make a distinction between an action being against a value, but not corrosive of the pursuit of the value. This situation contrasts with an action being directly contrary to the value, which would indeed be a corrosive act. The decisive moral issue in killing animals is the degree to which meat is necessary for the overall health of human beings.

Some people are vegans, and admirably so. Nonetheless, others argue that, as long as animals of certain types exist in sufficient abundance, one can eat "lower" animals and plants of these types. According to this view, the taking of nonhuman life, be it plants or animals, is permitted because this activity supports life at a higher level. Should there come a time when human beings could be healthy without eating other animals, they should not kill them for consumption. In our current society, however, a reasonable argument can be made that eating fish, poultry, and meat from other animals in moderation promotes the highest level of life, which is human life.

Sometimes the hierarchy within a particular value is contested. For example, some people treat human life in the womb as if it were different from human life outside the womb. However, fetal life is still human life and, with modern medicine, the fetus is only very rarely a physical threat to the health of the mother, and even in this case the life of the mother is not "higher than" the life of the baby. Just as you cannot kill innocent people, you cannot take the life of a baby in the womb. The DNA of a baby in the womb is the same as the DNA of the baby once born. Life in the womb is true human life and it depends completely on maternal and social protection.

Knowledge is also a fundamental value we are supposed to respect by telling the truth and avoiding lies. Sometimes it appears that by telling a small lie a life or many lives might be saved. The difficulty with allowing this type of exception is that truth is then treated as a means to some higher end. In this case, truth is no longer a fundamental value, that is, an end in itself. Also, by allowing a small deviation for the sake of another value, one is on a slippery slope. First, small deviations in seeking the truth may lead to large personal or societal deceptions. Second, small deviations in telling the truth to ourselves might lead to a willingness to act against, initially in small ways, other fundamental values. The more pernicious effect is the clarity of and respect for truth in society. Lies multiply and soon truth is no longer being respected in society. If compromises with the truth are easy to strike and socially acceptable, society loses the ability to educate children in the truth and even the ability to have conversations that mean something.

To overcome the difficulty outlined above, some societies allow small but significant distinctions to be made that do not undermine truth and knowledge as values. As we have pointed out, each value is important in itself and cannot be played off against other values, even the value of life. Because life is such an important value, some societies allow the distinction between a lie, on the one hand, and withholding the truth or making a misleading but still true statement, on the other. However, lying itself is impermissible because we are not supposed to act directly contrary to knowledge in order to promote life. In addition, in some situations one does not reasonably expect the truth. For example, a person telling a joke may initially start telling a story as if it really took place. But soon enough it becomes obvious that this is a fictional story which hopefully ends in a humorous way. Similarly, in order to be polite and not offend people, praise is sometimes lavished on things that don't deserve great praise. For example, a niece may respond very positively when Aunt Millie asks whether her rather outlandish hat is beautiful. In this case, the hat is perhaps not beautiful in itself, but beautiful for Aunt Millie because her niece knows what a good person Aunt Millie is.

It is also true that for some fundamental values, no objective hierarchy is possible. As we will see in the next chapter, fundamental values such as playfulness, religion, and some types of beauty are sufficiently social or personal that a predominantly personal hierarchy within these values corresponds to the value itself. In these cases, a personal hierarchy or a social one may be sufficient to protect the interests of all people in society and still show respect to the fundamental value.

Obviously, correctly identifying the hierarchy within a particular fundamental value can raise tricky issues. For this reason, all good societies look to clear-thinking individuals to sort through these various positional issues. They also rely on social groups that pursue the values in an exemplary way and avoid activities that undermine the values. Although in some cases in this book we offer reasons to justify hierarchies of actions, for the most part we will merely assume traditional ones exist. As valuable as a careful discussion about internal hierarchies might be, it is not the focus of this book.

CORROSIVE ACTIONS, ONCE AGAIN

In earlier chapters we presented diagrams that included an area labeled "forbidden actions," and when we spoke about large and small sins we referred to "corrosive actions." Having presented the fundamental values approach, it is now easier to explain why "forbidden" and "corrosive" can be used interchangeably.

First, it is important to point out who does the forbidding. Institutions always designate some actions as forbidden, but they do so with the experiential support of institutional members or participants. After all, adults can choose the institutions in which they participate. Authorities such as the Catholic Church, other Christian churches, other non-Christian traditions, or a code of law passed by a legitimately elected legislature may well forbid certain actions. Some individuals choose to avoid these actions because they concur with the judgment of these institutions that the particular action or practice undermines one or more fundamental values. Others accept the prohibitions as reasonable ways to pursue the fundamental values, even though they would prefer to deviate from the institutional norms. In both cases, the individuals at least minimally buy into the prohibitions of certain activities.

Institutions draw upon human beings to participate in society through specific practices. If institutions last for centuries, it is often because they fulfill an important social function. Deeply embedded in all of us are basic human yearnings that stem from our genetic make-up and are molded or encouraged by various institutions. We yearn for the fundamental values and institutions provide us with coordinated ways to pursue them. The institutions that do so most effectively endure.

Institutions can certainly be unjust, and for this reason the activities promoted by them must be examined regularly to assure they respect the fundamental values. Similarly, prohibiting certain activities should serve the purpose of engendering respect in society for the fundamental values in question. We cannot possibly respect knowledge if we are telling lies, nor can we enthusiastically support beauty while defacing a beautiful statue, painting, or building. Such activities undermine the values a person claims to support. If large numbers of people undertake such activities publicly, society has a responsibility to take some action that is likely to diminish the extent to which the fundamental value in question is being undermined or corroded in the public sphere.

The fundamental values themselves are abstractions. Life, friendship, beauty, et cetera, remain and continue to be fundamental values even when many people act directly contrary to them. Contrary actions do not taint or diminish the values in themselves, although they do impact the human perception of the values and perhaps the attraction of people to them. In a sense, the fundamental values are untouchable, because they are ideals, but not in the sense of being unreal. Despite the fact that we neither touch nor reach the pinnacle of the fundamental values, each one nonetheless has a real impact on us. They attract us and when we act in ways that participate in the value we experience satisfaction.

Participation in fundamental values comes through individual actions. As a result of these actions we come to understand that there are always other actions that enable us to participate more deeply in these values. From the series of actions we perform we gradually perceive an ideal goal, the result of an infinite number of increasingly deeper actions that each more profoundly participates in the particular value. So at the very least, our actions are an essential component of our ability to imagine the values and the exemplary actions that participate in them.

In figure 10.1 we have repeated the standard diagram to highlight two aspects of the pursuit of the fundamental values. First and foremost, the title indicates the diagram refers to a "single" fundamental value. That is, instead of a single diagram, there really should be seven diagrams, one for each fundamental value. As this chapter emphasizes, fundamental values are pursued through specific actions. For any fundamental value, movement toward the right side of the diagram often deepens our understanding of that value and perhaps other values as well. The reason is that most actions are complex ones that pursue several fundamental values. For example, a simple visit to a friend sick in the hospital may deepen our appreciation not only of friendship but also of life, knowledge, and playfulness. The second feature to note in figure 10.1 is that, in order to flourish as human beings, we have to avoid corrosive actions in each one of the seven fundamental values. The reasons are that a corrosive action in pursuit of a particular fundamental value actually moves us further away from that value, not closer to it, and corrosive actions cloud our perception of the that value.

Just as acts that participate in the fundamental values deepen our understanding, experience, and appreciation of the values, so too acts that are corrosive of the fundamental values distort our understanding, experience, and appreciation of the values. In fact, as we have seen, choosing a corrosive action is only possible within the context of some kind of distortion. In order to do something directly contrary to a fundamental value, we have to allow ourselves to be blinded by the immediate good perceived or convince ourselves not only that the action is

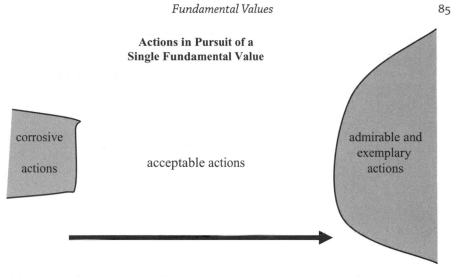

FIGURE 10.1 With two exceptions, this diagram is the familiar one used in earlier chapters. First, by including the word "single" in the heading, we highlight the fact that a similar diagram exists for each of the seven fundamental values. Second, for each fundamental value, there is a shaded region on the left labeled "corrosive actions." These actions move us away from, not toward, the particular fundamental value and they impede our ability to clearly perceive the particular fundamental value.

benign, but also that it will actually benefit us and perhaps also benefit others. Such confusion increases the likelihood we and perhaps others choose corrosive actions in the future.

If enough people in society participate in a pattern of corrosive actions, an institution itself may be corroded. That is, the institution may no longer be a carrier of one or more of the fundamental values. Instead, it may promote activities that undermine these values. And if enough institutions endorse corrosive actions, the culture itself can be corroded, in the sense that the culture is blocked from seeing the evil resulting from the actions of many, who may constitute a significant segment of society.

People also choose to avoid certain actions not only because they are corrosive in themselves but also because they have a corrosive impact on memory. We remember when we do things that undermine the fundamental values. If our undermining is serious, such as harming someone physically or emotionally, we feel guilty about it. We know we did something wrong and we want to set things right, but we don't know how to undo the harm. Unattended guilt corrodes because it keeps us tethered to harmful past actions and distracts us from concentrating on the present and the good and exemplary actions we should be about. Because guilt weighs us down, seriously corrosive actions cloud or impair our future actions.

POLITICAL AND ECONOMIC IMPLICATIONS OF THE FUNDAMENTAL VALUES

Behind the acknowledgment of the fundamental human values is a simple logic that is the basis for an important moral principle, the principle of solidarity. These values are *fundamental* because all people should seek to realize them and also because all people should be in a position to actually do just that. The particular ways people realize these values often depend on the societies or communities in which they are raised. But the various actions of all these communities aim at realizing the same fundamental values.

People participate in the fundamental values in thousands of ways. Which ways or specific actions are best for a person depends on his or her society, age, background, talents, interests, and degree of commitment to a particular fundamental value. Because people have such varied backgrounds and interests, they should have wide freedom to pursue the fundamental values in ways they see fit. This statement implies two important things. First, participation in the fundamental values flourishes in societies where people are free to choose the ways they want to realize the values, and, second, people committed to the fundamental values must play a role in creating such free societies.

Much of our emphasis has been how an individual pursues fundamental values. However, groups—teams, schools, clubs, churches and other religious groups, corporations, foundations—also pursue them. It is certainly true that the smaller a group is, the more freedom individuals within the group have to determine the specific actions they wish to undertake. Therefore, society should be organized in such a way that the smallest feasible groups are granted the freedom to pursue their own goals.

In any large society there must be an accepted manner of generating the goods necessary for or useful to pursuing the fundamental values. This means that anyone committed to the fundamental values has a general interest in making sure that most people have those requisite physical or financial resources. So, for instance, in order to pursue the value of life people need food, accommodations, and basic health care. What actually constitutes "basic" health care varies from society to society and is dependent on available resources. At the very least, however, health care should be sufficiently available to prevent high rates of infant mortality. Individuals committed to the fundamental values should work to assure all people in the society have access to such health care. Depending on the level of development of society, more health care services should be generated and allocated in some manner that is judged to be fair.

In sum, from the acknowledgment of the importance of the fundamental values for all people and groups in society stems a three-fold realization. First, all people should be able to pursue the fundamental values. Second, people should have the freedom to pursue these values in a manner that best fits their circumstances. Third, in order to pursue the fundamental values, people need some resources. Therefore, any society should strive to have an economy that generates goods in reasonable abundance and distributes them fairly.

11

Progress

DAVE WAS RELIEVED. Even though he left his apartment late, he was able to make up time by darting in and out of traffic and arrived at Maria's apartment right on time. When he rang the bell, she was ready and eager to go and he was delighted to see her.

They had agreed they would go to Sunset Hill, a spot in the western part of the city where a number of interesting shops and restaurants had opened during the past few years. After looking around Sunset Hill for a while and having something to eat, they would take in a movie and then get home at a reasonable hour, since the following day they both had to be at work early.

As Dave drove to Sunset Hill, he was cautious not to drive too fast and especially not to cut in and out of traffic. He knew Maria hated his more aggressive driving habits. The more Dave got to know Maria, the better he liked her, and the more careful he was not to upset her. So, when she was in the car, amber lights no longer meant "speed up" and whipping into breakdown lanes was not a clever way to get ahead of creeping traffic. Instead, he played by the rules, just like Maria.

Sunset Hill was lovely. The renovation of old buildings and the new structures went well together. After walking up and down various streets and in and out of shops for about an hour, they picked a restaurant that looked promising and sat down for an early dinner.

TECHNOLOGY AND RELATIONS

As Dave and Maria were settling in at their table, they ran through the little ritual they had developed. Whenever they sat down to eat or even to have coffee, they agreed they would turn off their cell phones. If either was expecting an important call, they would ask the other if it was all right to leave the cell phone on. Part of the ritual was an extended discussion about how important the phone call could possibly be and whether it really was in the interest of the other person to relent. But relent they always did after enjoying spirited banter.

Once their cell phones were turned off this particular evening, Maria said she was impressed by all the new and renovated structures and improvements in the area. That evolved into some conversation about improvements in general. Maria was a bit of a tech geek and always got excited about the latest technology. She was especially enthused with the new generation of phones and gadgets. She loved that these devices did everything but the laundry—and even that was probably not too far off.

Even though he was in a good mood, Dave didn't share Maria's enthusiasm for the latest technology. During the past week Dave had been on a lunch break and he was walking along a crowded street in the business district. Some person walking ahead of him had the type of cell phone on which the photo of the person at the other end of the line was visible on the crystal-clear screen. Whether the guy was having a bad day or whether he was always like this, he was screaming four letter words into the phone, which had the image of a pretty young woman on the screen. Apparently the young woman at the other end was up to the encounter, since the screaming curser would listen to her string of curses and then respond in kind. Dave described this event to Maria and then said, "Where's the progress in being able to shout obscenities in a virtual face-to-face encounter in the middle of a public street?" Dave mused that for every good use of the new technology there was always someone perverting it to increase the amount of rage, disgust, or rejection they could communicate to some other human being.

Maria agreed that technological progress does not always improve relationships. But, she said, technological progress could at least be used for good purposes. "These new phones," she said, "are already being used by expert physicians to help diagnose patients from afar and pass on their diagnoses to a doctor standing beside the patient."

RESEARCH AND RELATIONS

Dave didn't really disagree with Maria, but he explained how much his views had changed recently. He was now much less excited about "progress." Even if it made some things better, it always made others far worse. A particular incident had brought that home to Dave a few years earlier.

Dave always admired his Auntie Kath and Uncle John, who had three children. Mike is their youngest child and is about five years older than Dave. Mike was born with Down's syndrome. Auntie Kath loves all her children, but she has a special bond with Mike. Dave tells Maria what a wonderful "child" Mike is even though he is now in his mid thirties. Despite his age, there is a childlike quality about Mike that simply never ages. When Dave was growing up, just being with his cousins and Auntie Kath was a great experience, and he always felt better after he had been with them for a few hours.

In one of his sociology courses in college there was a segment on problems faced by parents of children with special neurological or physiological disorders. The professor was especially sympathetic to the challenges faced by these parents. He also pointed out that, via prenatal testing, it was now possible to inform a couple with a high degree of certainty whether the mother would bear a child with the chromosomal abnormality associated with Down's syndrome. The professor noted that statistics are kept on mothers who have the test performed on the chromosomes of the baby in utero. Over 90 percent of mothers who carry a Down's syndrome baby (confirmed through some medical procedure) choose to abort the child. Because Dave loves Mike and because he has met other loving and lovable Down's syndrome children, he could not believe the statistic was so high.

After he learned that statistic, he was curious about Auntie Kath's situation before she had Mike. Once when they were visiting, Dave told Auntie Kath he had learned about amniocentesis in a class he was taking. He said he did not want to pry, but was curious whether she had had amniocentesis before she had Mike. She said she did, since the doctor had recommended it. She was apprehensive about the results, but she had determined beforehand that, no matter what the result of the test, it would only increase her love for this baby. She had told that to the doctor before she agreed to have the test, and the doctor knew that after the results came in there was to be no discussion of further "steps to be taken." Dave told Maria he was elated when he heard this. It confirmed everything he knew about Auntie Kath. Auntie Kath was great on the topic. She told Dave she is always happy to talk about the challenge for parents of Down's syndrome children since she is always happy to think of her dear Mike.

Maria said she too admired Auntie Kath and hoped she herself would have the strength and clarity of vision to do exactly what Auntie Kath had done. But Maria also said that it makes sense to try to find a way via some medical intervention to reduce the likelihood of a couple conceiving a Down's syndrome child. Dave agreed, but he also pointed out how loving Mike is as a child. Maria was more hopeful that medical research could make progress, while Dave was dubious about whether decreasing Down's syndrome would constitute progress. They resolved they would talk to Auntie Kath about this at some family gathering where they could get time alone with her.

AUNTIE KATH

Thanksgiving was the next big gathering of Dave's family and Dave wanted Maria there. Not only did he want everyone to meet her, he also wanted to have a chance for both of them to talk to Auntie Kath. Dave had checked with Auntie Kath and she said she was happy to answer any of their questions. After dinner the opportunity arose for a conversation while Dave and Maria helped Auntie Kath with the dishes. The conversation went along just fine and eventually Maria told Auntie Kath that she and Dave wondered how to evaluate a medical innovation that was able to decrease the likelihood of a couple conceiving a Down's syndrome child.

Auntie Kath understood the issue. No one wanted in any way to diminish Mike's status as a totally valued and respected member of the family. On the other hand, the chromosomal abnormality is part of nature, but still statistically infrequent and something that causes parents to rearrange their lives. Maria wanted to know whether a drug that diminishes the likelihood of Down's syndrome represents a true advance.

Auntie Kath responded by emphasizing two things. First, any mother or father not willing to rearrange their lives for their child is not ready to have the child. This is part of what it means to be an adult parent: the child comes first. That's why many couples have their wedding in church. Bride, groom, and families are saying in public and before God that they are good to go with children, whatever it takes. Good parents understand this, and throughout their lives they are constantly adjusting for their children. Second, marriage involves unconditional love. Marriage begins with the unconditional love between husband and wife and then it is extended by the parents to embrace the child. "Frankly," Auntie Kath said, "I had some theoretical understanding of unconditional love at the altar when John and I exchanged marriage vows, but it was sketchy and ethereal, and it wasn't in the forefront of my mind. I knew I loved John and wanted to be with him forever."

Auntie Kath then switched her focus to Mike. "For all his developmental difficulties, Mike really knows how to love unconditionally. No matter what happens one day, he is ready to love all over again with the same intensity the following day. I know a lot more about unconditional love now, and a great deal of it I learned from Mike. Decreasing the incidence of Down's syndrome is a good thing. But people don't realize the great gift that comes to parents through a Down's syndrome child. It's not just that the child is alive and is their child. Down's syndrome children are cheerful, content, and eager to please others. Every day they demonstrate unconditional love, and over months and years they are imaginative in the way they show their love. Of course, because Mike is so dependent on me and his father, his unconditional love is a different type, but I have no doubt it is unconditional. If the syndrome were eliminated tomorrow, someone should quickly sit down with the parents of Down's syndrome children and record all the things the parents say they have learned from their children."

As is true for most Down's syndrome children, Mike likes routine, said Auntie Kath. He can handle special occasions easily as long as either his father or she is close by. But no matter how much fun he had the previous day at some special event, the following day always includes many long hugs. In his own way, Mike understands he has to get this relationship back to its central focus—loving Mom and Dad.

FIGURATIVE SPEECH

Maria and Dave's conversations above about technological progress find an easy parallel in the standard diagram we have been using. That diagram has areas designated by corrosive actions, acceptable actions, and exemplary actions. In a dynamically changing society, Dave and Maria are trying to situate particular actions. In the first case, Dave speaks about relationships (friendship). He questions whether smartphones really improve human relationships. Gadgets often seem at best to be neutral: they neither help nor hinder. In the second case of Down's syndrome, the discussion addresses the values of both friendship and life, but now the focus is on the special friendship of marriage. Auntie Kath, who is a very loving person, explains she really only learned the meaning of unconditional love (friendship again) when she had Mike. That is, her son Mike clarified some sector of exemplary actions on the right side of the diagram. All parents learn love from their children. Auntie Kath says she learned the best type of love—exemplary, unconditional love—from her Down's syndrome son Mike.

12

Pursuing the Fundamental Values

THE FUNDAMENTAL VALUES are naturally attractive, and throughout our lives
each one of us pursues them. What follows is a fuller exploration of each of the
values. Included for each value are many examples of the kinds of actions people
undertake in pursuit of the values. The examples are followed by an analysis of
how important each value is in society, an examination of how each value is experienced as infinite gift, and a discussion of how or whether objective hierarchy
operates within them. In general, examples are drawn from countries with developed economies. However, each society, culture, or institution has a multitude of
its own specific ways that people in that society promote the seven fundamental
values.

PARTICIPATING IN LIFE

Long before explicitly considering the importance of life, we take actions that lead
to a deeper participation in the value of life. As children we eat and drink, play and
exercise, sleep and look forward to the following day. We also worry when we or
our friends get hurt, we don't like being sick, and we are frightened when we get
lost. When we are very young we relish living and get excited when we experience
something new, as long as a parent or sibling is close by. When we feel threatened,
we become anxious. Some of these actions are socially and culturally reinforced

and supported, but the range of actions we fairly spontaneously undertake as children indicates a natural disposition toward welcoming life, reveling in it, and protecting it when we see it threatened.

When we get older and are ready to attend college or work for gainful employment, we become more seriously reflective. We often muse or think more critically about what we want to do in life, how we want to be as adults, and we try different approaches to living life. There are many sad cases when young adults are seriously troubled, depressed, and possibly suicidal, but generally when we are young we delight in life and the things we are allowed to do, unburdened by bearing the responsibilities of having to make a living or care for a family. That does not mean, however, that we are totally carefree. We do have to accept some responsibility at this stage of our lives. For instance, we realize that if we want to live long lives, we have to be cautious and take steps to remain healthy. We also look forward to getting older and having families and are willing to take some steps that move us along in that direction. We play sports or exercise and most people do such things as going to the dentist and make regular visits to the doctor. We embrace beautiful days in spring, fall, summer, or winter as a gift, and particularly on days like these we revel in life and share our joy and enthusiasm with friends and loved ones.

There is a darker side to this story of life enthusiastically embraced and cherished. In human history, millions of people have been the victims of genocide. Legions of men have been sent to their deaths in various wars. Children have been sacrificed to various deities and countless women, caught in the midst of conflict, have been routinely raped and murdered and their children savaged. Millions of people have been intentionally starved to death. In sum, there is contrary evidence that life is a broadly human and fundamental value. Instances of large scale brutality and genocide especially argue against the universality of life as a value. The fact that such brutality has occurred is roundly admitted. At the same time, however, in its aftermath, many thoughtful people point out the hatred that bred the brutality and they condemn it. They also highlight the tragic waste created by the brutal killing of so many innocent people. Without perhaps using the word *corrosive*, they clearly locate the taking of innocent lives squarely within the corrosive box of life. Even in the horror of genocide, life gets affirmed with the benefit of a historical perspective, and people try to understand how decent people could bring themselves to murder the innocent.

Life is admirable and to be respected at many different levels. Of course, we should try to protect all forms of human life. But humans are not the only ones who participate in life. Anyone who tortures or even kills a cat or dog is judged to have acted inhumanly. Life is not to be taken in an arbitrary manner. As human knowledge progresses, we appreciate how some species—such as monkeys and dolphins—have sensitivities and brains that are closer to humans than bugs, snakes, or birds. Life as a fundamental value means all life is to be respected. To take the life of even an animal requires an adequate reason. Just because someone "owns" an animal does not give the person the moral authority to kill or torture the animal; one needs an adequate reason. The large majority of adults and children understand this and abide by this rule.

PARTICIPATING IN KNOWLEDGE

Although some people are more inquisitive than others, we all seek knowledge of how the world functions. From the little child who constantly asks his parent "Why?" to the young adult who tries to figure out something on her own, even though it yields no tangible benefit, we human beings have an innate desire to figure out why things are the way they are. Knowledge comes to us in myriad ways—through friends, teachers, books, the Internet, newspapers, journals, magazines, television and movies, and a variety of other media. However, the institutions most clearly focused on transmitting knowledge or generating new knowledge are schools, academies, and other institutes.

Through different sources of knowledge, human beings focus on learning the way things really are or how they really work and interact. That is, their focus is on truth. Even when knowledge is passed informally from one person to another, if the new knowledge conflicts with the normal way in which a person understands how the world acts, the person then is alerted to determine whether his former way of thinking is true or false, or partially true and partially false. People don't just accumulate information; they seek true knowledge. Indeed, they seek truth itself. This is simply the way we are made; it is in our DNA. Some people seek more deeply than others, some explore more theoretically and others more practically, but each person wants to arrive at true knowledge and true explanations. Perspectives are insufficient.

Ordinary knowledge is acquired in conversation, observation, general reading, or watching television and movies. Higher knowledge, on the other hand, is not so easily acquired. Superior knowledge usually requires extensive schooling, as well as concentration, persistence, and effort. It is probably the case that seeking higher knowledge is not innate but socially determined and emphasized. Adults help us when we are young to appreciate that advanced knowledge brings deep satisfaction as well as greater opportunities for social advancement. Eventually, we learn to respect knowledge and to admire people who are knowledgeable and adept at learning. Even if the desire for higher knowledge is not innate, the acquisition of it yields deep human satisfaction. That is, the pursuit of higher knowledge conforms to our human nature.

Some of us are better at acquiring advanced knowledge than others, but we all acknowledge the importance of knowledge and of gaining more knowledge. After all, every one of us has experienced the joy that comes from finally figuring out something we have puzzled over for a long time. All human beings experience knowledge as a precious gift and one that can never be fully exhausted. It does not require a doctorate to recognize that knowledge is a fundamental value.

PARTICIPATING IN BEAUTY

Beauty entrances, whether it be in animals, nature, people, homes, art, architecture, music, dance, film, paintings, or drama. Participating in creating the beautiful is equally intriguing and satisfying. In the way we dress and present ourselves, in the gardens we keep, the homes we decorate, and the meals we prepare and serve, we invite the beautiful into our lives. We also participate in beauty when we paint, dance, sing, play music, or sculpt. Beauty fascinates, enriches, and satisfies the human spirit and we suffer in its absence or when it is assaulted. As humans, we are constituted to seek and respect beauty, and the attainment of beauty in whatever form brings human satisfaction.

Human beings relish the beautiful, but we can distort it as well. A "beauty culture" that elevates the superficial and idolizes youth and unnatural thinness distorts beauty, warps expectations, and leads to injurious behaviors. Nonetheless, beauty itself is something good, not evil, and it is admired and appreciated across cultures. When we craft something beautiful, such as a painting, a home, or a building, we are deeply gratified yet awed by the chasm between ultimate beauty and our participation in it.

Because beauty is often in the eye of the beholder and because the beholder is often influenced by the norms of the institutions of which he or she is a part, it is notoriously difficult to rank activities in pursuit of beauty independently of social institutions. Yet human beings spend a great deal of time establishing personal priorities with respect to beauty. In addition to private attempts, professionals play an important role. In any society, theatre critics, art critics, architecture critics, home decorators, and music critics, for instance, make their living by ranking aesthetic forms. Whatever the impact professionals and institutions have on our ranking of beautiful activities, each of us has strong convictions in this area. In our day-to-day lives we readily acknowledge that some vistas are more stunning than others, some environments more delightful, and some musical performances more moving or exalted.

PARTICIPATING IN FRIENDSHIP

Friendship or, more generally, sociability connects human beings one to another in varying degrees of intimacy and intensity. Some of our friendships are episodic and others endure for a lifetime. Marriage is a particularly intense kind of friendship in which couples commit to sharing their lives and promoting the wellbeing of their husband or wife. Within this unique kind of friendship children are born, nurtured, and raised. But friendship is not limited to relationships as profound and enduring as marriage or the family. Rather it, like each fundamental value, is broadly interpreted and includes a wide array of human connections. Living in the same city or town generates a form of amity, as does bearing the same national citizenship or school alma mater. These are admittedly quite distant forms of friendship, but there is nonetheless a bond that arises from sharing some things in common.

People affirm friendship as a value by having friends. We also expect everyone in our own culture and other cultures to have friends, and we respect friends and friendship. People usually treat friends of friends with deference, even if they are not close. We generally avoid doing anything that might break up a friendship. We see friendship as a gift with an infinite quality, since a friendship can always be intensified. We are delighted to have friends and we are humbled by the good and generous things our friends do for us that we hardly deserve. On the other hand, even in marriage couples recognize limitations and imperfections in their friendship, which can always be closer and more profound.

Hierarchy within friendship is determined by the closeness of the bond, the nature of the bond, and its duration. In general, it would appear that marriage is the highest institutional form of friendship, since the couple lives together, intends the good of the other, and promises commitment until the death of one of the partners. Friendships engendered by undertaking common risky or dangerous missions are also very intense, but they are usually of shorter duration than marriage friendships. Children who are friends can have extremely close bonds with one another, and parents respect such bonds. Nonetheless, although an eight-year-old thinks the friendship will last forever, many children move on to other friends as they mature.

Love is fundamental to human prospering and essential to friendship. To love someone usually includes having a feeling or sentiment, but that is not the heart of love. Rather, love consists in being committed to promoting the wellbeing of the other person. In this book we do not list love as a fundamental value; instead we call it friendship. Although it makes some sense to call love a fundamental value, there are big disadvantages to this. In American society, "love" too often refers to narrow, intense friendships that are expressed in physical and emotional ways. As a result, in popular culture "love" refers to something too narrow and constrained, too romanticized, or too sexualized, and it fails to convey the inherent breadth of a fundamental value. However, if the reader understands "love" in its proper breadth and acknowledges that love includes commitment as a central component, and if the reader allows for varieties of intensity and expression, "love" so understood is another legitimate name for the fundamental value of friendship.

PARTICIPATING IN PLAYFULNESS

Human beings are playful. Comic movies, television shows, plays, and stand-up routines are forms of play. Cartoons, jokes, funny stories—written or oral—good-natured teasing, cheerful banter, pantomime, spoofs, plays on words, clever observations, musicals and drama, rolling in the snow, splashing in the ocean, and whimsical play among children or adults are participations in playfulness as well. Board games, computer games, card games, arcade games all provide ways to play. Competitors involved in sports or other games participate in playfulness. Playfulness is almost synonymous with fun, but intensity is also compatible with having fun. Only when a particular game or activity ceases to be fun does it cease to promote the value of playfulness.

Even though some people are more playful than others, we all have our playful ways. The gift in playfulness comes through an unexpected but harmless turn of events. If, for example, the denouement of a comedic play is both unanticipated but also effectively ridicules a pompous individual in the play, the effect can be comical and delightful. Respect for playfulness is shown in part by the way we cultivate those who tickle our funny bone. Being funny is a special kind of genius. We are delighted by people who are truly funny and want to have them around. We also resent or disapprove of the killjoys among us who keep us from having harmless fun.

It is difficult to establish a hierarchy of actions within playfulness, because much of what delights us is a matter of personal taste. Some people enjoy the passive playfulness that comes from watching a movie or musical, while others prefer the active playfulness that expresses itself in sports or other types of games. Still others prefer verbal playfulness expressed by those with a good sense of humor and a rapier wit. The hierarchy that does exist in playful activities is based on amounts—the amount of fun people are having and the number of people having it. In the fundamental value of playfulness, if more is possible, it is always better, provided one has the time.

The fundamental value of religion acknowledges that our life, as well as the lives of other people, animals, and plants, stems from a being far beyond either what we can grasp or clearly articulate. This acknowledgment leads us to believe in something "wholly other," be that God or a Supreme Being by some other name. The giftedness of life calls some people to render thanks to God and praise him by suitable prayers, offerings, or reflections. Religious activities consist of a group of people giving public praise and thanks to God or requesting favors from God. As is the case for the other fundamental values, religion should be broadly conceived to include many types of activities which acknowledge a divine being active in sustaining our world.

Respecting religion as a fundamental value means allowing persons and religious groups as much freedom as possible to practice their faith. People who engage in religious practices are responding to what they perceive as a divine call. They express their gratitude, commitment, and hopes in communal prayer, sacrifice, praise, and other activities. Society should acknowledge the sincerity of their religious practices and allow religious groups to respond as they feel called to do, as long as their activities do not threaten the ability of others to pursue the fundamental values, including religion. Even people who practice no formal religion understand they should not interfere with the religious practices of others when such practices are harmless or pose little inconvenience to others.

Not every activity undertaken in the name of religion should be acceptable in society. In particular, we should not allow people to engage in activities that are harmful to others and directly contrary to the other fundamental values, no matter their justification. Just because some group feels called by God to offer a child in sacrifice or set off an explosive device in a crowded marketplace or destroy something of widely acknowledged beauty does not make it an acceptable practice or one that should be tolerated by society.

The basis of religion is the realization that human existence is a gift from a being or power or person far beyond our understanding. Participation in this fundamental value does not necessitate making any judgment about the underlying merits of a particular religion. For this reason, apart from personal conviction there is no objective hierarchy of particular religions related to the fundamental value of religion. A particular society may grant greater religious privileges to a particular religion practiced by a broad segment of the population. Despite such public preference, the acknowledgment should not hinder the practice of religion by any other group in society. To be more specific, in a Christian society, Jews and Muslims should be allowed to practice

their faith, in a Muslim society, Christians and Jews should be allowed to practice their faith, and in a Jewish society, Christians and Muslims should be free
to practice their faith.

PRACTICAL REASONABLENESS

Practical reasonableness helps us get our lives in order. Common sense is certainly
part of this fundamental value, but it goes further than common sense and includes
good decision-making. Whenever we think about the decisions we ought to make,
we are participating in the fundamental value of practical reasonableness. A more
specific example of participating in this value is making good use of available
information and resources when coming to a decision.

The focus in this book is on making good decisions with a primary impact on
one's personal life and the lives of others influenced by decisions in one's personal
life. Another realm in which practical reasonableness plays a vital role is ordering
activities in society. Any society uses institutions to help people strive for human
fulfillment. Some institutions are better conceived and developed than others. By
conserving resources, producing goods useful in the pursuit of the other
fundamental values, and employing human ingenuity to pursue the other
fundamental values, men and women participate in practical reasonableness. That
is, with the goal of enabling people to pursue the fundamental values, designing
and operating an efficient economy, a reasonable government, and all components
of a vibrant civil society entail the pursuit of practical reasonableness.

Because institutions involve large numbers of people, with various abilities, interests, and virtues, such institutions usually emerge through a process of trial, error,
and adjustment. Social institutions are too complex to be thought out in a single
grand scheme and then implemented. Because the impact of rules or policies affecting
large numbers of people is often uncertain, identifying corrosive actions in this realm
requires many more distinctions than are necessary at the level of the individual.

As central as government, the economy, and civil society are in daily life and the
promotion of the fundamental values, they receive little attention here. Rather,
our primary focus is on decisions made by individuals and nongovernmental
groups or institutions that have a primary impact on the way we order our lives.

DECISION-MAKING

Learning to make good decisions begins at an early age, with essential input from
parents and older authority figures. Because the methods for good decision-

making come through parents and others, these methods are themselves shaped by the institutions in which parents and adults participate.

Perhaps the earliest way in which young people participate in the value of practical reasonableness is recognizing, with much prompting by parents, they should share what they have with others and that they have to keep their living space clean and orderly. As we get older, other considerations have to be weighed when we are making decisions. Native talent is just such a consideration, as are personal interests. Time, effort, and resources—whether financial, social, or personal—required to implement a project are also considerations that have to be made when calculating whether to go ahead with one project or another. Perhaps one of the greatest challenges in decision-making is determining what types of personal resources are required to successfully implement a project in our life. For this, we need self-knowledge that is age- and situation appropriate.

When human beings deliberate and then decide what actions to take, they participate in the fundamental value of practical reasonableness. Of course, people are thinking all the time about what they should do. Every day they learn more about themselves, about the real world, and about the things that most excite them. As a young person becomes more experienced, she implicitly develops a framework in which she makes decisions.

The framework can be illustrated by describing a three-step process. Despite the particularity of three, we are not claiming that people go through the following process step by step, or that they think of what they want to do in the precise way we are about to describe. Rather, the three-step process offers a way to understand how we gradually develop a perspective on what we want to achieve in life.

Consider these three steps. *Step one:* we establish a hierarchy within each of the seven fundamental values. This is a fancy way of saying that we have to figure out which actions are exemplary ways of pursuing each of the fundamental values, which are good, which are reasonable but not particularly exalted, and which actions are simply off-limits, corrosive, or forbidden. *Step two:* we develop a plan for participating in the fundamental values over a lifetime. A life plan involves all the fundamental values individually, including practical reasonableness. It also involves the group of values as a whole. *Step three:* we make decisions about particular ways to participate in one or more fundamental values according to the manner in which it fits into a person's life plan.

Now let's consider a specific example that illustrates this three-fold process. Suppose a young man is taking an exam to qualify for a job. The young man desperately wants the job because he needs money to take care of his sick and impoverished parents. For the sake of his parents, he is tempted to cheat on the qualifying exam. As part of step one, he acknowledges that cheating is wrong because it corrodes truth, that is, it lies in the forbidden zone of the fundamental value of knowledge. As he ponders what to do, he enters the second step of making a decision. Taking care of his parents is presumably a part of his life plan. Therefore, he has to consider actions that definitely help his parents (improved health is part of the fundamental value of life) but that do not lay in a corrosive or forbidden zone of any fundamental value. In a speculative way, he knows what the proper decision is, but still his emotions try to convince him that cheating is the only way to help his parents, who are relying on him. His moral knowledge of what he should do with respect to life and knowledge is fed into the value of practical reasonableness. He is now in step three of decision-making when he will actually decide on a course of action. He will make a good decision if he finds a way to help his parents without cheating on the qualifying exam.

The fundamental value of practical reasonableness is in effect the "coordinating" value, and pursuing it therefore makes an enormous difference in how people lead their lives. This chapter is an exercise in practical reasonableness, but so also is this entire book. The process we use to sort out the various moral issues can help people better understand which factors should be considered when making moral choices. The book also grounds approaches to moral decision-making that people might already be using, perhaps tentatively, by relying on a broad and longstanding moral tradition. By making the process explicit, in many cases it gives people greater confidence about how to make moral decisions in the future.

HIERARCHY WITHIN PRACTICAL REASONABLENESS

In treating each of the previous fundamental values, we have discussed whether there is some objective hierarchy, relevant to a given society or institution and pertaining to the individual actions leading to participation in the fundamental value. Practical reasonableness involves making decisions and plans. Aside from good decisions versus bad decisions, it is difficult to think of a useful hierarchy involving such decisions. If we restrict ourselves to the types of decisions adults make, personal and institutional circumstances play such a significant role that we would be hard pressed to elevate one type of decision over another. For example, we might be inclined to say that selecting a marriage partner is among the most important decisions individuals make. While that statement is true, it omits many other companion decisions. Choosing to turn down a job because it would jeopardize family commitments, choosing a lifelong commitment to art or music and all that entails, deciding to give your life to promoting your religious faith—there are numerous examples of other equally important decisions.

It is very difficult to categorize specific decisions. Consequently, various groups find it more helpful to emphasize certain qualities of decision-making rather than seek to identify a hierarchy within a class of decisions. In particular, the Catholic Church has long identified four primary virtues with respect to decision-making that it terms "cardinal virtues." In this case, cardinal does not refer to the group of people who wear red robes and elect the pope. Rather, it stems from the word's Latin root, which means hinge or something on which something hangs or turns. The cardinal virtues are the ones on which much hinges, including the other virtues.

The four cardinal virtues are prudence, justice, temperance, and fortitude. Each of them refers to factors that should be taken into consideration when we make decisions. Prudence is the habit of taking all relevant information and perspectives into consideration and weighing them properly. The virtue of justice is the habit of making sure everyone is given due consideration and receives proper treatment in any decision which a person or institution makes. Temperance is the habit of carefully weighing the demands of the emotions or appetites, which often seek fulfillment in the short term, with what the intellect indicates is the correct course of action. Fortitude is the habit of making proper decisions no matter what the reaction of others or the adverse consequences that might be incurred.

SOLIDARITY, SUBSIDIARITY, AND THE COMMON GOOD

Since practical reasonableness is a fundamental value, we naturally strive to realize it in our lives and we have an obligation not to undermine any of the fundamental goods. The seven fundamental values or goods are collectively known as the common good when they are presented as the overall goals of society. Because the pursuit of the fundamental values only occurs via specific actions, "common good" is also used to refer to thousands of actions pursued by individuals and groups in society which result in participation in the fundamental values.

One insight of practical reasonableness is that all people should be able to participate in some minimal way, as judged by generous social standards, in the fundamental values. Each and every person deserves respect and should be able to share in the essentially good things of life, namely, the fundamental values. This realization is articulated in two principles: the principle of solidarity and the principle of subsidiarity, both of which were first raised conceptually at the conclusion of chapter 10.

Solidarity acknowledges that in society every person should have enough resources to pursue the fundamental values. Subsidiarity says that the smallest feasible group should be the one designated to choose and provide these needed resources for the members of the group. In some cases, the smallest feasible group can be quite large. For instance, in order to provide security to people in a particular country against foreign attack or aggression, armed forces of some type are required. In order to educate the young so that they learn to participate in knowledge, some system of schooling is required. In many varieties of knowledge, the smallest feasible unit is the family or the individual person, but when it comes to higher knowledge, larger and more extended institutions are needed. Many institutions of various sizes also conform to the principle of subsidiarity. For example, hospitals, educational institutions, voluntary organizations, and family businesses, as well as corporations, sports teams and associations, cultural groups—all these are institutions that promote various groupings of the fundamental values. Other institutions are broader than any single business or cultural group; these institutions distinguish themselves primarily by their activities, less by who are formal members and who are not. Marriage, honoring the dead, movies and television, music, fashion in clothes, public holidays—all these are also true institutions, although in a broader sense. Any society has many such institutions. Ideally, they are structured in such a way that they promote the common good.

People have plans to pursue beauty, friendship, life, knowledge, religion, and playfulness. In order to know what they need to pursue the fundamental values, people have to understand the full range of possibilities for pursuing them – be they straightforward or complex. We can divide the type of knowledge required into two groups: general social knowledge and particular personal knowledge. General social knowledge refers to the way in which the world works, the ways large groups of people interact, and general ways to safeguard the well-being of people. In order to pursue the fundamental values, people have to have some idea how the economy functions and whether most, many, or few people have sufficient resources to pursue the fundamental values. People have to understand how their government works and whether it functions in a reasonably fair manner. People have to know what types of educational systems work reasonably well and what helps human beings abide by laws which have been passed by various bodies of officials. We presume that most young people have this type of general knowledge or can fairly easily acquire it if they do not.

The second type of knowledge is personal knowledge. In order to lead an authentically moral life individuals need two types of personal knowledge: self-knowledge and knowledge of others. As we pointed out in an earlier chapter, self-knowledge comes neither easily nor quickly. Only after years of experience and serious reflection can we begin truly to know ourselves. This might seem counterintuitive; after all, we certainly know what we are feeling at any given time. We are also aware of our impulses and desires and at any given time we have a pretty good idea of what we want out of life. What we tend not to know, however, is the pattern of these feelings, urges, and desires. We are often hazy about the impact these patterns have on our ability to reach our goals. It is also difficult for us to discern patterns of our interactions with others, especially in pursuit of our goals. Self-knowledge of this type is difficult for everyone to discern. We return to the importance of self-knowledge in part III.

13

Getting It Together

MARIA WAS GETTING impatient. "That's ridiculous, Dave. Your nephew Ron is erratic and undependable. What he needs is moral and ethical boot camp, not some college course in ethics. No ethics course is going to straighten him out and make him more virtuous. I know you want to help your nephew, but thinking a course in ethics is the answer is pure fantasy."

"Come on, Maria, be reasonable," replied Dave. "I am not claiming the course will turn him into a saint, but it just might help him get a clue. Unless he changes, he is headed for disaster. He is constantly lying to himself and others. A course in ethics can't hurt. What do you have against studying ethics? You, the queen of the morality brigade, are you saying that an ethics course has little value? You certainly took enough of them yourself!"

THREE TYPES OF ETHICS COURSES

Dave has always been close to his nephew Ron and it is very clear Ron needs help of some sort. Currently a sophomore in college, Ron is drifting academically and socially. Dave and other family members know Ron is a pleaser. He says what others want to hear and he often agrees to things he knows are untrue. Ron acknowledges this fault, but the pattern continues.

In his junior year of college, Dave took an ethics course he found interesting. Dave tells Maria it was a wake-up course for him. He had never considered the many different approaches to individual problems. The ethics course addressed important issues in society, such as gay marriage, the environment, sexual infidelity, and embryonic stem cell research. It was interesting learning about the topics and the ethical issues involved. Most important, the course gave him a better understanding of how people could lead good and decent lives and yet differ from him substantially in their moral positions on thorny issues.

Maria did not think Dave's account of the value of his ethics course got to the heart of the issue. Maria asked Dave, "Do you think you acted more ethically after your ethics course, at least for a while?" "No," Dave replied, "but that was not the purpose of the course. The course was supposed to make us reflect on why we behave in certain ways." "But why reflect on your behavior," said Maria, "unless you're thinking of changing your bad behavior into good behavior? You went through the whole course and yet there was no behavioral change, other than being more tolerant of others. If the same thing happens to Ron, how is that supposed to help him?"

"Okay Maria, in your view, do ethics courses produce anything useful?" "Not really," Maria said. "Okay, maybe some of them do, but I think most ethics courses offered at colleges and universities do not address issues in a way that helps students order their lives better, much less behave better. But I admit some courses work better than others."

Somewhat tentatively, because she had not yet discussed the issue much with anyone, Maria said there might be three types of ethics courses in college. The first and by far the most common are what she tentatively called *ethical foundations courses*. Foundations courses are usually very general and focus on a handful of basic ways in which people make ethical decisions. Most philosophy departments offer such courses, and they can also be found in specific fields, such as business, legal, or medical ethics. Maria explained that the goal of these courses was to cover the terrain of moral problems in society related to a particular sphere of activity, such as business or medicine. The professor presents an account and perhaps a critique of three or four ethical systems and then uses each system to address particular ethical problems. Professors make no summary comparative assessments of competing ethical systems. One system is never proclaimed or proved clearly better than or clearly inferior to another system. Despite their name, these courses lack a firm foundation; they offer no vantage point from which the professor, much less the students, can judge one system better than another. At best these types of courses provide a very basic understanding of different ethical approaches. At worst, they merely improve cocktail conversation.

"In my view," Maria insists, "foundations courses provide no help or guidance; they are more like 'art appreciation' or 'science appreciation' classes. If a person has been given good moral training by his or her parents, this type of course should definitely not influence what a person does. Why should anyone change what they are doing in ethical matters just because you learn other people, according to their own lights, have plausible reasons for doing something different?"

Because the second type of course emphasized consistency, she used the term *consistent system ethics* to refer to this group of courses. These courses take one ethical approach and attempt to apply it consistently to an array of contested issues in society. For example, the course could assume that the natural law approach is valid, or it could assume that a utilitarian approach is the one which is most helpful in modern society. Whichever approach is selected, the professor explains the main assumptions of the approach and then applies this approach to a series of ethical issues. This course offers a systematic justification for various practices and it can help a student understand why her parents taught her certain things. If the course is taught from a natural law perspective, she may understand why one is never permitted to lie, even for the benefit of others. It may point to practices that are inconsistent with the main ethical approach in the course and in which the student has been raised. This type of course can lead to true insight because the student is already following most of the practices advocated by the ethical system. As a result of the course, the person may have a better sense of the correspondence between the theory and her practice. This may yield a clear view of true human fulfillment and it might highlight a few inconsistent practices in which the student engages.

"The third type of ethics course does not exist at colleges or universities," said Maria, "but it is the one your nephew needs. I would call it *basic training ethics*, and it teaches practices. If students agree to participate in the course, they agree to strive to act in certain ways. It is more like joining a sports team, which is all about behavior and performance. If you agree to be a member of a sports team, you have to work out every day, come to meetings on time, learn plays, and practice certain moves over and over again. In this type of ethical course, if it existed, the focus would be on actual behavior. The teacher in this course would be less of an instructor and more of a 'behavior coach.'"

In a sense, the basic training ethics course Maria described would be a remedial course in good behavior. Parents are supposed to help their children become well practiced in the ethical system they deem has the most merit. At the very least, by the time they reach college, teenagers are supposed to have a reliable set of moral skills. Teenagers may not draw upon their moral skills or fail to live up to their ideals, but they should have ideals they strive to reach. Their moral skills should also include qualities like gratification deferment, emotional control, impulse control, et cetera. If a college student lacks rudimentary moral skills such as these, the only thing that will help them acquire them is the kind of basic training course Maria describes or a peer group with outstanding moral skills and behavior that the student decides to imitate.

Dave had to admit that Ron definitely needed moral basic training and that the ethical foundations course would be pretty useless. But he wasn't so sure what he thought about the consistent system ethics course. It sounded a lot like a foundations course that dealt with only one ethical system. "I don't understand why the consistent system course is useful," Dave said. "Well, the benefit," Maria replied, "is that it can help correct missteps. It is so easy to be swayed by what other good people are doing or what is popular or common practice. We just do things without thinking about how they fit in with our own general ethical approach. Some actions may be completely inconsistent with our basic ethical approach, but because we don't think about it, we adapt and go with the flow."

Maria offered what she thought was a great illustrative example from a story that was carried in the national media. To promote awareness of the dangers of drinking and driving, administrators at a public high school in California worked with the local police department to shock students into awareness of the tragedy of drunk driving. On a Monday morning, police officers appeared in about twenty different classrooms of a particular high school to announce to students (the faculty member in each class was told about the hoax beforehand) that three teenagers, including one of their classmates, had died in a car crash over the weekend. Students were upset, distraught, and some cried. However, the crashes never took place. In fact, none of the students had died; the ones who were named by the police officers were in on the hoax.

Maria said, "This was a terrible message to give to students. It basically said it is okay to lie as long as you are doing it for a good reason. And this was the leadership of the high school saying this to students. It's clear they are utilitarians: if it works, use it. If lying potentially saves a life, tell a lie. Anyone who follows a natural law system knows that you cannot undermine one fundamental value such as knowledge in order to promote another, such as life. Or consider another case: a doctor should not lie to a patient because he thinks it will yield better results. Or, if a friend confides in you and asks you to keep the information confidential, you should not promise not to reveal the information but then decide to save your own skin by revealing it. There's no consistent ethical way to justify these actions by claiming that breaking the confidence leads to good consequences for me. This line of thinking, whether or not it is properly termed 'utilitarian,' is totally contrary to the natural law approach."

Maria also admitted that one of the things she likes about a consistent system course in ethics is that it enables a future mother to think carefully about how she is going to raise her child. A mom has to have concrete ways of getting things across to young children and then she needs good explanations when the child becomes a teenager. A consistent system course gets a future mom or dad thinking about these things.

"Dave, admit it. Your nephew needs moral skills. Practically all college courses in ethics are about knowledge, not about skills."

CONTEXT

The above exchange between Dave and Maria highlights two important aspects of living an authentically moral life. The most important point is that ethical knowledge alone does not usually lead to good ethical practice. Moral living requires solid ethical skills. In part III of this book, a variety of these ethical skills are analyzed and practices are recommended that can help young adults strengthen these skills. Maria does admit that a course in a particular ethical approach—such as the natural law approach—can help eliminate inconsistencies in what a young adult thinks is right and wrong. It can also offer satisfaction to a young adult since the course may reveal why certain actions are corrosive and others exemplary. Both goals are the aim of part II of this book.

The exchange also illustrates the danger of permitting actions that undermine one fundamental value because they promote another. We should not lie to save a friend from difficult consequences because in the end doing so undermines both knowledge and friendship. Indeed, friends could act in the same callous way towards us. Similarly, we should not kill a severely deformed infant in order to gain essential knowledge that might prevent terrible malformations in future infants. Such actions undermine both life and knowledge. Condoning such reasoning implies approving the killing of our own child so as to improve medical practice in the future.

PART TWO

Avoiding Corrosive Actions and Promoting Friendship

IN PART I we articulated the primary ways in which natural law is expressed. Our claim is that all humans seek to realize seven fundamental values: life, friendship, beauty, knowledge, playfulness, religion, and practical reasonableness. We emphasized the myriad and diversity of satisfying ways to pursue these values. We also noted that some actions or activities do not lead to deeper participation in any particular value; on the contrary, some actions or practices either block participation in the value or blind a person to envision effective and attractive ways to pursue the values. Human beings acknowledge that certain activities are forbidden or wrong because they impede progress toward participating in the fundamental value. The actions are corrosive because they eat away at a person's ability to participate in a particular fundamental value.

In part II we narrow our perspective and consider primarily the fundamental value of friendship, but with attention to the way it is pursued through actions also involving other fundamental values. As is the case for adults, young people pursue all the fundamental values, but friendship is especially significant for young adults. As older teenagers they make friends who are very important, because some of these friends will be good friends for the rest of their lives. Within the family, however, norms for natural law emerge long before children begin high school. Parents teach their very young sons and daughters how they are supposed to interact with one another. To a certain extent, rules for interaction between the sexes involve cultural values, but they also draw upon universal insights from the natural law about how men and women interact well together and show respect for one another.

Because fundamental values are important for all people, human beings have a responsibility to one another. Natural law indicates that each person should be concerned that other people can participate in the fundamental values at a socially determined minimum level and that groups of people should take reasonable steps to make it likely that this happens. To illustrate this general principle, in the next chapter we indicate in some detail the responsibilities of friends when one of them who has imbibed an excessive amount of alcohol seeks sexual intimacy.

Marriage is a very high form of friendship and many young people eventually hope to be married. That is, they intend to find a friend for life with whom they also hope to generate life, namely, children. The various activities of teens and young adults revolve around finding a suitable partner for life. Finding such a soulmate is no easy task. One reason it is difficult is that there are many pleasurable activities our modern society allows in the pursuit of a soul mate. According to the natural law approach, some of these activities—such as premarital sex—impede our ability to develop as deep friends and soul mates. Part II explores how what seems to be a generally accepted practice in American society—premarital sex—can blur the vision of young adults and diminish their ability to make a lasting commitment to love someone "until death do us part."

Life and playfulness are also fundamental values that enter into deliberations about the acceptability of various forms of sexual intimacy. We acknowledge that various types of sexual intimacy involve fun, pleasure, and the potential for new life. Nonetheless, an activity which is corrosive of any single value, in this case friendship or life, cannot be justified simply because it enables some participation in another fundamental value, such as playfulness or beauty.

Trying to find a spouse with whom a young adult can grow and have a family, and to whom they can remain faithful until death parts them, is a reasonable and common pursuit. The central issue is what behavioral patterns are more likely to make permanent marriage to a single spouse successful.

14

Drinking and Drugs

LOOKING OUT FOR YOURSELF AND YOUR FRIENDS

THE DRINKING SCENE is a central component of social life for college students and young adults in the United States. It is also a mainstay of hook-up culture. According to one of the students profiled in *Sex and the Soul*, people are less inhibited when they drink, and getting drunk enables them to do things they won't remember the next day—things they might well be ashamed of doing. While Donna Freitas, the author, found that most random hooking-up was not associated with getting drunk, drinking and often getting drunk are synonymous with socializing in the minds of most college students.

Of course, not all young people drink alcohol, and many drink quite moderately. Nonetheless, college students are familiar with the scene at many bars or off-campus parties: large amounts of alcohol available at low prices. This combination results in many young people drinking to excess. Most young people understand that someone who drinks alone has a problem. They might also think that a pattern of binge-drinking is worrisome. However, few seem to believe that the excessive drinking many young people do in their college years and beyond is a big deal, much less something requiring friendly collaboration.

PRACTICAL REASONABLENESS AND GETTING DRUNK

Excessive drinking is certainly a social issue, but it is also a moral issue that natural law helps us to understand. According to natural law, drinking alcohol is permissible.

Excessive drinking is not. One may be against drinking alcohol for good religious reasons or because drinking exposes a person to excessive dangers. But many people believe it is possible to drink in moderation without disastrous results.

In today's society, moderate social drinking does no harm and is often helpful in terms of cultivating the fundamental values of friendship and playfulness. Excessive drinking, on the other hand, undermines the fundamental value of practical reasonableness. In order to act (that is, be "practical") in a reasonable way, people have to be able to reason. Inebriated people are simply no longer capable of thinking clearly and, therefore, acting reasonably. Putting yourself in that position is seriously wrong because you can no longer participate in practical reasonableness. Getting drunk is corrosive and immoral. By so doing, the person abdicates reason, at least for a period of time. But simply saying that it is wrong will not keep people from doing it.

Confronted with the grim reality that drinking to excess is immoral, some young people will want to consider whether there are exceptions, even purely technical ones. For example, does this really mean that brides-to-be and grooms-to-be cannot get drunk at bachelor and bachelorette parties? Yes, that pretty much is what it means. Too many bad things can happen when people can no longer act reasonably, and certainly no one wants to mar the celebration of the wedding itself by altercations or scandals prior to the wedding.

So the natural law approach to drinking is fairly straightforward: don't get drunk, ever. Since both friendship and playfulness are fundamental values, the natural law approach would not necessarily discourage getting together with friends for drinks at a bar, although some religious traditions do not permit people to drink alcohol. Without elevating drinking in bars to the high status of "exemplary actions" we spoke about in earlier chapters, what takes place in a bar (provided it is not contrary to religious convictions) can be positive. In addition to fun and friendship, there is often good conversation that contributes to conviviality and getting to know one another. These are good things. Because all these activities and values can be promoted by moderate intake of alcohol, drinking is not an "off-limits" activity according to natural law. What is out of bounds is drinking too much.

Similar observations explain why using addictive drugs for recreational purposes is wrong. In the instance of recreational drugs, the positives that come from associating with friends at a bar do not occur. Learning about others, anticipating future events, integrating recent events into a broader spectrum, or listening sympathetically and with some understanding to the difficulties a friend encounters have no meaning since they do not get integrated into the lives of the individual when drugs are used. Especially if a person can become addicted by ingesting a drug one or two times, natural law says this is a forbidden activity. Taking such drugs is directly contrary to the type of practical reasonableness that is supposed to guide all human actions. Therefore, whether or not a drug is legal, if it is addictive, using it is corrosive.

College authorities are aware of the problem of excessive alcohol consumption and they try to address it in a number of ways. Most colleges or universities have "alcohol awareness programs" which try to persuade students to drink alcoholic beverages in moderation. They also take some steps to curtail alcohol consumption. Drinking is forbidden on many campuses or allowed only for students who can produce a college ID indicating they are of legal drinking age. In order to prevent students from taking advantage of any perceived laxity, colleges treat violations of this policy severely. Colleges and universities also provide a wide range of medical and counseling services for students who have drinking problems.

It's laudable for colleges to have programs promoting responsible drinking. But, according to a natural law approach, what initiatives in this realm should students themselves take when interacting with students who drink to excess?

INTERVENTION

In terms of practical reasonableness, the principle of solidarity means something both positive and negative. On the positive side, it means that every person should have a concern that people have opportunities to participate in the fundamental values. With respect to actions that are out of bounds, it means that every person should have a general concern to prevent them from occurring. It does not necessarily mean people are compelled to intervene. Whether or not intervention is warranted is determined more by the principle of subsidiarity. This principle indicates the degree of responsibility any individual or group has for any other individual or group. In general, the smallest feasible group should be the one to make decisions affecting the welfare of people in the group. And the more tightly knit the group, the greater the pressure to intervene. For example, in order to win games members of the school basketball team practice hard every day and rely on each team member being alert and able to respond quickly to circumstances on court. Compared to a political science club that meets once a week to discuss regional and national politics, the basketball team has a greater responsibility to intervene to prevent one of their members from doing something stupid and immoral the night before an important game than the members of the political science club have the evening before their weekly meeting.

An example drawn from the bar scene helps demonstrate the principle of solidarity in action. Consider the case of a group of college friends, all from the same residence hall, going out to a bar on a Friday night. Just to keep things simple and to avoid trivial objections, let us also make the unusual and unrealistic assumption that each friend in the group basically subscribes to the natural law approach to morality. They are there at the bar having a good time, with no one drinking to excess, except one member of the group, Matt. In fact, Matt has separated himself from his friends and is sitting over at a table chatting with an attractive young woman, who also has had too much to drink. All in all, a pretty familiar scene.

Does anyone have any responsibility here? Well, our focus is on Matt and he has the primary responsibility. Unfortunately, he is already drunk and is therefore no longer able to be reasonable, rational, and responsible. Matt's friends can see what is going on and have a pretty good idea of what is going to happen next. Matt and the young woman are probably going to take their leave, go back to her room, and end up in bed before the night is out. Matt's ability to make clear decisions is certainly compromised, and the same is true for the young woman who is in no position to consent to sex. If Matt has sex with her later in the night, not only will he do something that is morally wrong in a serious way, but he will also do something that may be life-changing. What to many moderns appears as the triviality of the sex act may in fact jeopardize Matt's future since, when she sobers up, the young woman may well claim that she was raped because she never consented to sex. It is also true that the young woman's future could change forever should she conceive a child. What to do?

Matt's friends like him. They are the ones closest to him in this situation. There are no parents around, which is of course one of the attractions of the college experience. Thus, friends have more responsibility in this setting than they might have otherwise. According to the subsidiarity principle, they constitute the smallest feasible group who could possibly intervene. But do these friends have a moral responsibility to act? Certainly Matt has the primary responsibility to act morally, but he is drunk and his tryst could be a life-changing event for both him and the young woman. Matt is now or soon will be in a near occasion of sin. Given this situation and the fact that it is easy for the friends to intervene, they have some responsibility to do so. In this case, what they should do is fairly straightforward. They should go over to Matt, surround him, and in a friendly, jocular way escort him back to the residence hall where the guys live. Of course he will object. But the friends can exercise persuasion and even some force. They might say, "Come on, Matt, we're all going back together" or "No, you will see her again tomorrow. You come with us back to our apartment." He will want to stay alone with the young woman to see how things develop. Nevertheless, if his friends act deci-sively, he will most likely go along. And if he doesn't, at least they tried. The same principle applies to the young woman's friends, who should be equally protective in making sure the young woman gets back to her own room where she can fall asleep alone!

A confirmation that the "natural law thinking" we have outlined here is indeed natural is to consider an alternate outcome. Suppose Matt and the young woman returned to her room and had sex. Then suppose two days later the young woman lodges a formal complaint of date rape. Or suppose the young woman becomes pregnant and Matt's friends find out that she had an abortion. They would rightly reproach themselves for having failed to act to prevent this harm or at least attempted to prevent it. In retrospect it would seem quite reasonable to them that true friends should have intervened. More precisely, it is what the natural law approach expects of good friends.

Many people in modern society resist the very idea of intervening in a situation such as the one described above. In their view, the responsibility to act morally adheres solely to the individuals directly involved. If Matt and the young woman want to have sex, that is their decision. This is a very common reaction in our modern culture. According to the principle of solidarity in the natural law approach, however, Matt's friends are interested in his welfare and they also want to prevent corrosive things from happening. If they can achieve this with some ease, according to the principle of subsidiarity they ought to intervene. In this case, without too much effort they may be able to prevent Matt from doing something that is poten-tially life altering and harmful, something that, if sober, he would not do.

Consider a related problem. Alcoholism unfortunately affects many families. In a family, it is usually an adult who regularly drinks to excess. The individual, call him Edgar, can still go to work each day perhaps, but the alcoholism has bad reper-cussions in the home, especially on children or spouses. Many people in the family understand that Edgar needs professional help or has to become part of an Alcoholic Anonymous group. The difficulty is getting him to admit he needs help. There might be a way to organize an informal intervention team that pushes Edgar to get help. What a family does depends on particular circumstances. But family members who are sober understand they have a responsibility to help Edgar. In this case, the family is the smallest feasible group.

The above analysis also applies to people who have friends, colleagues, or family members heavily involved with addictive drugs. Taking such drugs is immoral and the smallest feasible group, often the family or a group of friends, has some respon-sibility to attempt to prevent a young person from taking drugs or to get an addict into rehab.

SUMMARY

An individual has a moral responsibility to avoid drinking to excess. This chapter has highlighted the responsibilities of relatives and friends. As we saw earlier, excessive drinking inhibits rational thinking and undermines fundamental values, as does the use of drugs or other addictive substances. Unfortunately, excessive drinking and drug use are often considered socially acceptable by many young adults.

The specific issues of alcohol abuse and drug use raise two important issues: What are our responsibilities in the face of a friend's potentially damaging behavior and what moral skills do we need to lead an authentically good life? This chapter paid particular attention to two moral skills: self-control and practical imagination in promoting good or avoiding evil. The following chapters present reasons why young adults should avoid sexual intimacy prior to marriage.

15

Sexual Activity Outside of Marriage

INSTANT INTIMACY IS a fact of life for many young adults who ardently resist making any long-term commitments. There is almost nothing young people will not post on Facebook, and quick trysts or one night stands are fairly commonplace in their world. Yet they resist long-term relationships that might foreclose their options and limit their experiences. They want to be loved and cherished, but the whole idea of contending with someone else's expectations seems way too constraining. Most young people expect or hope they will get married and have families—someday. But many are none too eager for that someday to arrive, nor do they seem to understand that what they are doing in the here and now might actually jeopardize their chances of realizing these goals.

The natural desire for physical and emotional intimacy with another person is one of the great gifts of human nature. It propels us to participate more fully in all the fundamental values. For most couples, marriage results in the highest participation in life (through children) and friendship (through commitment to each other until death). The full enjoyment of this gift, just like any other, requires that we use it well. And that means choosing to do some things and avoiding others. If young men and women hope to have meaningful friendships and enjoy loving and enduring marriages, they have to act in ways that make that possible. They need to question the reasonableness of today's social mores and look for something more rewarding and fulfilling.

Figuring out how to navigate the relationship scene is complicated and infused with seemingly equal parts of anticipation, anxiety, and confusion. When we are young we often feel at a loss and ill-prepared when it comes to negotiating this part of our lives. But each and every one of us grows up in a social context within a framework of established norms. In many cases these norms are useful guideposts that help us get our bearings. Some of these norms set the boundaries for what is and is not appropriate in our interactions with the opposite sex. Because many are linked to age and development, they guide us as we mature.

SEX FOR FUN

Some young people are fairly casual about engaging in premarital sex, for which they have a full range of rationales. This is true even for those who want to lead good and ethical lives. "It's fun. What's the harm? No one gets hurt. There are no long-term implications. Every one does it. Having sex before marriage will have no impact on my eventual marriage. If anything, I will be more sexually deft, which will be a treat for my future spouse and will lessen my awkwardness and embarrassment."

First, let us briefly run through these rationales and suggest a few reality checks. Something fun is indeed alright, unless of course the fun comes at the expense of others or at one's future expense. Someone can get a rush out of stealing things from a store, but the fun part does not make it right. It can be fun to be the maid of honor at a wedding, but that should not be the primary reason for doing it. In addition to fun, it should be an honor and a responsibility to assist the bride in her married life. Is there really no harm in premarital sex? If the partner thinks sex means something, implies something like love or affection, might be a sign of a deepening commitment, and for you it is just recreation, the harm can be considerable. There can also be long-term implications, like a baby to care for and a child to raise. At the very least, fun sex enters into a person's memory bank. Who knows when or how that gets retrieved at some time in the future?

Do most singles do it? Most surveys show that fewer than 25 percent of young unmarried people are sexually active. Does having sex as an engaged couple really have no impact on the marriage? First of all, some engaged couples do not get married. Even if they do, a partner to whom I am eventually married can wonder in the ensuing years whether he married me because I was good in bed or because he was committed to me. A tragedy looms if he is committed to me because I am good in bed since the sexual component can be more prominent for one partner in the early stages of a marriage than in the later stages. In addition, there's always someone out there who is better at sex. Or, there's always someone out there who is better at sex for me at this stage of my life. The excuses for justifying sex outside of marriage are legion.

Premarital sex has consequences, but many young people choose to avoid thinking about such things.

Some young people are comfortable with hooking-up, or having friends with benefits. Others are more selective, restricting sex to a person with whom they have a serious relationship. But even couples in a long-term relationship other than marriage admit that their commitment can end at any time, unannounced.

BIOLOGICAL AND SYMBOLIC

For many young people, questions about why sexual intimacy belongs only in a marital relationship are less about obligations to potential children conceived in such a relationship and more about their own freedom. Prior to marriage, they do not understand why their freedom should be curtailed, nor do they think sexual intimacy prior to marriage is corrosive of the fundamental value of friendship. In the language of fundamental values, they simply do not see why premarital sex misdirects or corrodes the later goal of attaining friendship at one of its highest levels.

Evolution culminated in human beings who are conscious and who interpret actions in terms of large goals or values. The sexual act among primates is certainly a biological act. At the emergence of primitive humans who were precursors to Homo sapiens, the sexual act may still have been merely a biological act, pleasurable and perhaps productive, occasionally yielding a new child. However, in a gradual process, which may have extended over thousands of years, sexual intimacy became a symbolic act that communicated the complete commitment of the man and woman to each other.

For human beings, sexual intercourse symbolizes the total gift of self to another and the totality of that gift precludes it being granted to anyone other than the person to whom one commits oneself. This symbolic meaning is an integrated add-on to the physical pleasure of the act. That is, it is not absent prior to marriage and then suddenly infused when vows are exchanged. Also, it is not a few-thousand-year afterthought, raised by Christian denominations millennia after the emergence of humans to justify restricting sex to marriage. Rather, it is a meaning that emerges from the act itself. The physical opening of oneself expresses the personal, exclusive commitment to intimacy and love between these two persons. Yes, it may be that it took thousands of years for the meaning to emerge clearly. However, the meaning comes from the act, not from some religious doctrine.

There is also a kind of profound mutual vulnerability inherent in the act of sexual intercourse that demands total mutual responsibility. Without total responsibility, sexual intimacy exploits human vulnerability. Sexual intimacy between spouses who have committed to "love and honor" each other until death is, as it was for early Homo sapiens, a pleasurable and occasionally productive act. However, it also signifies and reminds them of their lifelong responsibility to each other.

The physical act of sex includes two real components, one biological and the other symbolic. Sexual intimacy in marriage expresses and deepens the fundamental value of friendship by reminding the husband and wife of their commitment to unreserved mutuality and union. Outside of marriage sexual intimacy is corrosive because it is wrenched from its symbolic meaning. When the symbolic component is misused, it corrodes the commitment to one's current or eventual spouse in marriage and it also communicates a false message to oneself as well as to one's partner of convenience.

We have previously emphasized the importance that memory and imagination play in the moral sphere. Not surprisingly, memory and imagination should play a positive role in sexual intimacy, which is an expression of full human exchange and commitment. For this reason, contemplating or imagining the sexual act with someone other than one's spouse introduces corrosion into the activity of sexual intimacy between husband and wife. That is, if a married man freely chooses to contemplate an attractive woman other than his spouse as a possible sexual partner, he has already entered corrosive territory. The same would be true, for example, if a married woman thinks of a sexual affair as a pleasant diversion from the disappointments of her marriage.

The claim that sex involves an essential symbolic component expressing commitment requires further exploration. This chapter and subsequent ones explore this aspect from various perspectives. Some young adults will find the emphasis on this symbolic component completely convincing while others will find it charming, naïve, or unrealistic. Arguments are needed to persuade most young adults that the sexual act embodies an expression of lasting commitment.

TURNING EXCLUSIVITY ON AND OFF

Some single people think fidelity in marriage is important, but they have no problem with recreational sex prior to marriage. They think that as long as sex before marriage is consensual it is no big deal. But it is a big deal because, as we already pointed out, sex outside of marriage is stripped of its symbolic content. Sexual union is just that—union of two persons, not just of two bodies. When one or both of the parties are unwilling to commit to each other, what is supposed to be a mutual act of self-giving becomes merely a loan. Sex in this situation is wrenched from its symbolic meaning and is a pleasant hoax. Usually in this situation, but not always, it is the young man who is unwilling to commit to the woman. He may be willing to engage in pleasurable sexual activity over a period of months or years, but he does not want the young woman to interpret this activity as leading anywhere or becoming more deeply involved. He is basically exploiting the body of the woman for his own pleasure while setting aside the thought of a lasting commitment.

Sexual intimacy involves making yourself vulnerable to your partner. If the young man sees sexual intimacy as a way to secure pleasure without commitment and ultimately walks away from the relationship, he takes advantage of the young woman's vulnerability and washes his hands of all future responsibility to her.

Lets consider a justification for sex before marriage that many engaged couples endorse by their behavior. Many approve of premarital sex when it occurs between an engaged couple who fully intend to commit themselves together for life in a marriage ceremony in the relatively near future. Sexual activity in this situation and time period, even though it occurs outside of marriage, is deemed good and acceptable by many couples. Despite the widespread acceptance of this practice, careful reflection reveals it to be a ruse.

Sexual intimacy prior to marriage involves both self-deception and deception of others. The decision of the couple to have a marriage ceremony indicates a desire to make a public commitment to one another. At the marriage ceremony, the couple state their commitment to love and honor each other their whole life long. As an engaged couple, they obviously have not yet made that commitment. Consequently, their sexual experiences prior to the wedding are symbolically dishonest because they do not involve a total commitment.

Suppose the engaged partners do not believe they will be making a substantial new commitment to one another in the marriage ceremony. They might claim they are now already fully committed to one another. What is lacking is that their total commitment has not yet been made public and celebrated by their families and friends. They would argue that any sexual intimacies at this point are completely self-giving and therefore noncorrosive.

For two reasons, however, their self-giving is neither complete nor socially responsible. First, some couples who think they are "totally committed" break off their engagements before the wedding. This reality alone means that couples cannot be totally committed prior to a public commitment. Indeed, this is why society requires that the commitment be public—either before a priest or minister or a justice of the peace. Only at that point does the total commitment become binding.

Second, even if both partners are sure of their complete commitment, they have a social responsibility to support the institution of marriage. Marriage is not just about the couple committing themselves to each other, as important as this is. It is also about how society understands marriage, supports marriage, and helps sustain couples who are married. As an institution, traditional marriage of one person to another person took long millennia to build up. Young people should be willing to exercise self-control and restraint to support the institution of marriage, an institution that will provide them with future protection, encouragement, and support to maintain their total commitment. Couples do not act independently of institutions. They benefit from good institutions, and they have a responsibility to provide general support to institutions such as marriage, especially when it imposes a small cost—self-restraint—on them.

The previous argument stresses support for the institution of marriage. Such support is directly related to the common good, that is, the good of everyone in society. Approximately 40 percent of children in the United States are currently born out of wedlock. In a large number of these cases, it means the child will be raised by a single mother, not by the mother and the father of the child. The law of averages shows that such children will, on average, be at a large socio-economic disadvantage as they grow to maturity. A strong institution of marriage helps both mothers and children flourish.

Reserving sexual intimacy to marriage and linking sex to lifelong commitment enhance the likelihood of couples raising children as couples and not as single parents. Couples who want to make a contribution to the institution of marriage in society will avoid sexual intercourse until they are married. If only one couple decides to forgo sex for this reason, the impact is negligible. However, if many couples adhere to the norm of sex only in marriage, it helps reinforce a standard for those who are inclined to risk having a baby outside of marriage. That is, supporting sex reserved to marriage promotes the common good.

The total self-giving expected in marriage is marred or blemished by what happens in previous sexual encounters. Via memory and imagination, our past is part of our present and future. In marriage, a spouse with former sexual experiences at least occasionally recalls those intimacies. For the single woman, the premarriage liaison was perhaps an attempt at securing commitment at least for a few days, months, or years. For the single man, the prior sexual relationship may have been an unjust avoidance of commitment and engaging in a sign of commitment he knew was false. The act erodes the singularity of his commitment to his current or future wife. The memory of the misuse of the act clouds the clarity of one's present commitment.

Sexual intimacy between couples before marriage undermines the very lifelong loving relationships most young people seek. That is why it is considered off-limits. Some couples decide to field-test marriage by living together. They want to find out if they are sexually compatible in the hopes they will not end up as another divorce statistic. Such an approach, however, is misguided. For one thing it makes sexual performance seem like one more skill to be rated rather than a way of communicating that mutual commitment and tenderness can grow more sensitive over time. Furthermore, research indicates that divorce is significantly more likely among couples who live together before marriage than those who do not. Certainly this is not a simple cause-and-effect relationship. Rather it suggests that those who choose to cohabit are somehow less willing to stick with marriage when they find it less fulfilling than they hoped. This may be because couples that cohabit do not look sufficiently for those activities that provide deep, long-term fulfillment in marriage.

In this chapter we considered some of the traits of marriage as an institution, an institution that requires support, and we also briefly considered a number of arguments used to justify pre-marital sex. Think of this chapter as a preliminary treatment of the main issues concerning sexual intimacy. In subsequent chapters we review most of these arguments from different perspectives.

Even the most basic ways in which men and women interact requires support and management. In the next chapter we look at the types of support and encouragement that parents regularly give children so that they mature to respect the important differences between men and women. Another way to express this is that "natural law" does not happen independent of society. Natural law assumes parents instruct children and then young people attend to reasons for various practices. The next two chapters explore the role family culture plays in promoting the natural law approach to marriage.

16

Girls, Boys, and Teenagers

ALTHOUGH THE RELATION between sexes is fairly complex, it is not difficult for children to recognize the contours of such relations or perceive the various norms that society establishes because children are exposed to these norms gradually. As the children mature, parents, families, and other institutions in society make increasingly clearer to children and teenagers the ways in which boys and girls are expected to relate to one another.

SOCIAL NORMS FOR THE YOUNG

The establishment of clear norms actually begins while children are quite young. Consider a few examples. When young boys and girls reach a certain age (five or six), they are no longer permitted to see each other undressed. Busy moms and dads often bathe their toddlers together in one tub, but by the time they are setting off to kindergarten, their sons and daughters have different bath times. It is also true that at a certain point in school boys and girls start using separate bathrooms. While the unisex bathroom scene might be prevalent at some trendy colleges and universities, it is not going to spread to primary and secondary schools any time soon.

All of us can remember the rather rough and tumble days of childhood; young children can be pretty physical with each other. In the early grades of primary school, up to and including high school, boys always seem to be hitting, poking, pushing, shoving, tackling, and wrestling with each other. Most of the time their carrying-on is playful, but occasionally it can get intense and angry. Girls, on the other hand, tend to be far less involved in roughhousing. They do, however, hug one another, hold hands, or walk arm and arm very naturally. While there is some rough play between boys and girls when they are fairly young (less than seven or eight years old), it tends to end well before their preteen years. As boys get older and bigger, male roughhousing increases and gets rougher. And as that happens, the boys are repeatedly told by parents, teachers, and other adults to keep their hands off the girls. An occasional shove might be overlooked, but the older boys get, the more insistent parents and adults become that the boys leave the girls alone.

Although much is permitted for boys among other boys, or girls among other girls, young people gradually come to understand they have to treat members of the opposite sex differently. Boys are rougher with each other than they are with girls, both in what they do and what they say. In this culture, the girls welcome this special treatment. Girls can easily compete with boys in many different activities, but in most physical activities the girls are happy to restrict their contact and competition to other girls. Similarly the boys are happy to compete primarily with other boys in sports. Nonetheless, even as they advance through high school, the boys have to be reminded not to touch the girls. For their part, girls themselves readily endorse this norm when they yell at some annoying boy, "Don't you dare touch me!"

Part of maturing for young men is realizing what is off-limits in the presence of women. They cannot use their physical strength against women. They also cannot gross them out or say sexually suggestive things to them. Now, what constitutes "gross" and "sexually suggestive" is pretty vague and in our modern society seems to get vaguer as time goes on. And it may well differ from community to community. Nevertheless, whatever the boundaries, young people understand them in their own community.

This description of how relations among pre-adolescents and adolescents pretty much operate in Western society demonstrates something very important. Society and the institutions in them understand boys have to be trained and formed in how they treat girls, and vice versa. If society fails in this task, girls and women can suffer at the hands of boys and men who are able to take physical advantage of them. With or without legal statues and codes, a just society must at the very least assure that practically all young girls and adult women are safe with men, both inside and outside the home.

Social norms that sustain and support the realization of the fundamental values develop over time, often in complicated and sometimes confusing ways. Take for instance the issue of women's fashion. At one time young girls were scolded for so much as showing their ankles because it was considered a sexually provocative act. Today young women are encouraged by fashion magazines to look "sexy," and clothes that are marketed to even the youngest teenagers leave almost nothing to the imagination. Absent the religious convictions of a community, neither of these extreme fashion norms is very helpful. By allowing only extremely "protective dressing" among girls, one needlessly encumbers women while almost encouraging men to make sexually crude or obnoxious comments. Similarly, encouraging suggestive dressing among girls points toward an instant physical intimacy that at the very least makes women more vulnerable. Whatever the fashion trends, parents, teachers, and other adults share in the responsibility of making sure that young men and women can control their inclinations toward sexual intimacy. In a well-functioning society, young men and women know when they are reaching a danger point in taunting and teasing one another sexually.

Society is heavily involved in forming young men and women. It has norms, and boys and girls are eventually expected to adhere to them. This is all part of forming "nature" according to natural law. Even if the norms are questionable or wrong, society forms young men and women. If the norms are wrong, society relies on people committed to practical reasonableness to criticize the social norm in question and convince society to make adjustments.

Communities understand that if they want practically everyone to be able to pursue the fundamental values, then social interactions have to be such as to allow women also to pursue these values. If women are to prosper morally, they cannot feel physically and psychologically threatened by men. This falls under the principle of solidarity. Women must also be allowed to pursue the fundamental values in ways that may be (in Western society, according to a woman's choice) quite different from the normal way men pursue the same values. Yes, it seems to have taken hundreds or even tens of thousands of years for a society to come to a reasonable appreciation of this realization. It is also likely that some societies are a whole lot better than others at establishing norms that create this supportive environment. What this means is that the implications of natural law, particularly those involving complex interactions of women and men in society, require extended periods of experimentation and evaluation. It also means some societies are going to be better attuned to the fundamental values than others.

Human beings have appetites, tendencies, and intellects that predispose them to seek arrangements that promote and protect the fundamental values. Our societies have to evolve to a structure that properly accommodates these basic components of a fair society. One significant institutional change in society can have an impact on how many other practices are eventually interpreted. For this reason, a society committed to the fundamental values requires regular evaluation and adjustments, as society attempts to promote the common good in a changing society.

The emergence of men and women from early primates was a signal development. Scientists usually mark this transition by noting changes in both the size and intricacy of the brain in Homo sapiens. The emergence of the unique gift of consciousness is another crucial aspect of this development. Consciousness in Homo sapiens enabled great insights, but it also complicated interactions between members of the species. With consciousness, communication was no longer just about making signs, symbols, and noises. Now it was about speaking and interpreting the speech in context. A human now had to figure out what the other human was thinking and what was not being said, as well as what was. This added complexity only increased the need for social experimentation to work out behavior patterns consonant with natural law.

NATURAL LAW AND MARRIAGE

In Western society there is broad acceptance that husbands and wives should remain faithful to each other, despite the fact that plenty of them have affairs. Almost any married person who becomes sexually involved with someone else understands that an extramarital affair is wrong, cruel, and harmful to both spouses. Married men and women solidly endorse the norm: in marriage, sex is limited to your spouse. Spouses readily acknowledge that if one of them is unfaithful, their marriage is in crisis. In most cases it will be possible to save the marriage only if the offending spouse is truly repentant and the infidelity stops.

Our focus in this book is on marriage between one man and one woman. Not considered in any depth is the issue of polygamy. One man with many wives was and still is considered by some to be an acceptable way for women and men to relate, have children, and raise them. Without exploring the reasons why polygamy may have made sense in earlier societies, most people in Western society would acknowledge now that the commitment of a single man to a single woman constitutes a higher form of friendship than commitment of a single man to many women. Much of the following discussion can be used to show that polygamy in modern, developed society is unfair to women and actually corrodes friendship in marriage.

Why, for all practical purposes, is the commitment to sexual fidelity between a married man and woman universal? After all, the prevailing moral norm in our modern, ultra-accepting society is: Do what you want to do, as long as it does not interfere with others. Why does infidelity interfere with the nonoffending spouse? With millions of people married in Western society, you would think there would be many more marriages of convenience with prior agreements that permitted some extramarital sexual dabbling. Routine infidelities may be the rule in some or many marriages. What is practically unheard of, however, is anyone saying before-hand that the bride and groom are committing themselves to a type of marriage that permits occasional extramarital liaisons.

Married couples understand that marriage demands a commitment of one partner to the other. They also correctly interpret intercourse as a natural sign of that commitment. Cheating spouses hide their transgressions, and with good reason. They do so because offended husbands and wives rightly interpret cheating as a dreadful blow to their marriage. Extramarital sex jeopardizes the mutual commitment of marriage partners. Indeed, in many cases of divorce, extramarital infidelity is the very reason cited to justify the divorce. We claim that, apart from a natural law ethic, modern society has no real explanation for why this under-standing is so broadly shared.

The tenacious social insistence that extramarital sex is anathema has persisted even in a rather sexually permissive society. This reality seems to fly in the face of the way many young people act and justify their behavior, especially when it differs from that of their friends or acquaintances. "You do what you want to do, believe what you want to believe, and I will do what I want." This prevailing modern atti-tude of unconstrained choice suggests there are no universal moral standards, only those that individuals choose. Precisely because that attitude is so prevalent, soci-ety's insistence that marital infidelity is taboo is striking. It must be that somehow married couples understand some basic things about marriage, beyond concern for children, which gives them this particular perspective. After all, the taboo on sex outside of marriage cannot be justified just as way to protect the children. Even women far beyond their childbearing or child-raising years maintain a commitment to sexual fidelity in marriage and expect their husbands to do likewise.

Natural law can shed light on what is going on here. As was noted in the previous chapter, sexual intercourse and other intimacies associated with it are more than simply biological acts. The biological act of intercourse occurs in a context of at least weak commitment and some openness to the other. Even in sex among sin-gles, the importance of commitment and openness to the other person appears to be present at least in a tepid way. If asked to judge how a sexual hook-up with someone else was, the judgment often includes the notion of whether there was an emotional or psychological connection made. The connection may have only lasted for the length of the encounter and meant nothing beyond it, but it still counted for the moment.

In marriage, sexual intercourse physically joins spouses, making them utterly vulnerable one to the other. In making love, spouses willingly accept this vulnerability while expressing love and commitment to their partner. According to the natural law, sexual intercourse should be in principle open to the conception of a child. And yes, there are all kinds of objections that immediately come to mind when we say this. We'll get to these objections later, but for now we are highlighting the claims of natural law. Natural law insists that a child should be conceived in a loving act and that the lovers should be open to accepting any child that comes from this love. Even though conception does not occur with every sexual act, openness to conceiving a child is the framework for each sexual act in marriage, according to natural law.

A married couple has no obligation to maximize the number of children they have; they can plan sexual activity around a woman's infertile times, for instance. In fact, in recent years natural family planning, which does not use pills or devices, has become much more popular. One reason for this is that it is much more reliable and respects the women's physical cycle, without adding chemicals to her body. Even with natural family planning, however, when one has sex one should welcome possible conception. Sex is an expression of love and every child conceived should start with an act of love, possibly carried forth to conception according to God's plan. Children should be born in love, raised in love, and taught to love first by their parents.

Natural law argues that sexual intercourse ought to be the physical act that occurs in a context of commitment, love, and openness to life. Because of the context, sexual intercourse is in fact a symbolic act. It is also an act that stimulates the memory and imagination.

The physical dimension of sex, which developed over millions of years in evolution among mammals, is the way a species propagates itself. Accompanying the larger and more intricate brain of Homo sapiens was a development in complexity, in consciousness. People belonging to the group Homo sapiens not only were conscious of their own being but also of others belonging to the same group. And they were aware that other members of this group were conscious of themselves and others. They knew they were in a world that they could represent pictorially. The world was "out there" and they were here.

As a result of this development, over the course of thousands of years, man and woman began to see sex in a different way, as a statement of love and concern for the partner. They also became conscious that children come to be through sexual intercourse. For modern couples with children, the sexual act has a unique connection to memory. It is a reminder and a remembrance of a time when they hoped to have a child and to grow their family. Depending on their age and other circumstances, that yearning for children might still loom in their love making. Sex is an act of the total person. Memory and imagination are activities of the intellect. Strange as it may seem to some, sexual intercourse engages the intellect, not just the body apart from the brain.

Nonhuman animals copulate. Human beings have sex. There is an enormous difference between the two types of intimacy. Copulation is a physical act, but not much more than that. Why does the physical act suddenly change when human beings are intimate with one another? First, at this point scientists don't have enough information to know why suddenly things changed. What makes humans human is their consciousness, their ability to reflect on themselves even as they are doing or thinking about doing things. Because consciousness is linked to self-awareness, language and consciousness are an expression of the soul, which is a person's principle of identity. Humans adjusted to consciousness. The process of adjusting to their new awareness of themselves (and their awareness that other humans are aware of themselves) may have lasted thousands of years.

Awareness, language, and consciousness gradually modified the sexual act. Copulation gradually added components of memory and imagination (as one human tried to imagine what his partner was thinking during or after intercourse). As memory and imagination played a larger role in intercourse, the couple understood better how the physical act links together not only their bodies but also their psyches, their souls, possibly also their hopes and fears. In this way, sexual intercourse as an expression of love and commitment became more widely understood and accepted. In addition, couples increasingly understood how playfulness also entered into sex. In short, what at the dawn of humanity was once primarily physical, namely copulation, over probably thousands of years became the more complex and layered action of sexual intercourse, which is what modern married couples engage in.

So, the sexual act is physical (or biological), symbolic, at times playful, and at least on some occasions engages the memory and imagination through past intimacies and/or those expected in the future. Most modern couples, despite being somewhat casual about moral approaches, grasp this reality in some important way. It is the only way to explain why married couples want to restrict sex to marriage partners, no matter the form of marriage.

According to natural law, a wife expects the husband to "husband" his sexual memory. He is to guard it so that no foreign sexual images enter it. Most important, no sexual images stemming from intercourse with another woman should enter her husband's memory bank. And the husband expects a similarly pure sexual imagination from his wife.

LIMITED COMMITMENT OR FOREVER

Social norms around marriage are in flux in Western society, and marriage now refers to at least two different possible arrangements. The first arrangement acknowledges the possibility the marriage may only last for a while. Even though almost all couples hope their marriage will last for a very long time, some know and acknowledge to each other either explicitly or implicitly that divorce is a possibility. Prenuptial agreements are obvious indicators of this view of marriage.

Realizing that the marriage will last a few or several or many years, some spouses develop legal or mental contingency plans. When the marriage reaches the point where one spouse would like to end it, perhaps because he has fallen in love with someone else, it is seen as painful and wrenching, but not completely unexpected. In fact, it falls within the bounds of what the couple originally promised each other. In their wedding vows they may have used language suggesting they would remain married to one another their whole lives, but those words conveyed more of a hope than a promise, maybe even only a wish, without any firm commitment to work things out in case of difficulties.

The other type of marriage is captured in the traditional Catholic understanding of marriage. In a Catholic wedding ceremony each spouse says to the other: "I take you to be my [husband, wife]. I promise to be true to you in good times and in bad, in sickness and health. I will love you and honor you all the days of my life." This is an unconditional commitment to remain true to each other until the death of either the husband or the wife. According to regular Church teaching, marriage is a solemn commitment and the meaning of the words counts. It may be that one spouse said the words but did not mean them or understood them to include divorce when something terrible happens. If convincing evidence for this personal interpretation can be produced, in the eyes of the Church the marriage never took place, even though families and friends of the bride and groom were there in the Church and heard the couple pronounce their vows. It never took place because the promise was deficient (if indeed the bride or groom did not intend to promising love until death). The bride or groom may have been full of emotion and very loving throughout the day and subsequent years, but what counts is the freedom, understanding, and intention of the commitment.

A necessary requirement for a Catholic marriage to take place is that each partner must promise and genuinely intend unconditional love until death parts them. Each partner has to say it and mean it! The priest who witnesses their marriage is responsible for carefully reviewing with the couple what the marriage vows mean and imply, and prior to the wedding ceremony the couple has to formally state (and sign a statement) indicating they understand marriage in this way.

The general norm for marriage, according to natural law, must be a commitment until the death of one of the partners. Certainly, this is the highest level of commitment one person can make to another. The natural law justification for marriage until the death of one of the partners is threefold. First, the complete acceptance and privacy of marriage is the best way to assure that the hopes, fears, confusions, and vulnerabilities of spouses are protected. Second, lifelong commitment is also essential because each man and woman is a complex creature, partly mysterious, partly predictable, and an inexhaustible source of comfort and companionship. That is, each person is an inexhaustible source of love, contentment, and friendship. Finally, commitment until death provides stability, love, and support within the family, that is, both the nuclear and extended family.

Two people communicate most deeply one with another when they share their fears, hopes, joys, satisfactions, and confusions. These are the interior joys and groanings of the self, perhaps not completely understood by individuals themselves. Part of the satisfaction of marriage is the freedom of knowing that these emotions can be fully shared with each other while remaining forever protected. A spouse might slip on occasion and reveal something very private he thinks his spouse might not mind his sharing with family or friends. But these missteps get corrected over time by means of gentle or not so gentle conversations between husband and wife. The point is, secrets of the interior life should be protected by loving spouses. A marriage to death provides a safe context for sharing such intimate information and thereby encourages the couple to be deeply honest with each other and to grow in knowledge together. This type of sharing can only happen in a relationship secured by lasting commitment.

Apart from how much is shared at this very intimate level, each person possesses a wealth of human possibility. Because part of being married is pursuing the fundamental values together, the common activities of the couple create satisfaction, joy, the basis for reflection and perhaps gratitude, and/or the basis for new ideas about how to pursue the fundamental values. Occasionally a priest will hear the comment from a jaded husband, "Father, there is nothing about her I don't already know. I'm bored with her." In effect, the husband is saying that her wealth is depleted; he has mined everything and nothing else is there to interest him. In fact, however, his spouse is still a treasure. The real difference now after so many years is that the husband has stopped looking for the treasure in his spouse. Fundamentally marriage is for life because each partner offers unlimited ways for the other partner to grow in love as a person, and each partner implicitly says this in the marriage vow.

The third reason marriage lasts until death parts the couple is a practical one. Whether or not a married couple is blessed with children, the couple becomes part of a larger family, including both the wife's and the husband's families. Even without children, the couple is woven into a larger friendship group. An aunt and uncle without children can play very important, helpful, and meaningful roles in the extended family. Via their lifelong commitment to one another, they them-selves become a gift to other members of the family, and their mutual commit-ment, lived out within the family, is also a gift to young children—nieces, nephews, and cousins—in the family. If the couple has children, their lifelong commitment provides clarity, stability, support, and love to their own children, and eventually, God willing, to the grandchildren as well.

Clearly, in marriage each partner should make an enormous commitment—a lifelong commitment—both to the other person as an individual and to the family of one's spouse. With respect to the fundamental value of friendship, this is an exemplary action that then is carried to fruition through a series of exemplary and loving actions.

17

Movies, Moms, and Norms for Teenagers

MARIA AND DAVE were waiting in the food court of a large cinema complex. The film they had come to see was not set to start for another twenty minutes, so they were sipping sodas at one of the small tables near the door. Usually the theatre was packed with young teens and tweens waiting to see the latest hit film. Today was a bit different because mixed in with the young people were a good number of adults. Maria said she thought most of them were coming to see a new R-rated film about young lovers. Maria had read about the new film in a newspaper. The review she read said the film was fairly raunchy and had a lot of gratuitous sex, but because the actors were popular with the 12-to-15 year-old crowd, this group of kids was clearly the target audience. None of the kids was old enough to be admitted without an adult, so they had obviously persuaded a good number of moms to accompany them to the film.

Maria told Dave she wasn't sure how she felt about it. On the one hand, she was depressed that so many mothers agreed to accompany their daughters and sons to see such a film. Even worse, a number of moms had brought their much younger daughters, some of whom could not have been 10 years old. She also thought it was interesting so few dads were part of the group and she wondered what that was all about. Asking one's mom to go to a film like this was awkward for a son or daughter, but maybe it was easier for the girls. Maybe the dads were at work and maybe they just weren't around very much. Maybe physical distance in the movie theatre made it easier to see this type of film with your mother. Maria imagined that, once mothers and children entered the theatre, the guys would leave their mothers, and similarly for the girls, and then sit with their friends in another section of the theatre. Perhaps the mothers sat together, and then there were pods of boys and pods of girls.

It was depressing that so many young kids were there to see a steamy R-rated film. But the event piqued Maria's interest; she was curious about what the mothers might say to their sons and daughters after the film. She told Dave she would love to be a fly on the wall for those conversations. She couldn't imagine these "chats" would be anything but embarrassing for everyone involved. Certainly the mothers would have to register some disgust with the film. Not to say anything would mean they thought it was okay. But they had to do something other than register moral outrage. "Well, that was immoral and outrageous" was not going to cut it. At the very least they had to point out what was immoral and outrageous. Maria was sure the moms would clarify what they objected to and also make abundantly clear what they would not tolerate from their children.

Dave smiled and told Maria she was being completely naïve. "The mothers are not going to say anything," Dave said. "A few might. But look at them. The moms and daughters are both dressed like gangster hos. They just don't get it. At best they might say nothing. More likely they'll endorse it in some way."

Now Maria was annoyed. "First of all, why are you looking at what the mothers and daughters are wearing? What type of clothing they wear should be of no concern to you. You don't go around judging how guys dress. So, cut the women some slack and let them wear whatever they want to. I would never dress that way. But I don't know where guys get off making comments like yours. Who knows why they dress that way? Anyway, at least the moms showed up with the kids. That's more than you can say for the dads!"

Since Dave and Maria's film was to start in a few minutes, they got up and walked to their theatre. When the film was over, they went out for a drink. Initially they recalled some of the funnier scenes from the comedy they had seen. But after a few minutes, Dave retuned to some of the things Maria had said just before the film began. He was a bit defensive because Maria had accused him of looking too much at the young girls and their moms. But still, he had a point to make, so he tried again to react to Maria's earlier comments.

Dave said he agreed with Maria that it is interesting to guess what thoughts are going through the minds of these seventh-, eighth-, and upper-grade students as they watch these pretty explicit sex scenes. Also, he agreed completely with Maria that their mothers should say something. It's just that, judging from appearances, it did not look like the moms would necessarily object to what the movie's messages about sex and romance.

"There, you just said it. 'Judging from appearances,' you said. You have no right to do that," said Maria. Dave agreed he should not criticize a particular mom or her daughter for what she was wearing, but certainly it was okay to observe that clothes convey messages. "You're allowed to note the obvious!" Dave could feel himself getting carried away a bit.

"After all," Dave said, "pornography works on some people because of what is worn and what pose people take. It is certainly true that young women and men dress and carry themselves in certain ways to attract attention." Dave was quick to add that the girls were innocent, but he also claimed they were becoming less innocent, in part because of the leadership and acquiescence of their mothers. "Maria, I know you are positive and you say God made us, he did not make junk, and our bodies are good. I agree with all that. But modesty in dress and behavior has to count for something."

After Dave had spoken for a while, Maria conceded the whole dress thing is problematic. "A woman's body is something good and beautiful. The Christian churches believe this. The problem is not that guys don't acknowledge it. They know women are beautiful. The problem is the guys want to use that beauty for their own enjoyment and on their own terms. They also say they want to be friends with a young woman, but many want to be friends just for the night or for a few weeks, months, or years." Maria also agreed that too many moms give in too easily to cultural norms they don't actually agree with. In raising adolescents, you have to pick your battles so you don't end up alienating your own children. As a result, moms say nothing about a lot of the hypersexualized clothes, lyrics, and media being marketed to their kids. "The result," said Maria, "is a culture designed for children by adults who refuse to act like adults."

Maria was feeling down, so she asked Dave for his opinion of what parents should say about sex to a teenage child. "The movie might offer a good occasion to talk, but the parent better be prepared to say something." Dave completely agreed. "If the parent doesn't weigh in, the child will listen to his friend, his teacher, or the media. Parents have a big role to play."

Dave admitted he did not know much about teenage girls and what goes through their heads. Although he has two sisters, he never talked with them about any of these things. Dave likes his sisters, but he just could not imagine discussing sex with them. Although he had no opinions about mothers and daughters, he was clear about what he thought should happen between parents and sons. "Teenagers need simple, direct messages, repeated many times," said Dave. "And the message should come from both the child's mother and father." Because there are so many permissive messages about sex appearing in movies, TV films and melodramas, magazines, and the Internet, Dave said it was important for parents to work as a team to present their own message and approach. He acknowledged that teenagers will make believe they are not listening or even disagree with their parents because they view their parents as so old fashioned. But the teenagers are listening and they do think about what their parents tell them. Furthermore, because teenagers are experiencing so many new things every month, the message has to be said a number of times.

"But what's the message, Dave? What would you say?" "Okay, okay, I'm getting to that. I think the parent has to say four things. The full message may not occur all in one session. And parents can be imaginative about how they bring it up. But with a son, the father should be the first one to address the issue. Some time later, the mom can say, 'Dad told me he spoke to you about relationships and sex. I want to know what you think and I also want to share with you what I think.'" Dave suggested that, for a daughter, it would probably be good for the mom to speak first to the daughter and then the father, but he told Maria he was not sure he would be able to speak about relationships and sex to a daughter of his. "I actually think it is a sign of love for a parent to address this topic with his child. I would love my daughter, but I think I would not know where to begin the conversation with her."

"All right, the daughter may be a more difficult case for the dad. But, David, what are you going to say to your son?"

Dave began, "Well, the dad and mom have to say the four things to their son, each in their own way. The first is: don't think about having sex until you are ready to have a child and care for the child. Second, don't have sex until you can make a promise to be faithful to a woman and keep it. Third, don't think about having sex until you are mature enough to figure out whether some young woman to whom you make a promise of love for a lifetime will be able to keep her promise to you of love for a lifetime. Fourth, pray regularly to God for help and insight."

Dave proceeded to talk for a few more minutes. He admitted that three of the four things he was recommending were negative. Also, part of maturing is that boys spend a lot of time thinking about girls, and vice versa. "It's not as if they can stop thinking about them," said Dave. "They just don't have to fixate on them." Still, Dave was sure teenagers need direct, uncomplicated talk. Sons in particular get really embarrassed with sex and relationship talk. A parent has to quickly get to the heart of the matter.

Any parent wants a child to avoid corrosive acts. Aside from terminal embarrassment, the real problem for teenagers is they have no sense of the future. For them, a lifetime lasts about a month. Dave does not believe they can think or plan much beyond that, especially when they are in the process of falling madly in love or are trying to win their next basketball game or be a great performer in the school play. "So telling a teenager 'never' really means 'not during the next month.' Then you have to repeat it a month later," said Dave.

Dave added that he thought the most difficult point for the son to understand would be picking a girl who can make a lifelong promise and keep it. Dave said, "When I say this to him, he will probably say, 'Duh, Dad, do you think I'm going to marry someone who is not going to be committed to me?' But I would tell him it is not easy to make good judgments in this area. I'll tell him that he cannot possibly make a good judgment about a reliable girl until he knows how to recognize a girl or woman whom he can't trust to fulfill a lifelong promise. In order to know the type of girl who can keep the promise, you have to know the type of girl who can't keep the promise."

Dave waited for a reaction and, after a short period of silence, Maria perked up. "I'm impressed, David. I had not thought about this. You clearly have. Your four things are very good. They might not be the four things I would say, but I am impressed."

CONTEXT

Society contributes to the formation of girls as women and boys as men, and society begins with the family. Especially in a culture that allows many discordant voices, a mother and father should be clear to their children about those views and perspectives they most treasure. The convictions of a mother and father come with years of experience, thought, and commitment as well as with deep knowledge or and commitment to their children. When their children are teenagers, parents should start talking about important, big convictions with them. This is the way a family reinforces and eventually hands on a culture.

18

Sex and the Fundamental Values

NATURAL LAW EMERGES from and conforms to nature, but when it comes to sex, it is also countercultural in the Western world. No matter where you turn in American society you are bombarded with messages about sex. From films and ads in fashion magazines, from hundreds of thousands of Web sites, from television shows and from the media and towering billboards that rise in our cities and on our highways the word goes out that everyone is doing it—or at least everyone who matters or is cool or successful does it. And if some are not doing it because they don't have a convenient partner, this can be fixed in a variety of ways: weight loss programs and pharmaceuticals, hair transplants and waxings, or with dating services, the latest cocktails, better make-up, sexy clothes, sexy cars, sexy jobs, sexy everything. Sex is fun and free. It's an anytime experience with almost anyone. The message is clear: everybody's doing it, what about you?

PREMARITAL SEX

Some young people are comfortable with hooking-up, or having friends with benefits. Others are more selective, restricting sex to a person with whom they have a serious relationship. But even committed (but unmarried) couples in a long-term relationship admit that their commitment can end at any time, unannounced.

Natural law understands sexual intimacy in a very different way. Sexual intimacy is not seen as an end unto itself. Rather it is related to participating in the fundamental values, particularly the value of friendship in one of its most profound expressions. It is also linked to life at its deepest level, namely, when new human life is generated. As a result, natural law locates sexual activity strictly within a committed marriage relationship.

Sexual intercourse is a physical act between a man and a woman. It is the means whereby publicly committed and lasting love is expressed and new human life comes to be. At least in Western society, most of the young people who engage in premarital sex are not interested in becoming parents as a result of their sexual liaisons. Many of them are ill-prepared for that role as well. Consequently most take some precautions to make sure they do not get pregnant. Having donned a condom or taken birth control pills, they dismiss the procreative nature of what they are doing and focus solely on their mutual satisfaction. Despite their precautions, however, abundant statistical data shows that many sexual experiences result in "unintended" conception with all its inherent consequences. And even in the vast majority of cases when conception is averted, the very nature of the sexual act as the normal way to generate human life has not changed. Similarly, the drive that their love be creative in some real sense remains unaltered even if not attended to.

Assuring children are born into viable, loving, stable, and lasting environments is important. But even if unmarried couples could be 100 percent sure that conception would not occur as a result of a particular sexual encounter, would there be any compelling reason for them to forego sex? The answer is yes.

Outside of marriage sex weakens and calls into question lasting friendship. Whether or not those involved want to admit it, sex changes relationships, something the *Sex and the Soul* study makes abundantly clear. Some students, more often than not the men, think hooking-up is just part of the experience of college, a chance to be spontaneous and try new things. Others, more often women than men, are at least hoping that a sexual experience will develop into a relationship. Many of these are the same women who think they are entitled to a little conversation and civility after sex—an attitude a sizable number of guys finds repugnant. Being "entitled to civility" in a relationship is not an aberration; it is a fundamental human expectation. Also, civility is one thing; how about genuine respect and honor for one's partner?

Three components of the sexual act have been singled out. Sex is physical, entailing the biological possibility of conception; it symbolizes lasting commitment; and it includes memory, imagination, and hope. Because sex is not only physical, but is also symbolic and recalls memories, it is hard to be casual about it. The act itself is anything but casual. After all, on the level of the purely physical sex requires the uniting of two human bodies. As is well known, anyone who engages in sex with multiple partners runs the risk of incurring a sexual disease. This reality, however, is not a deterrent for many because they are convinced they take the proper physical precautions. Nonetheless, the possibility of disease should be a reminder that our bodies cannot do everything. Since the threat of disease does not deter the determined, let us consider other important arguments against premarital sex.

On the symbolic level the physical uniting of the two bodies represents the total gift of self by two individuals to each other. A committed marriage provides the only truly appropriate context for this kind of self-giving. When two people engage in premarital sex they understandably hold something back because they are not fully united, and this is because their future together is in some doubt. Consequently, the symbolic meaning that is integral to sexual union is missing.

Furthermore, the symbolic component of sexual union is not a simple add-on, like an optional extra ingredient in a recipe, which can be included at will. This means that sex as a sign of commitment cannot be absent prior to marriage and then suddenly be infused or added like a dash of salt when vows are exchanged in the marriage ceremony.

HONORING ONE'S SPOUSE VIA A RESERVED ACTIVITY

Human beings draw meaning from actions and pour meaning into actions. In personal relationships, thoughts and words don't suffice, even though they may be consoling or inspiring. Thoughts without actions or activities do not sustain a relationship or even advance it. Actions are required.

When a man chooses a woman to marry (or a woman chooses a man), he wants to make it clear to her that she is special not just on the wedding day but for his entire life. Human beings grant a special status to another person by reserving certain actions only for that person.

What would be an action that would grant special status to the spouse? Consider a few possibilities. One might be a kiss. But in most societies kisses are for family members and friends, and they can even be for fairly new acquaintances. A husband might say that he only kisses his wife in a certain way. One would certainly hope that a man only kisses his wife in a certain way, but it hardly seems this is enough, especially since kissing in various types of ways often leads to much more intimate activity.

Another possible reserved action might be living together in a house, condo, or apartment. In fact, this is a type of reserved action. Marriage involves husband

and wife moving in together. In addition, if a crisis arises in a marriage, the wife makes a very strong statement by throwing the husband out of the house. And yet this proposed activity does not fit the way in which most societies are organized. In many societies, the extended family lives together in the same house or compound. That is, grandparents, parents, aunts, uncles, and cousins may all be part of a single household. In this case, in addition to a husband and wife, there are many other adults, albeit all related to one another. Furthermore, if friends visit from far away, one invites them to stay in the house and this is not considered some breach of marriage etiquette. In our modern society, many young people often rent a large space and live there together, chastely. It is a place of convenience; the young women like the security of having men around, and the men freeload a bit on the willingness of the women to tend to the apartment or arrange social events. Whether in a modern society or a traditional society, living together is at best an ambiguous reserved activity.

Certainly wearing a wedding ring is a reserved activity. Both the husband and the wife make an important public statement by wearing the ring. In some societies, a married person also wears a special type of dress or garment. Both the ring and the dress are fine ways to highlight the married relationship, but both of them are a bit removed from the individuals. That is, a ring is purchased and given at the beginning of the marriage; there's no new ring given once a month. Also, the clothing is in no sense precious; for example, it is not personally sewn by the husband or wife. Wearing a certain type of dress is not closely related to the love a man feels for his wife, or vice versa.

What is needed is an act that is an expression of love, an act that is recognized by others in society as a reserved act, an act closely related to marriage, an act related to children, who are the most treasured outcome of the love between wife and husband, and an act that is cherished by both husband and wife. The act that fulfills these conditions best is the sexual act. Marriage is certainly about begetting children and it is certainly a commitment of love. Sex is a great mutual marriage gift. Referring to sexual intercourse, the husband can say, "I only do this with you," and of course she can say the same.

Does a man have to be able to say that he has had no sexual intercourse prior to marriage in order to enter into a lasting marriage? No, that is not the claim being made here. Certainly, once married, he in effect says to his wife that sexual intercourse is an activity he voluntarily and happily restricts to his wife. Beyond this, however, the issue is: How does a man honor his wife in a very special way intimately related to their married life? He honors his future wife long before marriage by setting aside an activity that he will only engage in with his future wife. By so doing, he not only honors his wife but he also prepares himself to live a committed married life. He not only says beforehand that he restricts sexual contact to his wife, he also prepares and trains himself for this during the years of abstinence prior to marriage. Given that discipline and training, he has confidence he will be able to be faithful to his marriage vow. By being chaste prior to marriage, he prepares himself for marriage at the same time that he readies a wonderful gift for his wife.

Reserving sexual intercourse for marriage is, of course, a universal sign of special commitment. A man does not have to wait until he meets the young woman who may be his future wife to consult with her about whether chastity prior to marriage will be something she cherishes. He knows that this will be well received, and he knows that he would be equally overjoyed if his wife also offers that gift to him. Just like the diamond ring, it is a wonderful wedding gift.

The gift of chastity influences both the symbolic aspect of the sexual act as well as the components of memory and imagination. Chastity prior to marriage and reserving sex to one's spouse in marriage makes real the symbolic component of the sexual act. Because sex is a reserved activity, it not just a physical, pleasurable activity. Rather, because the act is reserved solely for one's spouse, it conveys commitment every time it is performed. Also, the act is "pure" in the sense that it does not come burdened by prior images in the memory and imagination of sexual intercourse with previous partners. On the wedding night, "memory" of sexual intercourse begins and in the future sexual imagination is now informed by memory of previous intimacies between husband and wife.

Reserving sex to one's marriage partner prepares the person to live a committed married life. Making sex a "reserved activity" reinforces its symbolic content, and it enables the memory and imagination to be rooted in one's spouse. This is a secure foundation for growth in love and commitment to one's spouse.

SEX AS SPORT

Absent the protective context of a loving, lasting commitment, sex is nothing more than sport. This kind of sport is dangerous, however, not merely for the couple but for others as well. Many a young man has entertained his cronies by making fun of what a young woman did with him in the previous night's sexual encounter. Young women are also not immune from regaling friends with tales of the prowess, the "potency," or the fumblings of some young man. Without commitment, it's just sport, complete with trash talking about competitors and highlights of the most interesting, hilarious, or inept plays.

Within the context of marriage, on the other hand, sexual intimacy deepens the fundamental value of friendship by reminding the husband and wife of their commitment to unreserved mutuality and union. Outside of marriage sexual intimacy is corrosive because it is wrenched from its symbolic meaning. When the symbolic component is misused, it undermines the mutual commitment of spouses in marriage.

Married men may look at other women as attractive prospects—virtual or real—for a sexual romp and consider this harmless. These fleeting musings, however, enter the memory and imagination and married men who regularly entertain these possibilities endanger their marriage. They are reverting to an adolescent yearning to sex as fun or sport, with little or no attentiveness to their marital commitment. The same is true for any woman who thinks of a sexual affair with someone else as a diversion from the disappointments of her marriage. In both cases the symbolic meaning of sex is perverted with nothing but dangerous consequences for all involved.

Some single people think fidelity is important in marriage but they have no problem with recreational sex before they are ready for marriage. They think as long as recreational sex prior to marriage is consensual it is no big deal. But sex outside of marriage is a symbolic perversion. It signifies a commitment that does not exist. Sexual union should express a union of hearts. When one or both of the parties are unwilling to commit to each other, what is supposed to be a mutual act of self-giving becomes merely a loan. In this situation the symbolic meaning is wrenched from sex and commitment becomes an illusion, which in many cases is a hoax with the larger negative impact on the woman.

Human beings have the gift of memory and imagination. When sex only occurs within marriage, what partners remember or imagine about sexual intimacy is focused on each other and draws them deeper into their union. Premarital sexual experiences, however, can operate very differently. Rather than being an advantage as some might suggest because it provides them sexual technique and expertise, these sexual experiences can actually be a burden in a marriage.

The memory of previous sexual encounters is something people always carry with them. Certainly memories of other sexual adventures can recede as a new relationship develops, but they do not disappear. As human beings, we are not made that way. Sex requires vulnerability. New vulnerability can awaken the memory of early vulnerability in intimate relations. The memory of earlier encounters remains for years and decades and can be the source of insidious comparison. Prior sexual activity does not torpedo a marriage, but it diminishes the full, unrestrained commitment that is a part of any good marriage. It can also undermine trust or increase self-consciousness when spouses wonder how they measure up against past sexual partners.

Marriage is a truly safe space for both husbands and wives. It is also safe and nourishing for both memory and imagination. Sex is a powerful force. In many marriages, its force diminishes at various points. However, memory and imagination preserve it as something attractive and satisfying even after sexual contact is no longer as frequent as it was earlier in the marriage. In marriage both the physical being and the personal interiority or inner self of each spouse is protected and nourished. Within this safe space both partners are free to share intimate knowledge and growth in this love and affection. In marriage, each spouse can trust their confidences are secure in the mind and heart of the other spouse.

We live in a society that cultivates a kind of restlessness that drives us constantly to search for the new and different, and to improve our experiences. This attitude can influence how married couples interact with one another. A spouse who comes into a marriage with a varied sexual history can either try to forget what went before or integrate one's previous sexual experiences into the current relationship. The latter seems a recipe for disaster and the former is not easily achieved if any of the prior relationships were at all meaningful. For this reason, the sexually experienced partner entering a new marriage can be easily tempted to recall and compare, or forget and suppress. While the latter is preferable, it is surely not ideal. Better still would be avoiding the dilemma by reserving sex to a lasting and committed marriage.

GETTING REAL

Casual sex is a reality for many young people. Even though most of them yearn to participate more fully in friendship at its deepest levels, they think postponing sex until marriage is unrealistic, unnecessary, and unnatural. But their assessment is wrong. What is truly unrealistic, unnecessary, unnatural, and untrue is the conviction that sexual activity outside of marriage helps them reach their own goals in terms of friendship and marriage. In fact the exact opposite is true. And young people's own experiences frequently prove the point.

In the present social milieu, postponing sexual intimacy until marriage looks like a whole lot of giving up and missing out that hardly seems appealing. But not all of what is being given up is so great. The way the social scene is configured nowadays, sex is often viewed as the price of admission that gets you into the game.

What's missing in this present arrangement is romance and relationship—a chance for young people to get to know themselves and others as friends and possible partners with whom they might one day want to share a lifetime and love and a family. When this topic is raised in the media, the emphasis is frequently on how difficult chastity is for young people because they then can't satisfy their sexual urges. But what about the many ways in which life is hard because sex is now so free and easy? It is difficult for young people when any attention from someone of the opposite sex has to be seen as an implicit expectation of sex. Instant intimacy undermines friendship and romance. Yes, sexual abstinence is not always easy. But what is easy about negotiating the sexual pressure cooker that masquerades as "social life" for young people today? There is a better, more romantic, but less sexual way. It requires some adjustments both in young people's outlook and in how they approach each other, but it has big payoffs now and for the future.

19

Living In and Moving Out

MARIA AND DAVE were not able to get together during the week, which was a bit unusual. The previous long weekend Dave and Maria both flew out to Nebraska to be with Maria's family for Thanksgiving. It was a nice event and they chatted about many things on the plane trip back. But during the week they had obligations at work and they just talked a few times on the phone.

On Saturday they got together to do some pre-shopping for Christmas, at least to come up with some ideas for gifts. They did not want to actually purchase things, just look and then have a relaxing meal at a place far away from the mall.

Maria was the one who knew the restaurant on the far south side. Nothing much, but it was quiet. Sandwich, salad, and chat—it was a relaxing combination.

After both had confirmed that no pressing calls were expected and cell phones were turned off, they started to reflect on the people they met at Thanksgiving. "Your cousin Anthony is interesting, and he certainly has a lively girlfriend. What was her name again?" "Samantha. They have been going together for about seven or eight years," responded Maria. "In fact," said Dave, "I was going to ask whether they were engaged, because they acted a bit like married people." "Well, they have been living together for over five years. But no marriage yet. Anthony has still not popped the question."

Because Dave knew that family matters were sensitive areas, he said to Maria, "Can I speak candidly about Anthony and Samantha?" Maria said not to worry, she would not be insulted. Even before he offered his views, she reminded Dave how short their visit was, much too brief to capture the nuances of relationships among various family members. Dave acknowledged that he had very partial knowledge about Maria's family. He also admitted that, even though he was talking about others, he was really reflecting on himself and Maria.

Dave said Samantha and Anthony seemed like a nice, energetic couple, fun to be with. What surprised Dave was the fact that they had been living together for five years. Even though Dave thought they potentially could be happily married, Dave said that hearing Maria comment on their situation was enough to convince him that Samantha and Anthony were not going to get married. "I don't get it. How can Samantha put up with this situation?" Maria was fairly philosophical about it. "Even though I would not tolerate it," said Maria, "this happens to a lot of young women. Samantha would like to get married, but Anthony is not yet ready. He will eventually come around. The whole family will be ecstatic when Anthony finally comes to his senses."

"But Maria, Anthony is 33 years old. How long can it take to come to your senses? How can you live with someone for five years and not ask her to marry you? It doesn't make sense. Is love really that calculating? In fact, I think it's pretty insulting to Samantha. What, she hasn't performed well enough in bed? Or, Samantha still has some imperfections and Anthony's waiting until she corrects them? I don't get it. It seems he's just using her."

Maria and Anthony usually spent summers together in Nebraska when they were growing up. So, she was fond of him. Maria has not had much contact with him since she went away to college, which was about 15 years ago. Anthony has always been pleasant and lively, and, without thinking much about it, she thought he and Samantha were a good pair and would eventually get it together. So, when she heard Dave's characteristically blunt comments, she was surprised. And in fact, she thought about herself and Dave, and decided to say so.

"Well, Dave, you're in an awkward position to be making comments like that. From all our past conversations and from your not-so-subtle comments and whispers to me, I take it you would be delighted with the prospect of getting in bed with me." Dave was embarrassed by this observation, even though he knew Maria judged him correctly. "Come on, Maria, don't make it so personal. You're too soft on Anthony. Maybe Anthony is a great guy, but why is he holding back? Living with Samantha and not being married to her is like saying she's not yet good enough. Implicitly he's saying, 'Give her a few more years to season and she'll be fine.'"

Maria replied that she didn't think that was true. "Anthony does love Samantha and he's just not sure he can commit his life to her. He needs a little more time. He doesn't think Samantha lacks qualities for marriage. He probably blames himself for not being able to commit."

"You have to be kidding," said Dave. Dave pointed out that if the fault is with Anthony, he should move out and consider whatever his personal failings or difficulties are. The way it is now it appears that Samantha doesn't have enough in her to entice Anthony for a lifetime. By implication, by staying with her he's saying, 'Okay, let's do some more things together, including sex. Maybe eventually I will get turned on completely with you.' That's outrageous. You would never tolerate that if I said that to you. 'Ok, let's have some sex and then I will tell you whether I want to marry you.' How insulting would that be? I admit, sex with you would be very fun, but I know that now. I don't have to try it out to be sure. Think back over our relationship. It's really only in my bad moments that I really want to get physical with you." Then Dave added, "How long have I been with you? After all this time, I have no doubt that sex with you will be great. Anthony can't be waiting for more satisfying sex. He can't be waiting for Samantha to change her ways. If Anthony himself is the one who has to change, he should be a man, move out, and focus on change of whatever type he thinks necessary."

Maria objected. "But I think they will eventually get married. It'll just take a little more time. Anthony should not do anything abrupt to disrupt the relationship. Moving out would jeopardize the whole relationship. My family likes Samantha and they think they will make a good couple."

"But Maria, if they do eventually get married, Samantha would necessarily be insecure about her position as wife. Samantha must be wondering, 'Why is it taking Anthony five or six years to come to a decision?' By his presence in their apartment, he implies the problem is with her, not with him. How secure of his commitment can she be in marriage? How much more intimate can he get with her? Does he need more evidence that he will be satisfied with her? It certainly sounds that way. If, as you say, the problem truly is with Anthony, what exactly is the problem? After the great moment of self-enlightenment about his difficulty comes, does Anthony ever tell Samantha what the resolution is? Suppose Anthony meets someone else and starts going out with her. Then Samantha feels like dirt. She gives herself to him for five years. All the while, Anthony is saying he is the one who has the problem. But then some nice, sassy new lass comes along and suddenly Anthony is ready to take the plunge. Samantha would rightly feel used and thrown out. I admit she's foolish to allow herself to be used in this way. Maybe she is the one to move out and leave Anthony to stew. Maybe that will knock some sense into him."

Maria was getting a bit impatient because Dave was being so idealistic. She could see Dave's point, but he seemed not to care about the impact of his approach on Anthony and Samantha's relationship. "Gee, Dave, do you really want that to end the relationship? How about just accepting the modern reality that many couples live together before getting married? I don't approve of this, but I really do think Anthony will make a good father, and I know that Samantha wants to have children."

This only got Dave more agitated. "Forget whether Anthony will make a good father or not. That's not the point. The primary point is whether he will make a good husband. As for Samantha, by all means she should have children. Is she so hard up that Anthony is the only option? If she chooses Anthony only because options are limited and her biological clock is ticking, Anthony will eventually realize this. How can a marriage like that possibly last?"

"Alright, I misspoke about Samantha and the children," said Maria. "Yes, she does want to have children, but, no, she should not marry someone just because she needs a partner to make children. I was wrong to bring that up. I was just try-ing to be sympathetic to Samantha. She is in a difficult position. Do you really think Anthony will be a bad husband?"

Understanding Maria's concern for her cousin Anthony, Dave said, "Anthony is a very nice guy. He certainly does not intend to be a bad husband, nor does he intend to hurt Samantha. But living together has many unintended consequences. By living with her and not marrying her, he is putting her down. In marriage, each partner commits to put the good of the other person first. As I understand your explanation, Anthony says the fault is his. But because he likes living with Samantha, he actually puts his own interests first. If Samantha were his first pri-ority, for one, he would marry her. At the very least, he should say something like, 'Samantha, I should not be with you in this intimate way when I am not ready to commit. It's my fault that I am not ready. Let's continue to go out, but I'm going to move out of here and into an apartment with a friend of mine. There is no other woman in my life. But I have to gain confidence that I can really commit my life to you in good times and bad.' If he said this, he would treat her correctly, even nobly."

"The problem is," said Maria, "that Samantha would be devastated if Anthony moves out. Also, Samantha once told me she really enjoys living with Anthony and 'all that implies.' When I heard Samantha say this, I thought to myself, 'Okay, I get your point.' So, if Anthony moves out, Samantha would be the loser. Maybe only in the short term, but it would be difficult for both of them."

Dave observed, "The reason why they both don't move out is that it would indeed be difficult. If it were easy, they would do it. That's another problem with living together. It has great, tangible, experiential benefits. Benefits to which one becomes attached. After a while, neither party wants to part with the benefits. However, beneath the superficial benefits is a pattern that undermines the confidence any spouse needs in marriage."

As often happens, the conversation gradually trailed off. They paid for lunch and walked around the area for a while. While strolling, Maria once again picked up the earlier theme, but this time from a different angle. "Dave, you clearly have thought about these things. I know I should not be surprised, but still I am. Just as I was surprised last year when we were talking about what parents should say to their teenage children about sex. You had some good points. It occurred to me during our lunch conversation that perhaps you think about these things so as to distract yourself from intimate thoughts about you and me. What do you think about that?"

"Well, Miss Maria, you are quite the perceptive one," said Dave. "But I think about these things not so much to distract myself. You are quite sufficient to distract me from many things. I think about these things because I know you are committed to staying chaste until a final commitment is made. So, since I want to think good things about you, I have to think of good reasons for your position!" Maria knew that wasn't the real reason, but she still liked his explanation.

20

Sex, Contraceptives, and Children

AN IMPORTANT COMPONENT of marriage is the generation of children. Until about forty years ago, desiring to have and bearing children was considered a normal activity in marriage. Even this, however, has become problematic in modern society. Many a developed society now experiences a negative population growth rate because couples, whether married or unmarried, are having so few children.

CONTRACEPTIVES

Human sexual desire and expression draw individuals outside of themselves into an intimate communion with another. As part of their love and commitment to one another, at least until recently, couples have experienced a strong desire that their love produce children. The commitment to each other is the source of the desire to have children and is the basis for anticipating that the couple will be able to care for children resulting from the sexual act. Sexual acts should be motivated by mutual commitment to one another and the acts should be open to God using this occasion to bring forth new human life and sustain it.

Children's lives depend on the readiness of their parents to accept them. We know that infants in the womb are influenced by the attitudes of the mother, whose attitudes are in turn influenced by the father of the developing child. The security and long-term commitment provided in a traditional marriage that promotes the well-being of children are missing when a pregnancy is unwanted or occurs outside the context of marriage. In addition, security, love, and desire for the child should be the attitude of the parents from the moment the child is conceived.

Contraceptives refer to the means, including devices, patches, or pills, used by a man or woman to prevent the woman's ovum from being fertilized or to avoid implantation of the fertilized ovum (or zygote) in the uterus. Using contraceptives to substantially lessen the possibility of conceiving a child usually involves deliberation and discussion by the couple. The difficulty is that the use of contraceptives appears at least to the couple themselves to say that children are burdens or hindrances, not gifts to be welcomed. Unless the couple discusses the reason even for the use of natural planning to avoid conception and clearly communicates to each other their deep desire for or at least openness to children, their actions may lead them in a direction that is contrary to nature and that weakens their marriage commitment. Furthermore, no method of contraception works all the time. If a couple desires to avoid having a child and the woman nonetheless conceives, it is very important that this contingency has been discussed beforehand. Love and commitment to the child should characterize the feelings, emotions, and sentiments of the parents from the first moment of conception. Parents may have legitimate reasons for trying to avoid having a child at this time in their married life. However, in this case they have to be clear in their discussions with one another as well as in their hopes and prayers that, should conception occur, they wholeheartedly and enthusiastically welcome this new life.

A woman cooperates in a special way with the creative activity of God in the generation of a new human being. Conception should be the result of a loving act; it should be welcomed and affirmed if it occurs. Although conception requires the loving cooperation of a man, the woman is not only the means by which the baby grows but also the conduit for the mutual feelings of the father and mother to the child. The woman's emotions, feelings, and expectations should be surrounded by love and acceptance of whatever new life is building within her. Of course, the woman does not know whether she is pregnant for several weeks after conception. Nonetheless, an embryo experiences important growth in these early stages, and, if indeed a baby is forming in her, the growth should occur with love and acceptance, not apprehension, by the mother.

Means to avoid conception are now so common in the United States that many, including Christians, do not even consider them within a moral framework. Although the Catholic Church opposes the uses of chemicals and devices to avoid conception, many people consider this a religious idiosyncrasy stemming from the Vatican or based on primitive understandings of human nature.

To be clear, the Catholic Church bases its opposition to contraception on natural law. In this treatment of natural law, we have consistently tried to present the norm of nature guided by reason not in terms of mere physical human nature but also the need for good order among individuals interacting in society. In our view, this view of natural law better reflects the tradition and responds with greater clarity and nuance to many issues facing modern societies.

Consider first the positive justification for not using contraceptives to prevent pregnancy. The sexual act itself stems from an innovation in evolutionary development hundreds of millions of years ago. Compared with asexual procreation, sexual procreation provides greater overall diversification, protection, and opportunities for development in the human species (as well as in other species relying on propagation via sexual means). Earlier in human development, various factors explained why most women chose to bear many children, if they could. The fragile health of babies, the need for assistance in the operation of the "family economy" (such as a farm, processing activity, or artisanal work), the need for protection, and care for the elderly all made large families a sensible way to pursue the fundamental values. Of these various reasons, the unavailability of effective health care was likely the most important. As recently as a hundred years ago many babies and young children died as they succumbed to various diseases or childhood accidents.

The human desire to participate more fully in the fundamental values has led to the emergence of many new or radically changed institutions. Universities, for example, did not first appear magically and for no known cause in the twelfth century. In order to be viable, universities required a certain level of urban population and economic prosperity; the urban centers and additional financial means allowed some people to gather in various groups (universities or learning groups) in order to focus more particularly on understanding the world and increasing human productivity of goods and services. Hospitals and modern medicine are new institutions, and efficient new medical centers have had large impacts on the way people arrange their lives. Parents take children to hospitals when they are seriously sick, always with the expectation that the doctor will find the appropriate cure or remedy for the child. Modern medicine is a good development. Expert but expensive schooling is another. Both developments in their own way exert pressure on parents to have smaller families than a hundred years ago.

Life is one of the fundamental values. When considering human life, a natural reaction is for an individual to think small, of himself and his family. However, as a fundamental value, human beings must at least be concerned that the human species continues to thrive.

Human intelligence and practical reason represent significant breakthroughs in the development of life. If humans were to become aware that the continuation of the species is in jeopardy, they would have a responsibility to take appropriate action. One threat to the environment stems from the large number of people in the world. A rational reaction is to institute measures that protect the environment so as not to recklessly endanger future generations. Another threat exists at a country and cultural level. Humans in different cultural groups have to be concerned that they are replicating themselves and that sufficient diversity exists in the gene pool. These are not everyday considerations for most people. Nonetheless, should groups of people become aware of these threats, the people aware of emerging macro dangers have a responsibility to develop effective responses. Modern sexual procreation for any married couple is situated in this larger framework.

The sexual act is straightforward, but sexual procreation is quite complicated. It depends on many factors. Many women who have used contraceptives and then decide to have a baby discover how difficult becoming pregnant can be. This reality alone is not an argument against the use of contraceptives, but it is a cautionary tale against disturbing the rhythms of the body. As was commented in an earlier chapter, the basic biological systems, including reproductive ones, have been developed over millions of years. Disrupting them via unnecessary chemical interventions can cause considerable problems.

Introducing hormones or other chemicals into the female reproductive system may cause long-term problems. For this reason, when considering the moral status of contraceptives, it is best to formulate the issues surrounding contraceptives in terms of those barrier devices known to raise the fewest and least onerous medical issues, namely, condoms and diaphragms. Based on natural law, what are the objections to using such devices?

First, as understood by human beings since the emergence of Homo sapiens, the sexual act includes procreation as one of its ends. In most instances, the sexual act does not result in a pregnancy, but the physical act sets in motion a process that can result in the woman becoming pregnant. This possibility belongs to the act itself. In a previous chapter, we argued that no young person should engage in the act unless he or she is ready to become the parent of a child and then raise that child.

The act is also a symbol of love and commitment as well as a storehouse of memory and a generator of imagination. But the love and commitment are intricately wrapped in the physical act itself, and the act includes the possibility of the woman becoming pregnant. Ideally, the woman and the man are open to the possibility of a child, and, from the first moment of conception, the woman should have some anticipative joy and satisfaction that she will bear a child who came about through an act of love and who will be sustained for many long years by the mutual love of husband and wife for their child. Affirmation and love belong to the physical act of sex.

An obvious objection to this line of reasoning is that one can arrange things in a marriage so that not every act of sex includes openness to procreation. For simplicity, suppose the couple discusses the procreation issue between themselves and they agree that they want to structure things to have fun and have children in moderation. Let's suppose they have two sexual acts (A and B) they perform with one another. Sexual intimacy A is just an expression of love and the pleasure deriving from sexual intercourse. Using a barrier contraceptive prepares the couple for sexual intercourse of type A, since it severely reduces the likelihood of conception. Sexual act B includes the full array of intentions and possible results, including conception. Sexual intimacy B stems from love, is an expression of love, and wholeheartedly welcomes any resulting pregnancy. Before the couple has sex, they simply decide whether they are doing A or B. If they opt for A, they use some contraceptive device that practically guarantees that their act, though stemming from love and mutual commitment, has zero likelihood of conception.

In fact, with one essential difference, the system of sexual intimacy A or B replicates pretty closely the natural family planning approach (known also as the ovulation method, the sympto-thermal method, or the Billings method). When the couple adhering to natural family planning wants to avoid pregnancy, they use a variant on sexual intimacy A, but one that does not involve a contraceptive. That is, they have sex during the infertile times of a woman's period. Otherwise, they use variant B, which is having sex during the fertile days of a woman's period.

The essential difference in natural family planning is that, as is argued below, calling it a contraceptive is erroneous. According to natural family planning, a couple abstains from sex a few days a month. In this method, there is no device or means other than avoidance of sex. The modern mentality unfortunately does not make precise distinctions. For many modern young people, natural family planning is a type of contraception and any couple gets to choose the means of contraception with which they are most comfortable.

For many young adults, the main reason sexual intimacy made possible via a contraceptive device appears similar to natural family planning is the intended result is the same. If both the outcomes and the intentions (preventing a pregnancy) are the same for both methods, what can be the objection to using a condom or diaphragm? Posing the question in this way requires the natural law approach to clearly state in what way the barrier method undermines or corrodes a fundamental value. If natural law cannot produce a clear answer to this challenge, both the barrier method and natural family planning should be acceptable methods for regulating pregnancy.

The first important difference to highlight between natural family planning and contraception is that natural family planning is not anything that occurs during sexual intercourse. It is not a device that has to be properly placed; it is not a pill or patch that has to be taken prior to or after sexual intercourse. For this reason it is not a contraceptive at all. A contraceptive is used during or surrounding the act of intercourse to prevent a sperm from fertilizing the ovum or to prevent the fertilized ovum from implanting itself in the uterine wall. The "contraceptive means" used in natural family planning involves no intercourse for a few days within the woman's menstrual period. Abstaining from intercourse does not interfere in any way with the natural bodily processes surrounding intercourse. If a light in a room is not on, one cannot speak of "dimming" the light. If a person has not eaten anything in the past seven hours, one cannot speak of the "digestion" currently taking place in the person. If one does not engage in sexual intercourse, one cannot speak of using a "contraceptive." Therefore, speaking of natural family planning as a contraceptive means is at best a very imprecise analogy. The general goal for abstaining is the same as the general goal for using the contraceptive device, but the means are not at all comparable.

Furthermore, both the motivation and intentions are distinct when one compares natural family planning with the sexual act modified by some contraceptive. In natural family planning, the man and woman are attentive to the natural menstruation period of the woman. The goal is not to change or regularize the period, but to learn it and accommodate one's practices to the natural flow within the woman's body. The goal is not to rearrange this rhythm, however variable or steady it may be, from month to month, but to track it and react to it. The woman uses a variety of measurements to calculate where she is in her cycle.

The couple using natural family planning that wants to avoid a pregnancy performs the sexual act with the full array of love, motivation, commitment, and openness to new life that make the sexual act what it is. Even though the couple performs the sexual act at a time when conception is unlikely, the couple is fully ready to accept and welcome a pregnancy, should it occur. In a genuine way, the couple remains open to conceiving new life.

Natural family planning allows a couple to have periodic sexual intercourse while anticipating with a high degree of probability a pregnancy will not occur. This method requires attentiveness to changes in the woman and it also requires the discipline of abstention when the woman reaches the point of ovulation. By restricting sexual intercourse to times when the woman is not fertile, the likelihood of conception is severely reduced. Indeed, every year more data emerges showing how highly reliable natural family planning has become. Nonetheless, a very low possibility of conception still remains. Thus, the couple adhering to natural family planning can and should be open to and completely welcome any pregnancy that occurs. In short, love, commitment, and acceptance of any pregnancy can genuinely be the motivation in sexual intercourse occurring within the context of natural family planning.

In this chapter an additional component of the sexual act has been explicitly introduced. In previous chapters although the generation of children was discussed we emphasized the physical or biological component, the symbolic component of commitment, and the role of memory and imagination. If you think something important was left in the background, you're right, and we are rectifying it right now. This chapter highlights a fundamental, central focus of the sexual act: conception. Since the possibility of conception exists within the physical act, it is important to highlight possible conception as an integral component of the sexual act. Thus, there are four components: the physical act, the possibility of conception, the symbolic expression of lasting commitment, and the role of memory and imagination.

Conception is vital for couples and societies. Unless millions of parents want to conceive children of their own, country or regional populations eventually contract. Couples using contraceptives effectively state they do not want children during the period the contraceptives are used. This means during this period they deny an essential component of sexual intercourse, a component that has been part of sexual intercourse not only for humans but also for all nonhuman animals which reproduce by mating of males and females. That is, they are denying a component that has emerged through evolution and God's providence over hundreds of millions of years. But this is an essential component of the physical act of intercourse; to deny it corrodes the pursuit of life on a personal, intimate level and also in terms of the broader public. At a personal level, one cannot remove one natural, integral component of the act and then add it at will at some later time. At a societal level, one cannot remove one natural component of an act that has been used by humans for hundreds of thousands of years and expect most everything to remain the same; use of contraceptives corrodes the pursuit of life. Society gradually becomes "group solipsistic," not caring whether the good practices inherent in this society have to be passed on to the next generation. So, both at a personal and a societal level, contraception is corrosive.

Openness to conception is an integral part of the sexual act. In terms of the fundamental values, the sexual act is an expression of friendship at one of its highest levels, it seeks to promote life, and the act often involves playfulness. Depending on the couple and their mood or circumstances, playfulness may or may not occur. What is central to the act, however, are the expression of love and commitment as well as the openness to new life. Removing the intention of being open to new life corrodes the value of life as lived by the couple.

REPERCUSSIONS OF THE CONTRACEPTIVE MENTALITY

Let us explore the societal impact more closely. Why not remove the possibility of conception? After all, in this case sexual intercourse still involves the physical act and its accompanying pleasure and it also includes the symbolic expression of lasting commitment as well as memory and imagination. However, by reducing the act in this way, one removes a component (the possibility of conception) that has already adversely impacted the future viability of some groups which make extensive use of contraceptives.

Until contraceptive devices started to be widely used in the West about sixty years ago, successful propagation of the human race relied on on the four central components we have highlighted: the physical act involving pleasure, a symbolic expression of commitment, the integration of memory and imagination, and the possibility of conception. The sexual act is closely connected with the stability of marriage and the generation of babies in a society. It is now clear that significant groups in Western society are not reproducing themselves. Because on average couples are having children below the replacement rate, societies such as Italy, France, Germany, and Japan are experiencing negative population growth rates.

Many factors can influence the negative growth rate, such as average income and the cost of raising a child. But the people who can most easily afford children—the wealthy—are the ones having the fewest children, and wealthier countries are now the ones most likely to experience negative population growth. Clearly, the phenomenon of negative population growth rates is not being driven by economics. The wide availability and use of contraceptives plays an important role, especially in the way that it modifies the position of sexual intercourse in marriage and society. In particular, removing the possibility of conception from sexual intercourse changes the impact of the act on population growth in a significant way.

The first impact is out-of-wedlock babies. In the United States now approximately 40 percent of all new babies are delivered by an unmarried mother. For teenagers, 86 percent of births were nonmarital, but 60 percent of births were nonmarital for women from between the ages of 20 and 24, and nearly one-third of births were nonmarital for women from between the ages of 25 and 29. These were the results for the United States. Sweden, Norway, France, Denmark, and the United Kingdom all had substantially higher nonmarital rates than the United States.

The percentage of out-of-wedlock babies born has been growing since the 1970s. Some of these nonmarital births are to couples living together but not married. However, many mothers are now resigned to being single mothers. Why this dual trend? Contraceptives give false confidence that the woman will not conceive. When she does, the father of the child often does not stay around to care for the child. He never expected the woman he loved at the time to become pregnant and, once she did, many young or adult men are not inclined to make a commitment to help raise the child. This reality challenges the notion that for these young men the symbolic component—lasting commitment—was ever a realistic factor in the relationship.

Contraceptives enable young and old to consider sexual intercourse as physically pleasing without the additional factors of commitment and generation. Many people in modern society no longer interpret sex as an expression of lasting commitment. The positive aspect of natural family planning is that the planning itself actually increases the sensitivity of the man to the woman and his need to coordinate his activities to fit her reproductive cycle. Contraceptives offer the illusion that no baby can possibly result from this pleasurable act. As a result, the act may be performed frequently with a single partner or more frequently with different partners. But contraceptives don't work 100 percent of the time and couples forget to use them or choose not to use them.

One cannot meddle with sexual intercourse in important ways and not expect large societal changes. The possibility of conception inherently belongs to sexual intercourse. To suggest otherwise is effectively to jeopardize the stability of a country, since it removes from the act itself a welcoming attitude to the possibility of conception. Contraceptives corrode society by dramatically changing the basic framework of sexual reproduction. For at least 100,000 years human sexual intercourse included the possibility of conception in the minds of those having sex. It belongs inherently to the sexual act. Suggesting otherwise to people leads to very negative and dangerous results.

One last point. Because children require lots of attention and training, modern society does not always view them as cute, engaging, and stimulating young persons. On they contrary, children are sometimes viewed as burdens—expensive and distracting challenges in a marriage. The regular use of contraceptives reinforces the negative perception of children. Contraception communicates a message: "We have to avoid a pregnancy and a child." But children are supposed to be welcomed and treasured as gifts from God. Especially once they become teenagers and enjoy greater self-awareness, children are not supposed to think they were a mistake. In an open society that discusses everything and that uses contraceptives, this message eventually will be communicated to children. Such a society is not a pretty one, nor is it a loving one.

Precisely because children come from God, they are not the product of human choice alone. Loving sexual intercourse between husband and wife includes the possibility of conception. If a baby results, it comes about through God. After all, the baby participates in Being, who is God. A new baby is not primarily the result of a decision by a man and woman. A man and woman should acknowledge this reality by being open in each sexual act to conception.

21

Sexual Variations and Misdirections

HOW TO UNDERSTAND and appropriately address the reality of homosexuality and bisexuality receives a great deal of attention in Western society today. This is hardly surprising, given that a commitment to individual liberty, freedom, and the pursuit of happiness, as well as to the protection of the rights of minorities, is part of the bedrock of our society. Because of this commitment, U.S. citizens, as well as those of other Western countries, are inclined to let individuals make their own decisions about what they want to do. Unless activities impede the ability of others to pursue the fundamental values, these societies do not interfere. That is true even when the majority of the society disapproves of the particular activities.

Seeking pleasure is often understood as a worthwhile goal that is part of an individual's protected right to pursue happiness. This chapter explores the extent to which seeking pleasure is a norm which, absent any other norms, is compatible with the natural law approach as articulated through the fundamental values. It also examines whether a particular form of sexual pleasure, between two men or between two women, involves undermining the fundamental value of friendship or the fundamental value of life.

SEX AND PLEASURE

Within the framework of evolution, sexual attraction and sexual pleasure developed to promote the propagation of the species. Man and woman appeal to one another through primary sexual characteristics. But secondary characteristics are important, as are clothing, gestures, voice, style, et cetera. Attraction between the sexes is intricate and works through many paths other than primary sexual differences. Attraction arouses the anticipation of pleasure, at the very least, pleasure in spending time with the opposite sex. The anticipation of pleasure from sexual intimacy clearly plays an important role in making sexual intercourse attractive and appealing. Whether or not sexual intercourse results in pregnancy or is very pleasurable, the anticipation of pleasure makes it appealing.

Prior to the emergence of human beings, sexual intercourse was primarily a physical act that perhaps included some component of memory and expectation. Even the physical act of sex, however, is in reality the final part of a more complicated biological process. This is certainly the case among human beings. Hormones react to perfume and other scents, appearance, expectation, touches, music, et cetera. For the couple, sex may be simple and straightforward, but it involves an array of physical and psychological processes.

The occasion of having sex may legitimately begin with the anticipation of pleasure. Nonetheless, in order for the act to be a human act, the emphasis cannot be solely on the pleasures of sexual satisfaction. At the very least, sexual partners must attend to the perceived fears, hopes, expectations, and sensitivities of their partner, who willingly becomes vulnerable as part of the sexual act.

Several times in this book we have indicated that, understood properly, sexual intercourse has distinct components: biological or physical (which includes the possibility of conception, which was highlighted as a fourth component in the previous chapter), symbolic, and a dual component consisting of both memory and imagination. The biological component, together with the possibility of conception, and the component involving memory and imagination emerge from millions of years of evolutionary history. These traits are tightly linked to the survival and prospering of the human species, which eventually emerged as a separate species from the higher primates. Sexual pleasure played an important role in this process since it was an inducement for primates to mate and propagate the species. As was described earlier, the symbolic component, memory and imagination (including thoughts of children), and possibly playfulness transformed copulation into human sexual intercourse, as human beings, endowed with consciousness, gradually came to understand the importance of lasting commitment to the well-being of children and the infinite wealth of riches contained in each spouse.

Because sexual intercourse can result in conception, the physical act should only be performed by a couple who have committed themselves not simply to bearing and raising a child but also to providing a loving context in which that child can develop. One reason marriage is the highest form of friendship is that the couple commits not just to raising the child but also to modeling for the child the highest type of loving commitment people can make. This modeling of unconditioned love, if successful, is one of the greatest gifts parents give to their children. By demonstrating their mutual love for each other in the context of the family, the couple makes a great gift to their children; via their actions and words, they teach their children how to live in a personal community of lasting love. Thus, the gift of marriage vows is more than a mutual promise, valid until the death of one of the spouses. In addition, their lived-out commitment becomes a demonstrative example of how their children can eventually make a credible, lasting commitment to some young man or woman.

The sexual act is one in which two human beings make themselves vulnerable both physically and emotionally to one another. Sex is supposed to flow from the deep commitment of one partner to the other. Being good at sex is not simply about being smooth and proficient. Rather, it includes a kind of attention and sensitivity to the signals a partner sends about his or her reactions, fears, and expectations. It takes self-knowledge and knowledge of the other to develop the depth of attentiveness and imagination that are necessary for mutually satisfying and enriching sex.

Being sufficiently attentive does require practice, but the main practice field is not the bedroom. Practice occurs in the far less passionate zone where young people who are interested in each other normally interact. If personal attentiveness does not exist prior to sexual intimacy, it is not likely to emerge at a time of consuming sexual feelings. For this reason, one night stands or hook-ups of limited duration are a parody of sex rightly contextualized and understood. For the same reason, sex performed by a man against the will of a woman effectively dehumanizes her and makes the man less loving and more compulsive. In this situation, part of what makes sex a deeply human act is trashed by the man who treats the woman as something nonhuman, casting aside all her sensitivities, fears, and expectations. In addition to being a grown-up, repulsive bully, a man who takes advantage of a woman sexually elevates his pleasure over all else and in so doing perverts what should be an integrally human act.

The types of good sensitivity indicated above clearly can be present in sexual encounters between two men or between two women. Two men are certainly capable of being sensitive to one another and are able to engage memory and imagination. Thus, in a core component of sexual intimacy, gays and lesbians can act in much the same way as heterosexual couples. Perhaps it is for this reason that many reasonable people today, be they religious or secular in their views, condone or at least fail to condemn sexual relations among gays and lesbians. But let us explore whether the view of these reasonable people are in fact justified.

SAME SEX ORIENTATION AND SEXUAL INTIMACY

Although most people are attracted to the opposite sex, some are sexually attracted to members of their own sex. Whether this occurs primarily due to the DNA of people with same-sex attraction or primarily due to the impact of culture is not yet known. Coming to a definite conclusion in the nature/nurture debate will take serious and objective study over a long period of time. Sexual attraction has to be understood culturally and scientifically. Understanding it fully will require comparing over several generations emerging cultural patterns, on the one hand, with DNA sequencing in genes associated with sexual attraction, on the other.

Whatever the outcome of the debate, gays and lesbians are human beings who should be given and enjoy the same respect and interest due other human beings. This claim for respect and reverence is even more pressing within a Christian natural law framework, where people with same-sex attractions, like other human beings, are understood to be made in the image and likeness of God.

The question being asked in this chapter is not about the inherent dignity of gays and lesbians. Rather, the issue here relates to whether certain actions are corrosive or contrary to the fundamental values. Are homosexual acts permissible within a natural law framework? Or in terms of the language of this book, do homosexual acts promote or undermine the fundamental value of friendship and/ or life?

To judge from published data, whether or not to have sex with one another is not a vital question for most gays and lesbians. If it was at one time, most gays easily resolved the issue in favor of sexual intimacies. Most gays and lesbians choose to be sexually intimate when they want and they look upon prohibitions against homosexual sex as old-fashioned and indicative of narrow-minded attitudes. The issue of whether same-sex intimacies are directly contrary to the fundamental value of friendship or life is probably a more pressing moral question for heterosexuals than it is for people with same-sex attraction.

Even prior to deciding whether same-sex intimacies are corrosive of friendship, it is important to re-emphasize the distinction between a moral answer and a legal regulation. Whatever might be the moral guide established by natural law, society and natural law may (and, one can reasonably argue, should) allow gays and lesbians great freedom in the way they interact in private and in public. That is, the answer to the natural law question about the morality of an act does not uniquely determine the laws a society ought to enact. Even according to natural law, not everything that is immoral should be made illegal.

The factor that differentiates heterosexuals and homosexuals is the gender of the people to whom they are sexually attracted. Both heterosexuals and homosexuals have many friendships involving no or very little sexual intimacy. Their relationships that do have a sexual component are not the only types of friendships and acquaintances they develop. Gays have many friends with whom they engage in nonsexual ways. That is, much of their lives are similar to the lives of heterosexuals. The controversial issue focuses on sexual intimacy with members of the same sex.

Some homosexuals (and some heterosexuals) will only have sex within a committed relationship. Some homosexual men and women eschew commitment as a necessary condition for sexual intimacy. They justify having sex purely on the basis of it being an activity that is fun and gives them pleasure. This approach is identical to that taken by many young heterosexuals who justify fairly promiscuous sexual behavior with the observation that it is satisfying and fun.

Playfulness is a fundamental value. Therefore, before offering an evaluation of same-sex attraction, it is important to consider whether within the framework of the fundamental values fun and pleasure alone are ever an adequate justification for having a sexual relationship. But first, in the next chapter we look in on Dave's curiosity and his and Maria's reaction to gay marriage and gay children.

22

Unnatural Interests

ON FRIDAY, DAVE got together with three of his college classmates who live not far from downtown. They went to a bar and watched some basketball games, but mostly they talked about what they were doing. The following day, a rare spring day with the temperature in the 50s, Dave picked up Maria and went to a popular exhibit at the impressive Cultural Institute, after which they walked around in the downtown area.

Sitting on a bench, looking across at the skyline formed by the buildings along Michigan Avenue, Dave was telling Maria about the little gathering he had last night with former classmates. Dave said it was good hearing what people were doing. "They all have interesting jobs, except George, who has a very well paying but boring job. Unfortunately," Dave said, "I probably was a little too curious to hear what Jeremy was up to. Jeremy is super-smart, got very good grades in college, and now works for a large financial firm. Although we always enjoyed being with Jeremy, he did not spend a lot of time with us. In college he had his gay friends. That was fine by us, but we made sure to invite Jeremy to most of the events we went to, in case he wanted to join our larger group. But he usually politely said he was going out with other friends."

"At the bar, I was curious, but not inquisitive. Even though I wanted to know whether Jeremy was in a relationship, I said nothing and did not ask any questions that went in that direction. Still, as the conversation meandered through our different friends and hangouts, Jeremy said he was very happy because he and his friend Brian were planning on getting married." Dave then told Maria that he had a "Maria moment" similar to the one which Maria had once mentioned to him. That was when Maria was overly consoling with her college roommate Amanda, who had made a big mistake and had an abortion. Dave remembered Maria's account and then said to her, "I managed to keep my mouth shut and say nothing about gay marriage. I just said I was happy for both of them."

Dave admitted that, although on the one hand he was pleased he said nothing offensive in response to Jeremy's announcement of marriage, he did have qualms about whether he should have risked a gentle objection. Maria agreed that she probably would have kept quiet as well. Even though both Maria and Dave are opposed to gay marriage, Jeremy was not asking for their opinion. On the other hand, Dave admitted that he did not have to congratulate Jeremy. It would have been enough to say "Oh, that must be exciting for you." Maria, who is a stickler for the truth, thought that would have been better, but admitted she probably would have avoided any abrasive reaction.

Maria acknowledged these were difficult issues, but, she said, "It's not as if you have to agree with everything somebody does. It's a free country, and that cuts both ways. One is free to do certain things, and other people are free to object to free actions undertaken by others."

Dave and Maria had addressed this topic on a number of occasions and they were of similar minds. They did not approve of homosexual activity because it was against their convictions. However, they also thought private activity among gays should have the protection of law. Both Dave and Maria had a few friends with same-sex orientation. Most of these were good, loving, and well-intentioned people, and both Maria and Dave enjoyed being with them. But under no circumstances were Dave and Maria going to agree that their actions were ones they would support.

Maria admitted that her firm, clear thoughts concerning same-sex attraction wavered every once in a while when she thought about being a mother. "Girls think about being a mother fairly often. In our modern society it's hard not to think about what I would do if a child of mine turned out to be gay. Of course, I would still love him. But I suspect I would also be more defensive of him, not just of him personally but of his views. I suspect I would gradually grow silent about my opposition to same-sex intimacy. Maybe I would want to see my son in the best possible light. I just couldn't bear not to see my son, if I'm blessed with one. And, of course, I would want to have a loving relationship with him."

Dave listened and acknowledged the problem. No one wants to lose a son over a small matter. "But," said Dave, "the matter is not so small and sometimes the gay person is not really convinced he's gay. You know how college kids like to experiment with different types of personalities. Not everyone who feels an occasional homosexual urge turns out to be gay. Maybe it's important for parents to be honest and say what they think to their son or daughter."

Maria and Dave then talked about the extent to which same-sex inclinations are genetically determined. Neither thought it was, though neither was confident they knew the relative weight that genetics and both the family and ambient culture play. Maria said it probably differs from person to person. Maria then added, "Frankly, I suspect we will not know how important culture is relative to genetics for at least another 100 years. Culture is constantly changing and at the most genetics may say some people are partially inclined to same-sex attraction. Who knows? The issue will be with us for a long time."

Maria then asked, "Do you think homosexual activity is a big deal? Is it a significant issue?" Dave replied, "To my way of thinking, gay intimacy is certainly not as important as gay marriage. For me, children, sex, and commitment are all involved in marriage between a man and woman. Marriage as an institution has developed over several thousand years. We in society should protect our important institutions, not change them dramatically in a relatively short period of time. I don't want to be against individual gays, but I am allowed to be against policies that many gays promote. My goal is to protect traditional marriage. As much as possible, children should be raised by a mother and father. In the family is how they begin to learn how to relate to men and women. I'm allowed to say that. But would I say it to my own son or daughter if I knew he had strong same sex attractions? I don't know."

Maria agreed, though she admitted that she would express things a bit differently. "I think homosexual activity is unnatural. Yes, I admit that is politically incorrect language, but I think you know what I mean. Getting a facelift is unnatural in some way too, but there is a big difference. The facelift enhances nature. It may be a waste of money, but it is an awkward or even misguided attempt to make someone fit better into society. Homosexual policies, on the other hand, are trying to change the basic way in which people relate to one another. Or at least their policies seem to have that effect."

Maria does not usually get exercised about social issues, but this one aroused deep sentiments in her. In a strong voice she was now almost confronting Dave. "Homosexual activity can be tolerated by society, but it should not be approved as being normal. No one can convince me it is normal. If it turns out that my son is not normal, fine, I will deal with it and I will love him, no matter what. But I don't have to deny what I know to be true, that homosexual activity actually corrodes those involved in it and corrodes those who approve it."

"'Unnatural' seems a strong term to me," said Dave, "though I know what you mean. Discarding garbage on the side of a highway is polluting the environment, the same as smokestacks emitting noxious chemicals. If that is true for physical nature, actions inflicting damage on valued social institutions such as marriage can also be called unnatural. But 'unnatural' has to be understood in a narrow sense. When you use the word, you have to be careful to acknowledge that it refers only to certain activities in which many gays engage. Gay people themselves are not unnatural."

Maria wanted to stick with the contrast between natural and unnatural. "Think for a minute," Maria said, "about unnatural things. Maybe guys are more tolerant of pornography as 'natural' than women are. In one sense it is natural, since many people are attracted to it. But I think a large majority of women are convinced that pornography is evil, precisely because it is unnatural. Nature is not just the physical world. It also includes the way we human beings interact. Pornography should absolutely not influence the way we interact. It's evil, it's unnatural. Most of it involves showing naked young men or young women involved in sexual acts. Sex is for adults who are committed to a relationship. Pornography glorifies a fixation on flesh, sex, and youth. It's lethal in our society. I don't like to think about it, but it is everywhere in our society. Isn't that polluting society, isn't it being unnatural, or at least against nature?"

"Even worse," Maria continued, "if I think in personal terms, I would be very distressed if my son at a young age got into pornography or, in some sense even worse, turned to pornography regularly in his adult years. I would think that I had failed to bring him up correctly. I would worry the rest of my life whether I had been too lenient in tolerating certain behavior or things in the house."

Dave concurred. "At this point, no one says there's a gene that predisposes some people to pornography. Maybe there is a gene that gently influences the degree of attraction to that stuff. But most of it occurs because people don't control their desires. Being an adult means being able and willing to control your desires, not yielding to them. People attracted to pornography have to take serious measures to get out of a rut that will ruin them."

"Still," Maria said, "I agree we have to be careful with that word *unnatural*. After all, many good people find pornography alluring and they have to work hard to control their desires. As you point out, there has to be something 'natural' about the attraction, otherwise so many people would not be drawn to pornography. I guess it's because the human body is appealing and human intimacy is very desirable. What is out of kilter is the desire to do this apart from commitment and the possibility of conception."

Maria then added, "I am definitely not saying gays are evil or unnatural. But it certainly seems to me that some of their actions are unnatural, just as pornography is against human nature properly understood." Maria looked over at the skyline and was delighted that a heavy coat was unnecessary today. "Are we gloomy or what?" she said. "I admit all these things are very disturbing to me. Even though it's important to consider them, thinking about this stuff gets me anxious. Let's walk over to the cathedral and say a prayer there. We have to make sure that we are adult in our desires and that we are reasonable to handling these issues in our life."

23

Same Sex Orientation

AS WAS NOTED earlier, it is not immediately apparent that using fun or pleasure as a justification for action is directly contrary to the fundamental value of friendship. As a result, many people who are otherwise attracted to a natural law approach (including many Christians) are laissez-faire with respect to gays and lesbians. Many heterosexuals are inclined to let gays and lesbians do what they want to do. If gays and lesbians are not hurting anyone else, why even raise the moral issue, especially since many gays are dismissive of it?

The moral issue is important for a variety of reasons. First of all, truth counts, and second, parents have to respond reasonably and thoughtfully to questions posed by their teenage sons and daughters about this issue. Just as critical, any sophisticated moral system should be able to determine whether some action is acceptable, admirable, or corrosive.

Although in a natural law context fun or pleasure may initially seem like a sound reason for same-sex sexual intimacy, pleasure as the primary justification or norm for sex does not withstand scrutiny. Pleasure is too weak a foundation on which to base the freedom to engage in sex. Pleasure plays a role, but it is not enough. Once one admits pleasure or fun as the primary justification for acts of friendship, without reference to other fundamental values, it becomes impossible to confine similar acts to the realm and meaning of friendship and life.

PLEASURE—AN INSUFFICIENT NORM

For the sake of argument, assume fun or pleasure is a sufficient justification for sexual intimacy. Such an assumption, we argue, extends the normal borders of admissible sexual activity far beyond what most people, including gays and lesbians, would consider acceptable. For example, most people—be they gay, lesbian, or straight—abhor bestiality and in no way condone it. However, if a moral system allows pleasure as the primary criterion for sexual activity, those who get pleasure out of performing sexual acts with animals have a warrant to perform such actions, no matter what the rest of society thinks. But such activities certainly do not lead to greater participation in the fundamental value of friendship and even less so in life.

This example indicates that pleasure alone cannot be an adequate justification. Does pleasure plus commitment to another human being justify the moral worthiness of sexual intimacy? Actually, it does not. Just because two people are committed to each other and enjoy their sexual activity does not mean that sexual activity promotes friendship. After all, this combination allows for sadistic or masochistic sexual activity, and that type of sexual behavior always denigrates human dignity. Sadistic and masochistic activities use sexual pain not to express love and commitment, but arouse sexual feelings. As we have emphasized in many previous chapters, the sexual act is an integral human act used to pursue friendship and life. It includes the biological act, openness to children, the symbolic component of exclusive commitment, and the dual factor of memory and imagination. Sadomasochistic sex is corrosive because its focus is not on the sexual act but on sexual pleasure. It takes human aversion to pain and uses it to increase sexual pleasure. That is, it tries to transform the bodily signal of pain, something that has developed in animals over millions of years to alert humans to danger, into a means of pleasure. It is first and foremost corrosive of life. But also, because it uses the pain of another person or oneself for one's own pleasure, it is contrary to friendship, which must begin with love of oneself as a human being to be respected.

Up to this point the arguments that sexual intimacy among unmarried people are corrosive apply equally to heterosexuals and homosexuals. But there is a very basic distinction between heterosexual and homosexual activity that has important implications. Same-sex sexual relations lack the natural context of procreation that is present in heterosexual relations. Admittedly, a woman beyond her childbearing years can still get married. But even in this case, she is open to bearing a child, because the act itself implies this. In other words, the act itself expresses openness to conception, even if conception cannot take place because a woman no longer ovulates.

The difficulty with trying to justify same-sex intimacy within a natural law framework is same-sex intimacy does not proceed from any process of procreation consistent with same-sex activity. That is, same-sex attraction is not generative in any genetic way. Gays or lesbians may claim that because same-sex orientations sometimes appear in various species of nonhuman animals, gayness is "natural." But an occasional aberration in some animal species is not the same as being natural. Furthermore, the occasional appearance can only be that. Same-sex activity, of course, does not generate children. That is, nature itself has a way to prevent such activity generating children with a likelihood of having the same sexual orientation as the couple performing the act. If one assumes same-sex attraction is at least partially genetically determined, one must conclude that, absent genetic manipulation, it cannot intentionally be passed on.

Given the pace of genetic discoveries and developments, future possibilities may offer very difficult choices. For example, it may turn out, after decades of research, that sexual orientation is determined to a large extent by genetic factors. Suppose the field of genetic medicine develops to such a point that a woman could take a pill that increases substantially the likelihood she will bear a child with a genetic inclination toward the opposite sex.

In a free society, the woman can choose. Would the woman face any genuine ethical constraints that she might admit are binding on her morally, though not legally? Yes. One constraint is to take those steps that promote the best chances for her child, whatever gender it might be, to thrive in its pursuit of the fundamental values. If moral authorities, including the Church, were to agree that this pill is morally acceptable based on what it does, many women would take the pill because they understand a basic complementarity between men and women exists, is worthwhile, and enables both men and women to thrive.

The point of this highly theoretical example is to underline the importance given by most human beings to the ways in which men and women complement one another physically, emotionally, intellectually, and spiritually. From everything we now know about how DNA functions, the emotional, intellectual, and spiritual aspects of our lives rely on physical operations and then extend beyond them. That is, the physical provides a foundation, but then many other factors beyond the physical DNA also play a role in our formation.

SAME SEX SEXUAL INTIMACY UNDERMINES FRIENDSHIP AND LIFE

Suppose one does not admit the force of the arguments above. Same-sex couples might make the following claim, which has a certain appeal in our culture. While it is true that homosexual acts of love cannot result in children, they don't under-mine the fundamental value of friendship. Same-sex activity is just another acti-vity of friendship, perhaps not as socially significant as heterosexual marriage, but still worthwhile and definitely not contrary to friendship. While the sexual act in this case cannot result in children, it can be a valid sign of love and commitment.

The desire for sexual contact, gays would argue, appears to be as strong in homo-sexual couples as in heterosexual couples. Therefore, according to this argument, there must be something natural about it. Many committed couples of the same sex believe sexual intimacy is a sign of commitment and therefore they restrict their sexual activity to the person to whom they are committed. Whether or not the state acknowledges it to be a marriage or grants it a distinct status as a civil union, what can possibly be wrong with a same-sex couple making a commitment until death parts them and then enjoying the pleasures of sexual contact?

While personal commitment between two persons of same-sex orientation can be at times a high form of friendship, the underlying problem is the sexual expres-sion of such commitment. For same-sex friends who engage in sexual intimacy, one notes very few boundaries to the sexual activity and certainly no natural bound. In traditional marriage, the boundary is the desire to have children. In a same-sex physical relationship, given the sole justification of pleasure, the sexual activity can include almost anything imaginable. In saying this, we are not sug-gesting gays or lesbians seek novel expressions of sexual intimacy. Rather, we are simply highlighting the fact that, once sexual intimacy is removed from the con-text of procreation, there are no longer any moral barriers to novel forms of sexual intimacy. Any particular couple's motivation or intention may truly be of a very high form of friendship. The difficulty is that, absent the physiological framework of the traditional act of sexual intercourse, sexual activity brings with it such a wide warrant for sexual activity that it not only jeopardizes the symbolic meaning of traditional sexual connection but also threatens to extend sexual activity to areas far beyond the realm of friendship.

The natural bounds in traditional sexual intercourse between heterosexuals stem from one of the primary purposes of sexual intercourse among human beings, namely, procreation. In terms of statistical frequency, procreation may not be as significant a motivating factor as desire to express love or experience plea-sure. Nonetheless, human reason can perceive the central role played by sexual intercourse in the generation of children. This physical act is the normal means for "making a baby." Linked to this physical activity is the human desire to hand on the best of human values to the next generation. Human beings pass on their most treasured values via culture and common understandings. The way for children to come to understand the central importance of love, friendship, and commitment is to realize, once they reach adolescence or adulthood, that they were conceived in love, just as they were surrounded with love from the very moment of their birth. In this ideal circumstance conception emerges from loving friendship, and the loving friendship of the husband and wife provides the optimal context in which children mature—first becoming adolescents, then adults.

In many families, the ideal of conceiving in love and nurturing the child in love over many long years may be far from reality. Even in the context of damaged or difficult love, however, parents teach children how a man and woman relate to one another. This imperfect modeling of married love for their children forms a foundation from which the child starts to understand love and commitment. As the child matures, her notion of love and commitment will undoubtedly change. But it begins with what the child has learned in the family.

Same-sex couples may claim that they are just using sexual intimacy in a slightly different way than the customary use of heterosexual couples. They mean no harm by their nonstandard sexual intimacy and they do not intend to sleight in any way the majority population, consisting of heterosexuals. That is, their intent is not to undermine the value of love or procreation.

Good intentions are not enough. In the area of sexual intimacy, if sex becomes separated from a loving openness to accept a child as a possible consequence of the sexual act, sex no longer carries the message of conceiving a child in love and mutual commitment. This is bedrock foundation, necessary to produce a society that affirms children conceived in love and commitment. As we have argued, this is a very valuable understanding that likely took Homo sapiens millennia to develop. A society undermines this understanding by approving sexual intimacy that by its very nature cannot result in the conception of a child. Society may choose to place minimal legal restrictions on private intimacies. But a society that wants to instruct its young in the complementary love of a woman and man and the importance of procreation should not grant formal, public approval to sexual intimacy unrelated to the possibility of procreation.

A DIFFICULT NORM

A natural law approach admits the moral dilemma faced by gay friends. It acknowledges the genuine force of sexual attraction among some same-sex people, but also requires that they maintain chaste relationships. Although the same-sex attraction may be forceful and may proceed from a genetic predisposition, the attraction is still deemed misdirected or disordered according to natural law. The reality of the attraction is admitted, but in some important way the lure bespeaks a significant deficiency. The attraction does not include a procreative aspect. Because it lacks this natural component that is central to the development of the human race, same sex attraction must be managed, not acted upon.

The arguments above will be unconvincing for gays and lesbians and likely also unpersuasive for people who, without engaging in the theoretical argument, are inclined to let gays and lesbians do what they want. Nonetheless, these arguments are forceful and fairly represent a natural law approach. According to natural law, homosexuals enjoy all the respect due any human person. They can also form close friendships with members of the same sex or the opposite sex.

Heterosexual unmarried couples are expected to avoid situations likely to lead to sin or corrosive actions. Indeed, the stricture to avoid putting oneself in situations where sin is likely applies to all human beings, since all human beings are called to avoid corrosive activities related to any fundamental value. In particular, because sexual attraction is a strong human drive and because it is more easily acted upon when couples live in close intimacy and privacy, heterosexual couples should not live together prior to marriage. Similarly, same-sex friends with a same-sex attraction should recognize the power of sexual attraction and not live together.

Natural law allows that friends with same-sex attraction may enjoy happy, productive lives as friends who undertake many activities together, much as heterosexual friends would do. People with same-sex inclinations make many contributions of great value to society. But society has a vested interest both in the complementarity of man and woman as well as in procreation. For this reason, it is important that society express its support for traditional heterosexual marriage, which means a permanent commitment of heterosexual couples in marriage. Society may accept private behavior contrary to these values, as was the case in the culture of ancient Greece and Rome. In its public stance, however, it should support sexual complementarity and procreation.

This public-private distinction should not be used unjustly to disenfranchise or disadvantage same-sex friends who engage in public displays of private commitment. In particular, the distinction should not be construed to mean that gays have to lead essentially private lives. But what society permits is not the same as what morality requires.

According to natural law, legal statutes should provide general support for the pursuit of the fundamental values and prohibit corrosive actions that undermine the social pursuit of the fundamental values. Practically, this means that a society can permit those corrosive activities that fulfill three conditions. First, the actions are not easily controlled by public authorities; second, the actions do not physically harm or materially disadvantage individuals or groups in society; and third, the actions do not seriously undermine the pursuit of any or all of the fundamental values. As was pointed out above, even without political action groups, same-sex activities tend to undermine the institution of traditional marriage. However, to the extent same sex activities are mostly private, they may be permitted. Nonetheless, any society that promotes adherence to the natural law must strongly support traditional marriage and should not elevate same-sex commitment to the same status in society that heterosexual marriage has.

Society's reluctance to endorse same sex relationships by granting it the same status as traditional marriage does not, however, imply ingratitude to homosexuals as a group. Society may have many good reasons to acknowledge the significant contributions gay and lesbian individuals make in a particular city, town, or country. These contributions can be truly impressive and worthy of genuine praise and approbation.

Our many distinctions appear to constrain the life of gays or lesbians. Therefore, one can reasonably ask: What prospects does the natural law offer to two same-sex friends who have a same-sex attraction? Doesn't the natural law approach imply a fairly dreary, nonsexual existence for such friends? This is a plausible interpretation if one thinks sexual intimacies are among the most important activities in life. According to natural law, however, same-sex friendship is indeed a high form of friendship and, if one brackets out sexual intimacy, laudable. Two men or two women who work together, collaborate on various projects, or spend time together pursuing the arts or other interests can enjoy the benefits of deep and lasting friendship that is affectionate and deeply rewarding, but not sexual. Similar to heterosexual friends who work together on projects but are not married, they can make significant contributions to their community. Depending on how close their friendship is, the same-sex friends can play important roles in the life of their respective blood families. Similar perhaps to uncles and aunts who share in various functions and celebrations, the two friends can be valued members of the extended family. Like aunts and uncles who are generous with their time and resources, they may be considered valued friends who assist their nieces and nephews. They can make enormous contributions in the world of business, the arts, education, media, and politics.

All these activities can be undertaken with a devout commitment to God expressed in part by participation in a Christian or other religious community of worship and service. The active participation of these same-sex friends is welcome and should be applauded in a natural law approach. In trying to live out their commitment as the best of friends, it is hoped they will be admirable children of God who are loving, attentive, and contributors to society. According to the natural law approach, however, they have an obligation to be realistic in pursuing a chaste relationship. In particular, they must maintain enough physical and psychological distance to make chastity a reality in their relationship.

PARTNERLESS SEX

Some people and groups promote auto-eroticism. Masturbation and other forms of auto-stimulation are considered playful, pleasurable activities. Such pleasure, it is argued, can even be enhanced by use of pornographic materials. Even without auto-eroticism, some would argue that pornography is simply fun, harming only the practitioner, if anybody at all, and it therefore should not be considered corrosive.

The previous section has emphasized the inadequacy of pleasure as a justification and basis for sexual activity in the context of pursing the fundamental values of friendship and life. The case for partnerless sex is even weaker. Although partnerless sex may be considered an act intended to pursue the fundamental value of playfulness, it is an act directly contrary to the fundamental values of friendship and life. Human beings are called to interact in natural ways with other human beings. They are not intended to remain isolated, creating fantasy worlds of sexual attraction. Fantasy worlds are a legitimate part of any child's maturation process. They are not a reasonable way for adults to seek or find comfort and satisfaction.

Pornography has become a worldwide scourge. The Internet makes the images easily available around the world. Western society's focus on privacy and personal choice means the government only polices the use of pornography when it involves the use of minors. As a result, the availability of pornographic materials increases steadily. Because of this easy availability, parents and many cultural institutions have to work hard to instill in young people the ability to resist the encroachment of pornography in their daily lives.

Pornography rattles and disturbs both memory and imagination in a person. Young people have to develop skills to curtail capturing images in their mind that corrupt their memory and distort their imagination. People who regularly engage in viewing pornography run the great risk of distorting and ruining both their outlook on marriage and family as well as their performance as spouses and parents. The young man who regularly indulges in pornographic material will gradually change the way he views children and adults, since so much of this material emphasizes their role in providing sexual satisfaction. He may think this aspect of his personality will always remain part of his deeply private life, inaccessible to others. However, in marriage practically everything becomes known. But, worst of all, years of engaging his fantasy with pornographic material will adversely impact the way he looks upon his wife and their children. Even if he controls his urges toward his own children, he will not be able to curtail the images and fantasies about his own children. Young people have to understand the likely devastating effects that pornography can have on their future life, especially on relationships they will eventually value deeply. If a young man deeply immerses himself in pornography, he acts directly contrary to practical reasonableness because he seriously distorts or corrupts his memory and imagination, both of which play vital roles in the exercise of practical reason. A future husband who regularly views pornography will fill his memory and imagination with such distorted images of children and women that it will likely impair his ability to relate to wife and children in a whole-some way and in a way that promotes their wellbeing and development.

PART THREE

Moral Skills and Religious Practice

THE PREVIOUS TWO parts outlined the natural law approach. Although natural law speaks to the minds and hearts of many, to put it gently, not everyone is convinced. There are many intellectual and social reasons why natural law is not as convincing as it is intended to be. So, we first explore them and then in the following chapters we give a glimpse of what Christianity adds to the natural law approach.

The three important elements that Christianity add to the natural law approach are affirmation, enhancement, and motivation. First, the Bible as interpreted in a tradition offers assurance that natural law does unveil moral truths. Second, Christian belief and practice enhance moral skills that make it more likely that people will be able to follow consistently the natural law approach. Third, because baptism and the other Christian sacraments offer a share in divine life, they motivate Christians to strive for exemplary actions in their lives.

Parts I and II identified and justified the fundamental values as truly universal human values. Part II considered particular actions in pursuit of marriage, one of the highest expressions of friendship. Actions related to sexual intimacy were shown to be corrosive if they did not attend to and respect the four central characteristics of the sexual act: the physical act itself, an openness to new life, an expression of lasting commitment, and the engagement of memory and imagination. If this is not the context of acts of sexual intimacy, they are corrosive of the values of friendship and life rather than conducive toward participating in those values.

Applying general principles requires experience, reflection, and loving perception, which are ways to participate in practical reasonableness. How to do this in particular circumstances requires good will and imagination. The chapters on Dave and Maria continue to offer specific ways to talk about and pursue the fundamental value of friendship in a relationship that is gradually tending toward a lasting commitment.

In part III the focus is on acquiring moral skills that are useful to young adults as they live their lives, but especially as they prepare to make a permanent commitment to another person. We contrast two paths to the acquisition of moral skills. By the time young people finish high school, practically all of them have acquired a basic level of important moral skills. These skills enable a young person to clearly distinguish right from wrong, or acceptable from corrosive actions, and then to make the correct decision. A young person has a good set of moral skills if she can consistently determine which action is at least acceptable and then reliably decide to follow the path that leads toward fulfillment of the fundamental values.

We first name four important moral skills that help people determine what the correct action is and then actually do it. We then list activities and experiences through which young people usually acquire at least the rudiments of these moral skills. The final step is to explore how various Christian religious activities enhance these same four moral skills in young adults.

Christianity is, of course, the Good News of and about Jesus Christ. However, part of this good news is that, through religious practice in the Christian community, Christians are more apt to behave the way in which natural law indicates all people, with or without religious faith, should act. One could say that part III offers the "moral value added" of Christianity. Aside from offering some clarity in times of doubt, the main value consists in two significant benefits. First, religious belief and practices give young people greater self-control and self-knowledge; they also enhance a person's ability to make and keep a lasting commitment while properly managing his or her memory and imagination. The second benefit is that religious belief and practice greatly expand a person's imagination and hopes. As a result, a young person may aspire to perform a new array of exemplary actions. Christianity is a religion with benefits in the moral life.

24

Why Doesn't Everyone Agree with Natural Law?

IF THE NATURAL law appeals to all people of good will, why don't more people get with the program? Many people have never heard of natural law, and many who know something about it either find it confusing or disagree with the norms that flow from a natural law approach. With respect to contested norms, consider the following instances, all of which have been addressed in previous chapters. Many young people do not consider it wrong to have sexual relations prior to marriage, whether or not they are committed to the person with whom they are having sexual relations. At least in Western society, both the morality and legality of abortion are widely contested. Many young people do not consider drugs and getting drunk corrosive or against their conscience. Some young people may choose not to indulge in these things, but many of them do not hold it against those who do. That is, although personally opposed, they do not believe the activities diminish the moral stature of the person who does indulge.

The main reason why natural law does not prompt spontaneous agreement by most in a modern community is that moral codes are not just theoretical norms that can be perceived objectively by any person. They are norms lived in actual communities and the experience of abiding by the norms provides insight into the reasonableness of the norms. As we have pointed out many times in previous chapters, many people live in societies that endorse practices contrary to natural law. However, for people living in such societies these practices, although contrary to the norms of natural law, seem plausible and reasonable to them. In most instances their attraction does not stem from a careful review of moral arguments. Rather, it stems from the fact that many of their friends engage in these practices.

The fact that "everyone is doing it" does not constitute a good reason for doing it. Our claim is that some societies or groups within society have popular practices that are seriously flawed. Depending on the degree and pervasiveness of corrosive practices in a community, the explicit or implied norm arising out of specific practices may blind members of the community to ways in which the practices are corrosive.

As we pointed out in the earlier discussion of sin, some actions appear to be good or reasonable to us because we perform some mental gymnastics to convince ourselves of this. With time we may come to realize that such actions actually impede our progress toward a fundamental value. This phenomenon can also occur in an entire community. The actions of a community in one or more areas may dull the consciences of people in the community. The comfort of performing the action, which enjoys the support of the community, may prevent many people from realizing the compelling force of a natural law argument that highlights how the practice undermines the pursuit of one or more fundamental values. In a particular community, the practical norm acquired from the repetition of an action either by one's friends and/or by well-regarded members of society can blind people to the way in which an action is corrosive.

Whether this constitutes sin in the proper sense depends on the extent to which the person really suspects the activities are questionable. If the person gives no serious thought to a particular action and just follows along with the cultural masses, the requirements for these activities to be considered personal sin may not be fulfilled. ("May not" because people always have the responsibility to form their consciences.) On the other hand, if one reviews the various contested activities listed above, it is difficult to imagine young people not thinking seriously about whether premartial sex, abortion, and drugs are wrong in themselves.

THREE TYPES OF COMMUNITIES THAT SUPPORT A CORROSIVE ACTIVITY

The previous explanation is highly theoretical. Therefore, considering three particular examples will provide greater clarity about the relationship between social practice and social conviction and what impact this has on how compelling a moral norm is. The community in which the norms are lived or violated might be either large or a small subgroup of a larger entity. To gain perspective, let us consider two examples for a large community or culture and another for a smaller subgroup of the larger community.

In the United States, a good percentage of the population does not consider it wrong or corrosive for a couple to live together prior to marriage. In previous chapters we presented strong reasons why this type of behavior is corrosive of people who pursue the fundamental values. If these reasons were as compelling as we think they are, fewer people would approve of couples living together prior to marriage.

We claim that a collective blindness exists on this issue. This is true even though people who disagree with the natural law approach can be very reasonable and some of them are highly intelligent. Native intelligence is not the decisive factor here; deceit is the issue. Primarily it is an issue of self-deceit, but in this case it must involve collective deceit or deceit on a broad scale. How is this possible?

Sometime after 1960 a larger group of people started to experiment with new types of intimate relationships prior to marriage. This did not happen suddenly, and it is not the case that prior to 1960 the norm for chastity before marriage was adhered to by practically all young people. Nonetheless, sometime prior to 1960 the rule of no sex before marriage was a broadly accepted norm, and for a couple to live together prior to marriage was deemed a serious infraction of the moral order. Consequently, most couples living together before marriage did not advertise the fact, either to their families or to friends.

For a variety of complex reasons, the social consensus concerning appropriate levels of intimacy prior to marriage changed in the 1960s and 1970s, and continues in flux. Gradually, more couples chose to live together before marriage and did so in a public manner. As a result of the openness of their premarital relationship, this information became available to other young couples coming of age in American society.

People in the United States are well informed about various practices relating to sexual intimacy because there has been increased interest and coverage by newspapers, television, movies, and the Internet. Without necessarily intending to, these media report on moral norms. Reports about activities have their own dynamism: the activities reported may become advertised and promoted activities. These in turn may be imitated by many Americans, and what previously had been only a local norm may become more widely accepted. The media report not only on liaisons between actors and actresses, but also on extramarital intimacies between businesspeople and their lovers. As for college students and their escapades, much of this is documented more or less thoroughly through behavioral surveys. If the reporting is sufficiently frequent and favorable or simply nonjudgmental, some people are persuaded to make these forms of behavior their norms.

This appears to be what happened. Young people gradually got the impression that living together before marriage was accepted. Although living together prior to marriage is certainly not required by society, it is no longer an activity frowned upon by society.

Of course, a process like the one sketched above can happen in reverse; a community can move from blindness to sight, from bondage to freedom. Slavery, the second illustrative case, was an established institution at the inception of the United States. Many lawmakers were uncomfortable with it, but it was perceived as necessary for the good of the union. Gradually people raised their voices against the practice of buying and selling slaves, and then against ownership of slaves. After much argument, toil, and blood, the United States reached a new plateau where slavery was officially prohibited. But then it took another 100 years for blacks to secure effective rights normally accorded to non-blacks. We would describe that process as an ongoing one, which moved from corrosive behavior toward an increasing consensus to allow blacks as much freedom in pursuing the fundamental values as non-blacks enjoy.

Our third example involves a smaller group and it helps illustrate the role played by a local community in the formation of norms. Because behavior influences the way people think, and because together behavior and theory produce norms, behavior can have a bad impact in a small community as well as a large one.

Students in college write papers and take exams, and for many students cheating is a realistic option. Cheating is an activity deemed corrosive by natural law (because it undermines the pursuit of knowledge), but in many cases it is an option. How much cheating takes place at the undergraduate level depends to a large extent on a particular college or university. Some institutions may encourage faculty to monitor tests carefully in order to decrease the amount of cheating. At a particular institution, some students, perhaps because of their socioeconomic or religious background, may be very opposed to cheating and they speak out when they see students who cheat. But if an institution becomes tolerant of cheating, the amount of cheating on exams tends to increase. Students who were unsure about whether the activity is corrosive may adopt a more pragmatic approach. While acknowledging that cheating is wrong, they may argue they will fall behind in life and lose out to less qualified students if they don't engage in cheating. As a result, in a tolerant academic atmosphere the likelihood is that cheating spreads. To preserve their status or prospects for success, students otherwise not inclined to cheat join the cheating brigade. This example illustrates a larger point: communities in which one grows to maturity have a significant impact on the type of person one becomes.

In sum, behavioral patterns in community tend to influence the way people act, perceive, and think. As a result, some quite solid arguments advanced by the natural law approach may have little traction with some people. The reason is less theoretical than behavioral. The people hearing the arguments are attached to another way of acting. In this scenario, the behavior proscribed by natural law seems normal in the community. As a result, behavior that should be seen as corrosive is accepted as part of the ordinary way of doing things. To cite another example, bribes are corrosive of solidarity and the common good; they yield favors to people who, though less qualified, are willing to purchase access or influence. In some political environments, however, bribes are generally perceived as pathways to success rather than as corrosive of one's stature as a human being.

The reality of fundamentally different practices between communities can be expressed in another way. In order to objectively assess whether an activity is corrosive, one has to be able to fairly evaluate the argument. One does not have to agree with the argument immediately, but one has to be open to understand how an activity that may appear harmless can undermine not only an individual's pursuit of the fundamental value but also the community's pursuit of that value. If a person is absolutely convinced that a few sexual liaisons prior to marriage are a good thing or at least in no way harmful to marriage, that person cannot objectively evaluate the argument that premarital sex treats sex as fun and pleasurable and totally separate from personal commitment to an individual. Appreciating that engaging in sex should involve personal, permanent commitment is at the heart of the natural law argument. In order for the argument to work or at least have a chance at working, the person must minimally consider seriously that premarital sex may indeed undermine commitment in marriage.

RANKING GOODS

Another reason why people may not agree with the conclusions of natural law is that some groups or subgroups may rank social goods in different ways. Consider, for example, the fundamental value of life. No action should be taken which "undermines a fundamental value." This means that actions that work directly contrary to the value rather than promoting it are forbidden because the actions are corrosive.

Some people identify freedom as a fundamental value. We argued earlier that freedom is a value, but not a fundamental personal value since a person should not strive to have as much freedom as possible. People should be free to pursue the fundamental values in ways they choose, but in order to pursue any value, a person has to choose one way rather than another. He cannot remain open to all ways. On the other hand, freedom is a very important societal value. Society should be arranged so as to allow individuals much freedom in pursuing the fundamental values. Because this is true, society has to promote freedom at the same time that it protects people in society. But social freedom never comes ahead of human life. Society does not allow a person to exercise his personal freedom by killing another person. Rather, a system of laws and police forces exists both to prevent assaults and to bring to justice people who have assaulted others.

It may appear obvious that life has a priority over freedom and that freedom is primarily a social good. Societal freedom allows people considerable room to choose the ways in which they wish to pursue the fundamental values. But societal freedom does not enjoy a higher status than life itself. Life, especially human life, should be protected.

Freedom, however, can confuse people. A person who is free may decide he is free to end his own life. But committing suicide corrodes a person as well as ends the person's life. Suicide is directly contrary to the fundamental value of life. Taking the life of a fetus also corrodes anyone involved in making the decision or implementing it. Humans are made for life. Choosing against life makes them less human and makes it more likely they will not correctly evaluate future activities involving life.

Abortion is a contested issue in American society. Natural law is clear in supporting human life in all its forms. Nonetheless, many people accept abortion as a private act that anyone is free to perform. Such people may be caring, thoughtful, and sensitive human beings. But they appear to place societal freedom above the fundamental value of life. These thoughtful, caring people wind up approving something that is only apparently caring and sensitive. In fact, because they wrongly give greater stature and status to the freedom of the individual woman and consider the life in the womb less than a full human life, abortion continues to be a tolerated practice in many societies.

THE NOVA EFFECT

As a star gets older it gets larger and eventually explodes and generates many small remnants. The eminent philosopher Charles Taylor uses the image and name of *nova* to refer to the modern phenomenon of many different ethical and philosophical systems. Until the nineteenth century, there was general agreement on the broad norms that constrain people's actions. That is, there was one large supernova, the natural law approach embedded in humanism. For a variety of reasons, cultural forces caused the supernova to burst. The remnants are small, ethical novae. The group of localized gases or nebulae are the new, almost individualized, competing ethical or spiritual systems. The great consensus no longer exists. Instead, according to Taylor, people adhere to a perplexing variety of moral and spiritual systems.

Many people select their individual norms almost as if each norm were an item on a multipaged menu for a popular local diner: yes to vegetarian, no to nuclear power, no power sources which emit pollutants, no gas guzzling automobiles or trucks, no sexually alluring clothes, no religion, yes to drugs, et cetera. Time was when people adhered to only one or two moral systems. Natural law was one of these, as was pragmatic realism. The current drive to pick and choose falls within a general approach first developed by the philosopher Nietzsche, who advocated that we should define ourselves by making whatever choices we want.

One implication of the nova effect is that many norms do not get improved or refined by the broader community over time. The reason is twofold. First, the norms tend to be so particular that no large group (or even subgroup) of people abides by approximately the same set of norms. Second, because people tend to pick and choose, many people do not attempt to conform to a logically consistent ethical approach. If a community does not articulate reasons for norms and if a community abides by a great variety of norms, people can easily wander far from moral consistency, both in theory and in practice. More to the point, modern practices may induce people to perceive natural law as an attempt to enforce an old-fashioned moral consistency.

In short, the nova effect results from the decomposition of a moral consensus that prevailed in previous centuries and a new, much greater emphasis on societal freedom. The result is not merely the multiplicity of norms. Due to the great variety of systems, individuals have to work harder to abide by whatever norms they select because individuals lack a visible community of similar adherents.

DOES NATURAL LAW CHANGE OVER TIME?

Although the fundamental values remain fixed, society constantly develops new ways to pursue the fundamental values. Computers, iPads, iPhones, iPods, air conditioning, plastics and polyester, cheap air travel, space stations, thousands of electronic computer games, new types of museums, high definition TV, innovative medicine—all these offer new ways to pursue the fundamental values.

Society always needs intelligent and wise people who reflect on various innovations to explore the extent to which they lead to higher realizations of various fundamental values. Consider a development mentioned earlier and likely to be realistic sometime in the next fifty years. Suppose in the not too distant future eating meat is judged to be no longer necessary for a normal person to remain healthy. If this turns out to be true and a consensus develops around it, an implication for the natural law approach would be that, so as not to undermine life, one should not eat meat. Eating vegetables, fish, or dairy products would be acceptable, but eating chicken, turkey, pork, lamb, veal, beef, and other meat products would be considered corrosive acts, since they require taking the life of a creature that is fairly high in the cycle of life. Wise and intelligent people would have to deliberate what role eating fish plays in maintaining a person's health. It would have to be determined whether fish is a necessary or at least advisable component in a healthy diet. It is at least conceivable that most people could keep themselves healthy and satisfied by eating just fruits, vegetables, and dairy products.

If vegetarianism on a large scale should be deemed to be healthy for most people and a consensus of opinion developed around the view that people could remain healthy without eating meat, natural law would say people should avoid eating meat, so as to honor and preserve life. This would certainly represent an enormous change in our eating habits. However, all the principles of natural law would remain the same. The difference would be where a particular activity is located in the standard diagram we use for each fundamental value. Eating meat in the future would be considered a corrosive activity because no longer would killing these types of animals be necessary to sustain human life, which is a higher form of life than chickens, pigs, and cows. That is, eating meat would be moved from the area of "acceptable" to the left-hand area marked "corrosive." However, the reason for designating an activity as corrosive would not have changed; in addition, the fundamental value of life would remain the same.

Natural law is natural in the sense that it conforms to the way humans and the world are made and because it is established in its broad outlines. The fundamental values are part of our make-up as human beings and we are hardwired to pursue them, even if at times societies are blinded to certain corrosive activities in which they regularly engage. What changes are the ways in which we can pursue the fundamental values. As the ways to pursue values change, we adjust our behavior. However, it would be misleading to claim that these adjustments represent a change in natural law.

25

The Christian Difference

CHRISTIAN BELIEF AND practice do not change the natural law approach. That is, the fundamental values remain the same, as do the corrosive activities. However, Christian belief and practice do add three components to the natural law approach: revelation in the Old and New Testaments, enhanced moral skills, and the selection of exemplary goals.

In all Christian churches, the Old and New Testaments are normative for belief and practice. These sacred writings, however, confirm the basic framework of natural law. It is true that the Catholic Church as well as some other Christian groups have traditions of authoritative teachings concerning faith and morals. The religious teachings on matters of faith are rooted in the Old and New Testaments. Similarly, the ethical or moral teachings of the Catholic Church and many other Christian churches are influenced by the Old and New Testaments. However, the Catholic Church justifies its moral norms primarily by invoking natural law. In particular, when questions arise whether a certain practice is "corrosive" or "acceptable," the Catholic Church uses natural law reasoning.

In the previous chapter, we pointed out that the plausibility of natural law is influenced by the practices of the community. Christians are not perfect in their practices and this can result in wrongly classifying certain activities. Nonetheless, the leadership in the Catholic Church always calls its members to correct practice, since practices are so important in perceiving whether actions are corrosive, acceptable, or exemplary. With respect to religious doctrines of the Catholic Church, the teaching authority of the Catholic Church, represented at its highest level by the pope, relies primarily on the Old and New Testaments for justification. But when it comes to deciding whether certain practices are acceptable or corrosive, the Catholic Church invariably invokes reasoning based on natural law.

The second benefit Christianity brings to moral living is that Christian belief and practice enhance and reinforce essential moral skills that are needed to act in accordance with natural law. With particular reference to corrosive actions or sin, religious practice helps Christian believers to avoid corrosive actions.

The third value-added component of Christian belief and practice relates to the boldness with which each believer forms a life-plan. This issue was discussed in chapter 4. A life-plan is a tentative plan, subject to frequent review and revision, which identifies a personal way to realize the array of fundamental values. By listening to and praying over the Old and New Testaments, as well as by receiving the sacraments of Christian practice, believers seek to develop their relationship with Christ. Their faith is that human fullness is found in Jesus Christ, who is the new Adam, the man God intends us to imitate. In their religious communities Christians seek to develop a relationship with Christ. Regular practice of the faith deepens this relationship so that it impacts all the various dimensions of Christian life. Christians' familiarity with Christ influences the actions they seek to perform as they strive to realize the fundamental values more fully.

Religious confirmation of the natural law approach through revelation, assistance in securing moral skills, and a more focused and ambitious life-plan are three important ways in which Christian belief and practice supplements and makes more specific the natural law approach. This chapter provides brief descriptions of these complementarities between natural law and Christian belief and practice.

SCRIPTURAL ENDORSEMENT OF NATURAL LAW

In the Christian tradition the Old and New Testaments constitute the written part of Divine revelation. These are God's words transmitted under the inspiration of the Holy Spirit to human authors. The words of Holy Scripture are to guide people and the community in their relations with God and one another.

The fundamental values receive biblical support in many tales and accounts of the various books of the Bible. As is noted below, the Bible also contains some difficult exceptions to what at this stage of social moral development are considered exceptionless corrosive practices. But emphasizing positive support, perhaps the most striking endorsement of fundamental values, which are central to natural law, comes in the Ten Commandments (Exodus 20:1-17 and Deuteronomy 5:1-21). These commandments certainly contain injunctions specific to the Jewish experience, such as the order to "keep holy the Sabbath." But the commandments also highlight activities that are corrosive for Jews and others. "You shall not kill" endorses life. "You shall not commit adultery" addresses the limits on a committed relationship (friendship). "You shall not steal" encourages freedom and subsidiarity in the pursuit of the fundamental values. "You shall not bear false witness against your neighbor" requires honesty in the pursuit of truth and knowledge. Specifically, this means one should not lie when a lie can injure another person's wellbeing. More generally, it is an injunction to speak the truth to people in circumstances when truth is the norm. (In telling jokes, one is allowed to deceive another for a short period of time, after which one reveals that it was just a joke!)

The New Testament contains a number of passages that suggest or come close to stating that morality is written in the minds and hearts of all people. In his letter to the Romans, St. Paul states: "For when the Gentiles who do not have the law [Torah] by nature observe the prescriptions of the law, they are a law for themselves even though they do not have the law. They show that the demands of the law are written in their hearts, while their conscience also bears witness and their conflicting thoughts accuse or even defend them on the day when, according to my gospel, God will judge people's hidden works through Christ Jesus" (Romans 2:14-16). This passage has often been cited by Christians to justify the claim that all people know there are some actions to be avoided and some actions they are obligated to perform.

Despite some Scriptural endorsement of the natural law approach, the confirmation of natural law in the Old or New Testaments is not specific. Many passages in Sacred Scripture speak about the commitment to life, friendship, beauty, knowledge, playfulness, religion, and practical reasonableness. Admittedly, many passages are fairly general in extolling these values. Alternatively, some passages specifically allow things (polygamy is one example) that we, today, would designate as corrosive. The presence in the Old and New Testaments of passages pertaining to moral behavior does not eliminate the need to think carefully through the hierarchy of good actions within any fundamental value or the need to identify carefully which actions corrode an individual's pursuit of the fundamental values.

One example of the need to think through implications values is the fundamental value of life. The commandment "You shall not kill" means that one should not take the life of a person unjustly. How do we know the correct biblical interpretation involves qualifying the broad formulation against killing with the qualifier "unjustly"? This is a necessary interpretation since there are many passages in the Old Testament in which God tells the Israelites they are to kill their enemies. Some passages are disturbing or even scandalous to Christian and modern sensibilities. For instance in the battle against the Midianites, Moses ordered the army to kill children and mothers and not take them as prisoners (Numbers 31:13-18).

In the time of Moses, norms for "just wars" had not yet been articulated. In fact, the development of a theory of just wars developed when Christian thinkers, such as St. Augustine, tried to reconcile Old Testament passages with Jesus' calls for peacefulness and "turning one's cheek" to abuse. Obviously, neither the Old nor the New Testament says anything directly about modern issues such as nuclear deterrence, in vitro fertilization, or removing life support when a person is in a persistent vegetative state. The Christian approach is that these issues have to be decided by reasoning carefully about the fundamental values and drawing on important insights contained in the Old and New Testaments.

SUPERNATURAL VIRTUES LEADING TO ENHANCED MORAL SKILLS

One becomes a Christian by being incorporated into a Christian community. This occurs through baptism. The original rite of baptism involved being submerged in water. This was a symbolic representation of death. In baptism, the newly baptized dies to the old, worldly culture of sin. In rising up from the water, the Christian is "born again" to a new life of love—love of Christ and love of neighbor.

Through baptism one not only becomes a member of a Christian community but also receives supernatural gifts. "Supernatural" gifts do not contradict human nature. Rather they enable Christians to share in a life that is "beyond" or "higher than" human nature. These are gifts from God that enable Christ's followers to participate in and imitate God's love. That is, our own efforts do not secure the gifts, nor are they rewards for good behavior. Rather, they are part of God's outpouring of love for those who are called to follow him. Most essentially, we are baptized into the divine life of Father, Son, and Holy Spirit.

Grace builds upon nature. The facets of nature that correspond to the supernatural gifts of faith, hope, and charity are the natural activities of faith, hope, and charity. Virtually everyone, whether or not they are Christian, regularly practices the natural gifts (as potential skills which have to be developed, they are given to humans as a package deal with the natural law when they are created, body and soul) of faith, hope, and charity.

Natural faith occurs when a person believes someone will continue acting in a way consonant with the believer's wellbeing. A wife trusts her husband to be faithful, a boss trusts one of her workers to be honest and forthright, et cetera. Natural hope occurs when a person looks forward to a positive outcome, even though current circumstances may not indicate such an outcome is likely. A mother hopes her son, who is currently in a bad relationship, will meet and marry a good woman who brings out the best in him; a businessperson hopes that her new fledgling business will one day be a grand success; a high school students hopes for a high grade on an important standardized exam. In a religious context, charity is another word for love, understood not primarily as a feeling or something physical but rather as a desire to promote the wellbeing of the other person. A person demonstrates natural love when one does good things for the beloved (parent and child, husband and wife, friends, cousins) and remains faithful even during difficult times. A young man may "fall in love" with a young woman while the young woman is still unaware of his affection or while she remains appreciative of, but not yet committed to, him. In this case it is better to say that the young man is hoping for a natural love relationship, since one has not yet fully emerged.

Supernatural gifts of faith, hope, and charity build on the natural gifts, but they differ in their source and the specific action involved. The gifts are "supernatural" both by origin (they stem from God who bestows them freely) and due to the activities they enable. The three supernatural gifts bestowed through baptism are faith, hope, and charity.

Supernatural faith, hope, and charity are potential ways of seeing and acting bestowed at baptism. But a more encompassing and traditional way to describe the gifts is as supernatural virtues. A virtue is a habitual way of acting. The challenge of the Christian life is to turn the potential of supernatural faith, hope, and charity into virtues, that is, habitual ways of acting. Each supernatural virtue enables a regular activity that is beyond an individual's human ability acting on his or her own. That is, the activity moves a person beyond human nature, without conflicting with it, and enables him to live partly in a higher sphere while continuing to be a part of the natural world.

The supernatural virtue of faith enables a Christian to believe, first and foremost, that Jesus is the Son of God and sits at the right hand of the Father and that the Holy Spirit has been given to all Christians to lead them to full humanity and high holiness. Faith focuses on Jesus as God and man, the fullest possible revelation of God in human form. Furthermore, a person of faith accepts the Old and New Testaments as Divine revelation that expresses the truth that Jews and their Christian heirs are part of God's plan which reaches its fullness in Jesus Christ. Christians have a brother in Jesus Christ. Because faith is a supernatural virtue, it is a disposition to recognize and affirm with confidence the important ways in which God has revealed Himself to us in human history. Above all, it enables the Christian to see God's saving action in the passion, death, and resurrection of Jesus Christ. But this disposition to see God's saving action in Christ is not merely the conviction of something that occurred long ago. Supernatural faith believes Christ's healing and saving work continues today through Christian communities of belief. Despite many lapses on the part of individuals and leaders of the Church, supernatural faith affirms Christ's continued, saving, and vivifying activity through the Church.

The supernatural virtue of hope is the disposition to trust that Jesus will come again in glory and welcome into His Kingdom those who trust in him. Supernatural hope endures setbacks which, from a purely human perspective, suggest the promise will not be fulfilled. For example, even if the Christian herself or a family member or friend experiences things such as serious sickness at an early age, a disastrous marriage, persecution, the loss of an important job, or other serious mishaps, the supernatural virtue of trust means the person remains confident that God does not waver in his love for us and in fulfilling his promises. Alternatively, the Christian with unwavering hope is not unnerved by persecution of Christians or societies that do not praise or even respect God.

The root meaning of charity is love. Through baptism Christians share in God's love and even his glory: "And I have given them the glory you gave me, so that they may be one, as we are one, I in them and you in me, that they may be brought to perfection as one, that the world may know that you sent me, and that you loved them even as you loved me" (John 17:22-23). The supernatural virtue of love is first of all focused on God. A baptized person is incorporated into God's life. A person with this virtue is attentive to God's voice and seeks to do what God wants in his or her life. Following the inspiration of the Holy Spirit, the person is called to imitate the Father and the Son in loving creation. All this is to be done in an ordered way, loving and caring for those people whom God has entrusted to our care. It is a supernatural love because it is focused on loving selflessly, desiring the wellbeing of others, and loving others as Jesus loved his disciples.

Because the supernatural virtues are habitual dispositions, they are inclinations that may lie hidden or dormant for periods of time before they flower in different ways. Also, a virtue does not mean that a Christian is never tempted or that Christians never succumb to temptation or that they always choose the best possible activity. The supernatural virtues are not failsafe mechanisms from on high. They enable activities directed to God which are compatible with, but still beyond ordinary human nature. Although the supernatural virtues enable us to participate in God or God's life, our human nature remains with us. As such, we are subject to occasional doubts about Jesus and his sayings, worries about the future, and failure to love as God wants us to love.

Virtues are dispositions. In order for virtues—human or supernatural—to be activated in our lives, we need moral skills. Moral skills are abilities a person has and can call upon when needed. Virtues provide a general direction to our actions, but we still have to develop skills in order to pursue the fundamental values effectively. In the next two chapters, we turn our attention to moral skills. It turns out that our moral skills can be greatly improved by activating the supernatural dispositions we have from the supernatural virtues of faith, hope, and charity.

HOLINESS AND AIMING FOR MORE EXEMPLARY ACTIONS

Since Jesus is the fullest possible expression of God's love, a Christian can do no better than focus on Christ when formulating a life plan, that is, a general roadmap to pursue the fundamental values. Christians are called to imitate Christ. This does not usually mean doing exactly what Jesus did; rather it means understanding what motivated Jesus and using that motivation in our own lives.

Jesus said many things that point to rich fulfillment of the fundamental values. In the context of human and natural beauty, he said: "Why are you anxious about clothes? Learn from the way the wild flowers grow. They do not work or spin. But I tell you that not even Solomon in all his splendor was clothed like one of them. If God so clothes the grass of the field, which grows today and is thrown into the oven tomorrow, will he not much more provide for you, O you of little faith?" (Matthew 6: 28-29). Other sayings of Jesus address our specific relationship with Jesus himself. In the context of life, Jesus says, "I am the bread of life; whoever comes to me will never hunger, and whoever believes in me will never thirst" (John 6:35). Jesus' criticism of the Pharisees and other groups remind Christians that they are called to follow Christ and in this way rightly order or align their desires. By the grace of God Christians' desires are more exemplary or exalted. Their desires aim for complete human fulfillment, available only through God's grace.

For a Christian the Gospels and the life of Christ as revealed in other New Testament writings establish a fulcrum which is the basis for reading the Old Testament and other parts of the New Testament. Whatever Jesus said and did must be interpreted in light of his most important saving action, namely, his passion, death, and resurrection, which also are a divine confirmation of his preaching and wondrous works. The passion, death, and resurrection constitute the prism Christians have used through the centuries to understand the meaning of life and the meaning of the entire Old and New Testaments. Illuminated by the Holy Spirit and the tradition of the Church, Christians are attentive to Sacred Scripture. Based on a prayerful reflection on Sacred Scripture, Christians decide what activities they will undertake to spread the Good News of Jesus Christ. All this happens in a context of both private and community prayer as well as a readiness to follow Christ in his path to the Father.

Not surprisingly, a Christian focus on Jesus changes what Christians strive for and how they react to adversity. In terms of our early diagrams, specifically figures 4.2 and 4.3, Christian revelation changes what Christians consider to be exemplary actions with respect to each of the fundamental values. It may also serve to modify what Christians consider to be reasonable actions that move us toward exemplary actions. Finally, our focus on Jesus may clarify why actions on the left side of the diagram corrode our pursuit both of Jesus and of the fundamental values.

PRACTICAL MORAL SKILLS

The next few chapters focus on the acquisition of practical moral skills, with particular reference to types of modern friendships that may include a dimension of physical intimacy. Of course, anyone reading this book already has some moral skills pertinent to this area. In addition, any reader knows how problematic this whole area is. Most people aspire to deep, lifelong friendships, but personal quirks, stubbornness, and sin prevent people from realizing their goal.

No one's perfect. One implication of this is each of us has to recover from personal sin or honest mistakes and then move on. The next chapter looks candidly at the modern situation of young adults looking to become friendly with someone who might become a spouse for life. We make some specific recommendations about practical strategies concerning how to proceed. If one fairly consistently adheres to these practices, a good spouse is not guaranteed, but progress toward eventually finding a good spouse is much more likely. The recommended practices we describe in the next chapter establish the proper framework for modern relationships that are in conformity with natural law. Once we have articulated these, in subsequent chapters we will highlight specific moral skills related to courting.

26

Basic Strategies in Modern Relationships

YOUNG MEN AND women who want to lead moral lives often struggle with the issue of sexual intimacy and what role it should play in their relationships. The choice too many young people wind up making, however, is far more likely to be determined by strong cultural influences and the "heat of the moment" than by any reasoned process of discernment. To prevent hormones, impulses, current trends, or emotions from dominating their decisions, young people need to do a couple of things. First, some intellectual clarity is needed. We addressed this issue in parts I and II. Young adults also need to develop the moral skills necessary for making wise choices, no matter the circumstances. Given this very real challenge, we offer three relational steps or practices for their consideration: (1) accept working hypotheses that suggest the need for a cautious perspective when entering a new relationship; (2) engage in a process of personal introspection and investigation; (3) make a strategic revelation about personal hopes and expectations in a friendship that might move toward marriage.

WORKING HYPOTHESES

The first practice focuses on what researchers call *working hypotheses*, which are hunches researchers have before they are completely clear about the pattern revealed in a number of events and why the pattern occurs. Three realistic working hypotheses for young men and women as they approach relationships are as follows.

Working Hypothesis 1:   For most young unmarried men sexual inti-
                           macy is not a sign of commitment.
Working Hypothesis 2:   For most young unmarried women sexual inti-
                           macy is either simply fun or part of a strategy
                           employed to secure long-term commitment.
Working Hypothesis 3:   For most young people romance is disassoci-
                           ated from sexual intimacy and is primarily
                           about communication.

These hypotheses offer a general interpretation of modern interrelationships among young people in matters relating to dating and sexual intimacy. They are not intended to reflect necessarily the perspectives of the readers of this book. They are simply helpful generalizations.

Young men and women seek one another's company because they enjoy it and because, ultimately, they would like to commit themselves to loving and living with another person. Familial social gatherings as well as the high schools and colleges young people attend still are important contexts in which young single women and men meet. Nonetheless, new venues for social interaction have emerged. Whatever the venue in which young people meet, social constraints on sexual intimacy prior to marriage are far less strict now than they were prior to the 1960s.

In the marriage bazaar of modern society, young people should be able to get to know one another without committing themselves to sexual intimacy. As hypothesis 3 suggests, young people fundamentally understand that. Unfortunately, they live in a topsy-turvy world that puts the cart before the horse when it comes to sex, romance, and marriage. Romance is soothing and fulfilling, whereas sexual intimacy at the start of what might eventually be a wonderful relationship is too much, too quick, and at once too superficial and too intense. Sexual "intimacy" should suggest a time lapse before someone is admitted to an intimate sphere. An expression of intimacy binds together two people who have come to know and understand and cherish each other. It is not an introductory ritual that may or may not lead to true intimacy, should their coupling develop into a more substantial relationship.

Working hypothesis 1 is that young men would like to have sex with the young women they get to know. For them, sex is something fun and pleasurable, and they presume the young women with whom they have sex feel the same. For most of these young men, having sex does not signal they are committing themselves even in the short-term to the wellbeing of their sexual partner. Within this hypothe-sized framework, "conscientious" young men take steps to reduce the probability that pregnancy will result from their sexual unions. But even conscientious young men do not in general interpret sex as a sign of enhanced commitment.

Working hypothesis 2 is that young women have sex with the young men they get to know in part because it is pleasing and enjoyable, but many women also con-sider it a strategic move. They understand that having sex does not necessarily lead to long-term commitment. But they also know that not having it will likely send many young men looking elsewhere and put an end to any hope the relation-ship might last. By agreeing to have sex, young women hope to keep the relation-ship going long enough to eventually secure a commitment from either the young man of the moment or maintain her reputation as someone willing, but not too willing. Those young women who accept this kind of a social framework usually take measures that minimize their chances of conceiving a child as a result of their sexual encounters.

Working hypothesis 3 is that both young men and young women have romantic ideals and they see a strong connection between love and romance. They do not, however, necessarily connect sex with either. Romance is all about finding a soul-mate and a deep sense of connection with someone you respect who also respects you. It is an experience of being cherished by someone for who you are. Sex, on the other hand, is more about immediate pleasure seeking or satisfying the expecta-tions of others or positioning oneself as available, but not too frequently. A romantic framework for a couple is completely relaxing because young women are able to talk about their romantic aspirations. Young men may feel uncomfortable even admitting they have romantic aspirations, but the young women can tell when the young men respond well in a romantic situation. The real difficulty is that, in most cases, neither the young woman nor the young man finds a social milieu conducive to romance rather than sex.

Many young people do not have the attitudes or approaches described by these working hypotheses. Nevertheless, hypotheses 1 and 3 are helpful for young women and hypotheses 2 and 3 assist young men interested in leading good, authentically moral lives. The three hypotheses are also a helpful starting place for initially evaluating social interactions and also for developing certain moral skills, particularly the skill of personal knowledge of self and others.

These hypotheses are descriptive, and as such they pretty much capture what passes for the dating scene among many young adults today. That said, two caveats should be noted. First, in no way is it recommended that young people act in accor-dance with these working hypotheses, nor are those who do so to be commended! Second, these working hypotheses should not suggest that most young men and women are immoral. Many, if not most, young people whose attitudes match these hypotheses do not believe they are doing anything wrong when they have sex. And as was pointed out earlier, Catholic teaching maintains that although premarital sex is objectively wrong, if the participants do not think it is wrong, it may not be subjectively morally wrong for them. (The action, however, is likely to be morally wrong to a serious degree if the couple can rightly be faulted for not taking appropriate steps to form their consciences about such an important issue.) According to Catholic teaching, you cannot commit a serious moral wrong unless you intend the wrong. What these young people fail to realize, however, is that this pattern of premature sexual intimacy outside of a committed relationship is corrosive and undermines the very things they want or hope to one day have—romance and committed, long-lasting, loving relationships.

For young people who commit themselves to leading good moral lives, the working hypotheses suggest that caution is needed when meeting other young people. Many young people endorse these hypotheses. Therefore, those people whose romantic aspirations don't conform to the hypotheses need to be both cautious and also provide some signal that they are seeking a distinctly different type of interaction. That is, young men who don't seek social contact based on these hypotheses must give clear signals to young women that they have a different perspective. For their part, young women who are not casual about sexual intimacy should share this message in some appropriate manner. Working hypothesis 3 suggests that both young men and women who don't put sexual intimacy anywhere near the front end of a relationship be alert and imaginative to arranging dates or meetings which focus more on sharing of ideas and sentiments and much less on physical intimacy.

Consider first the young woman who is trying to be authentically moral. At the earliest stages of friendship and relationship, caution is necessary. Such a young woman clearly has no interest in turning away all potential young men. Open and alert are the code words. A new male acquaintance may come strongly recommended or be close friends of friends trusted by the young woman. They might be thoughtful people, admirable people, accomplished people, or religious people. Whatever their gifts, talents, or recommending characteristics may be, however, in the early stage of a relationship, a young woman should be cautious how she interacts.

Being cautious does not mean being suspicious. Young people who enjoy each other's company should not hesitate to spend time together, go on dates, and have fun together. However, the time they spend together should be designed to help them get to know each other, not get into bed with each other. That means avoiding situations that cry out for intimacy. In other words, being cautious means giving "no" a chance when it comes to sexual intimacy. This is especially true for young women who often feel coerced by a social scene that assumes sex is part of the bargain if they want to continue seeing someone they like.

Many if not most young men socialized in our present culture will push the sexual envelope pretty early in a budding relationship. Young women need to know they can push back and resist dating patterns that assume sexual compliance. This is difficult in today's society, especially when young women are hoping a relationship will have a future. However, it is a manageable situation for a young woman with a plan.

Any objective observer would have to admit the practical effect of working hypotheses 1 and 2 is a social scene in which young men are permitted to exert enormous, unjust, and immoral pressure on women. In this social environment, women are being coerced to offer sex shortly after the first meeting just to keep the relationship going. This puts an absurdly unequal and unjustifiable burden on women in relationships. Nonetheless, it is the way of the social world for most young people these days, and young women have to be prepared to operate in this culture.

In order to operate realistically in the world of modern social relationships and still remain committed to a natural law framework of development, young people should assume that any young people they meet in social circumstances are likely to operate according to hypotheses 1, 2, and 3. In the face of reality described by these working hypotheses, young people who personally do no behave according to these hypotheses need effective practices. In particular, a young man has to provide signals to the young woman how his expectations differ from the prevailing ones, and he has to be alert to signals coming from the young woman. Of course, the young woman must do the same. In particular, two practices involving signaling are recommended.

PRACTICE 1

Practice 1 urges young men who want to lead an authentically moral life in conformity with the natural law approach to make it clear to new female acquaintances what the young men are not expecting. Most young women these days assume sex is a requirement to keep a relationship going. It may not be expected on the first encounter, but, absent other signals, the pressure for sex grows with each subsequent meeting. Therefore, it is incumbent on young men who understand how unfair and unjust this coercion is to provide early, clear signals (but not glaring in neon lights!) that they neither expect nor welcome that approach.

Though the signals must be clear, they do not have to be very specific. A young man can say to a young woman he met perhaps an hour or two ago and whom he finds fun, attractive, and engaging that he has to leave the party early but hopes he will see her again in a few days. Or, he might say that he has to leave early but he would welcome her email address. Or that he will be in contact with a mutual friend to try and arrange another common social evening together with a number of friends.

Whatever approach he uses, he is communicating clearly to the young woman that he likes her, that he wants to see her again, and that he does not expect any sexual intimacy. In other words, he is not looking for sex without commitment and he is signaling that the young woman should not use sex to prompt a commitment.

Clear messages like these would be both a compliment and a relief to most young women, who would actually like to be courted. For the most part young women are not looking for instant intimacy. If the young woman gets the message from a young man that he is neither looking for nor expecting sex during courtship, she should affirm him and indicate that she feels the same. More than likely, most young women long for the kind of intimacy that is cultivated over a long period of time. There is safety, mystery, and enchantment in getting to know someone gradually, by putting together small pieces of a large and complex puzzle. Courtship is a process that helps young men keep their mind off sex, or, at the very least, it helps young men for whom sex is near the forefront of their imagination to focus on other very alluring and captivating aspects of the young woman. Courtship sensitizes the young man and expands his horizons, while doing something similar for the young woman.

Instant intimacy lets young men off the hook by truncating the development in communication and imagination that should be occurring during courtship. Most couples who are thinking about marriage share a lot of information with each other. That does not mean, however, that they have developed the deep communication skills that serve marriages well over the long haul. Those skills are best cultivated in courtships without sexual intimacy. This kind of courtship is especially important for young men since it helps them get outside of themselves and inside the mind and feelings of the young women they love. And because this type of courtship eliminates sexual coercion by placing the focus on having innocent fun together in full view of their friends and relatives, these types of courtships are more richly satisfying for young women as well.

A few more observations about communication are appropriate, especially since in our modern society good vibes and solid communication are assumed to be the basis of all good relationships. The author has enjoyed performing wedding ceremonies for many young couples and helping them prepare both for marriage itself and the wedding ceremony. In the preparatory meetings, he asks each young couple some questions, through which he tries to help them develop their readiness for marriage and the skills they will need to avoid divorce, something none of them want.

One of the early questions to the future bride and groom is: Why do you think your marriage will not wind up in divorce when so many other marriages do? With a handful of exceptions, the standard response to this question from both the young man and woman is: Because we communicate well together. This answer is given with much love and conviction, but their mutual observation clearly cannot be a convincing answer if practically all couples—those who eventually get divorced as well as those who don't—give the same response! The couple would not be getting married if they did not "communicate well" together, in the sense that they candidly share their feelings and reactions to one another.

Deep communication between partners usually takes many years to develop. It requires that each spouse be able to anticipate the feelings, attitudes, and reactions of the other, whether they are positive or negative. That is, even young spouses should be able to read some of each other's unspoken or explained emotions, anxieties, hesitancies, or reticence and respond to them either in words or deeds. Similarly, they should be aware of things each other hopes for or wants to achieve in life. The hopes and aspirations, as well as the fears or reticence, change over time and an astute spouse has to regularly spend time thinking about what is going on with his soul mate. Just because they are soul mates does not mean they know how the other person is going to react in particular circumstances. Life is complex and so are people, especially spouses.

Young couples cannot expect to communicate at this deep level right away. It takes good will and effort by both over many years for that to happen. However, they can begin to develop this kind of communication in a courtship that is focused on a full array of interests, fears, talents, perceptions, emotions, feelings, and sensitivities in the other person rather than on achieving or experiencing sexual intimacy. This type of courtship is truly satisfying to both the young man and woman. But it is especially important for the young man, since it forces him to get inside the mind and feelings of his fiancée. Furthermore, this kind of deep knowledge will help the young man behave in ways that support, reassure, encourage, and calm the young woman he loves. She will then have greater confidence in him and his ability to provide her with emotional support for a lifetime.

A related point is that good communication involves imagination and insight. A number of classic comedy routines focus on a wife speaking to her husband about something the couple was planning to do. She says to him: "Well, I said 'yes' but you should have known that I meant 'no'!" The comedian then does riffs on trying to understand this seemingly baffling woman. A variation on this theme is the husband saying to the wife, "Honey, just tell me what you want and I'll do it." Meanwhile the wife is steaming because she has given her husband dozens of hints about what she wants and he does not even get close to understanding what the issue is.

The two situations depicted above suggest how important imagination and insight are in good communication. Without them, deep communication is practically impossible. Furthermore, "personal imagination" can only develop as a skill if on a consistent basis one sympathetically tries to figure out what is going on inside the head of one's partner. Asking the partner outright for an explanation may be the surest way not to find out. For some very important things you have to piece things together and use your imagination. For a wife to say to her husband, "You know that my 'no' meant 'yes'," is not that unreasonable. After all, the couple has been living together for years. People in close relationships develop their own language. You do not have to be a rocket scientist or a linguist to figure out the syntax of this personal language. Just being a sympathetic listener who reflects on what is said and tries to imagine what is prompting it will go a long way toward improving communication.

The type of deep communication described above comes about after many years in good marriages, but courtship is a very good preparation for sympathetic sharing in marriage. In courtship the man and woman become experienced in pleasing and surprising each other precisely in ways that have nothing to do with physical intimacy. And it's fun and very satisfying.

A simple, quite specific thought experiment underscores the point. Suppose a young man is asked to consider relationship A and relationship B. Both A and B involved real young women whom he knew and very much liked for about the same amount of time—at least a year. For a variety of reasons he eventually broke up with both of them. Relationship A was based primarily on courtship, with no physical intimacy. Relationship B, on the other hand, was primarily sexual. Here's the thought experiment. Years later, after he is happily married with another woman, which prior relationship will he recall with greater satisfaction and delight? One can't say for sure, but most people would suspect it would be relationship A. Courtship without physical intimacy is about discovery and friendship and it can be great fun. It is also a social ritual that is rooted in mutual respect but does not preempt marriage or slight a future life partner. It is even something the young man can share with whoever his future wife turns out to be. He does not have to be embarrassed to share some of the things he learned in relationship A.

By engaging so many of our human dimensions, courtship helps create the true intimacy between men and women that sexual intimacy eventually expresses in a new dimension. This is a natural sequence of things with sex coming only after the playful, sensitive, imaginative, surprising, and pleasing interchanges that help acquaintances become deep friends and, over time, possible long-term lovers. Discovering which activities together are hits and which ones are misses, getting a clearer sense of what charms and what dismays – all of this is part of the captivating experience of building deep friendships.

PRACTICE 2

Most young people who have not done considerable soul searching are not ready for a lifelong commitment. Although this statement is statistically true, every year many thousands of young people get married and many of them will remain faithful to one another for a lifetime. The important issue, therefore, is not necessarily age or whether a person in a budding relationship is in love, but whether the person has reflected for a considerable time on the relationship. In order to be ready to "take the plunge," it should be the case that via reflections that extend over a year or more the person makes a confident judgment that the relationship will deepen significantly over time and will last.

Three important factors enter into reaching the conclusion that this new relationship is "the one." First, the person has to be confident she has enough self-knowledge to know what she wants and needs in life. Without reasonable self-knowledge, the decision that someone is "the one" could be a serious misjudgment. It is also important that the person be a good judge of character who can fairly assess the strengths and weaknesses of a person they think they love. The third factor entering into the calculation of whether this person is the one is confidence that the young man or woman pondering whether this is the one is able to make and keep commitments. This refers not only to the major marriage vow but also the many smaller commitments that are part of marriage.

As a self-test of whether he can sustain a long-term commitment, a young man who is serious with some young woman should, for example, over the period of a few weeks actively contemplate the possibility that he might find another woman more appealing to him. In particular, in his mind he should entertain thoughts of boredom or annoyance with his current girlfriend and then see whether this prompts him to look more eagerly or favorably on other young women he knows or doesn't know. Perhaps this type of imagining is not sufficiently realistic. However, in some way he has to test himself and she has to test herself. They owe this to one another. If he has doubts about remaining committed to his potential wife in good times and bad, in sickness and in health, he should wait. A man and woman can still continue to maintain their friendship. However, a less than confident partner should put the friendship in a holding pattern until both the young man and woman are confident of their ability to keep a major commitment.

To be clear, practice 2 means not letting a relationship develop too deeply if one is not yet ready to make a major commitment. Allowing the relationship to proceed toward greater romance and satisfaction can cause considerable hurt and disappointment to the other party if a person is shaky about his or her ability to commit. Alternatively, it may result in a decision to make a verbal commitment that is not in fact a real commitment.

These are complicated issues and most young people find them difficult to navigate. Seldom is it very clear how much we know about ourselves and others or whether it is enough. Nevertheless, without such knowledge, it is fair to say that young people will have great difficulty making wise choices about relationships. The next chapter examines more carefully the ability to make and keep a commitment as well as three other moral skills. These are described as crucial skills for aiming at and achieving exemplary actions in marriage, as well as in other moral endeavors.

27

Basic Moral Skills

MAKING DECISIONS IS a pretty basic part of life, and the decisions we make shape the kind of life we end up leading. The purpose of this book is to help people make decisions that lead to a flourishing moral life. This chapter highlights four attributes or skills that contribute to making sound moral decisions: self-control, knowledge of self and others, the ability to make a commitment, and the ability to manage memory and imagination. These four moral skills help us to excel in the moral life and they also help us avoid getting derailed along the way. In terms of the fundamental values, they strengthen our ability to formulate realistic plans and move toward exemplary actions. They also provide a kind of protection, keeping us from engaging in corrosive actions that undermine our ability to reach our ultimate goals.

SELF-CONTROL

An essential requirement of the moral life is the freedom to make decisions. We cannot fully exercise this freedom, however, if we are controlled by things, including our own impulses, that we allow to dictate our decisions. Our make-up as human beings is complex and includes appetites and emotions that are often strong and compelling. Following these impulses is sometimes a perfectly reasonable thing to do, but not always. Our desires can get out of hand, usually through a kind of intellectual sleight of hand that overwhelms the will. As we have seen, when this happens, the intellect, working in tandem with our desires, essentially reclassifies corrosive actions that will derail our plans to lead the moral life. It transforms them mentally into positive or nearly positive actions, linking them with various appetites. In order to lead an authentic life we have to be able to control these appetites, acknowledging their power but resisting their compulsion.

The first of the moral skills is self-control. Using our terminology from earlier chapters, appetites in themselves are good. However, an appetite often gets connected to a plan, and when this happens we call it a desire. Since the desire may be either good or bad, desires should be moderated by reason. But desires and passions can be very demanding; they want action, not reasoning. If a person allows strong urges, passions, desires, or compulsions to push reason to the side, the person no longer operates under the sway of right reason. That is, the person is not engaging in practical reasonableness. The result is a corrosive action.

Gaining control over our various appetites is a lifelong project. One can make a plausible argument that gaining self-control is considerably more difficult in our modern society, primarily because so many pleasurable activities or things are readily available to us and, precisely because they are pleasurable and soothing, they make insistent demands on the intellect and will. Many people in modern society struggle mightily to gain control over their weight, smoking, drinking, drugs, or visual delights. We understand we would live a healthier and more reasonable life if we could control these things, but intellectual awareness alone is not enough to secure control of our desires and appetites.

Modern developed societies offer an abundance of attractive and pleasurable things. As a result, even our "consumption desires" can take many forms. People may overindulge or, for corrosive activities, simply indulge in movies, television, music, clothes, food of various types, gadgets, cars, homes, drugs, alcohol, sex, gambling, or pornography. Some of these things are less harmful than others, but lack of control over any one of them spells trouble because it can lead one to neglect important responsibilities. Adults seek to control their lives or at least free themselves from compulsive or impulsive decisions.

SELF-KNOWLEDGE AND KNOWLEDGE OF OTHERS

The second skill we need is personal knowledge, both of ourselves and of other persons. By far the more difficult knowledge to attain is self-knowledge. But we also cannot fulfill our responsibilities in life unless we become good at judging the types of things people need and the types of things they may not need but which bring them satisfaction.

One insight of practical reasonableness is that all people should be able to participate in some minimal way in the fundamental values. Each and every person deserves respect and should be able to share in the essential good things of life. This realization is articulated in the two principles of solidarity and subsidiarity. As indicated in an earlier chapter, solidarity acknowledges that in society every person should have enough resources to pursue the fundamental values at what society or a person judges to be some minimal level. Subsidiarity says that the smallest feasible group should be the one designated to decide how needed resources should be used to pursue the fundamental values. These principles articulate our commitment to others in pursuing the fundamental values.

In order to strive for the fundamental values, one needs personal knowledge, that is, self-knowledge and knowledge of others. How we understand ourselves is an important part of gaining self-knowledge, but so too is grasping how we are perceived by other people. This kind of knowledge is both hard to get and difficult to assess. Asking someone outright what they think about us is the least likely way to get useful information. Most people asked that question simply would not give a straightforward answer for fear of being hurtful. Even if a seemingly unvarnished response were forthcoming, it would be difficult to know if it was an accurate assessment from a wise observer, a prettified response to avoid hurting someone, or a jaundiced view from someone with an axe to grind. The best way to find out how we come across is through astute observation and reading between the lines. Of course, a person with those abilities already has a fair amount of the very kind of self-knowledge they seek. Although difficult to attain, self-knowledge is crucial for the moral life as well as for everyday interaction with others.

Self-knowledge also involves the recognition of personal sin. As was pointed out in previous chapters, people can easily deceive themselves to think they are doing something good when they are actually corroding the pursuit of the fundamental values in their lives. Since personal deception is easy, we noted the importance of avoiding the near occasions of sin. The theme of the book is physical and emotional intimacy; hence our example for a near occasion of sin involved a man and woman close to one another in either a public place or a very private place. In this case, the near occasion of sin involved the sexual appetite. However, the concept of a near occasion of sin has many other applications. It can be applied to other appetites, such as the desire for food or drink, on the one hand, or revenge or caustic comments, on the other. Many people understand their weaknesses in these areas. As a result, keeping certain foods and drinks out of the house, or staying away from certain stores, lest a person consume or purchase too much, is a prudent way to act. Similarly, a person prone to revenge or caustic comments may develop the practice of using an excuse to impose a cooling-down period on himself. For example, if he is involved in a group discussion and realizes he is getting annoyed at someone, he might excuse himself from the group, explaining that he has to make a telephone call. In fact, the telephone call is to himself, allowing him time to calm down and get a grip.

The concept of near occasion of sin also has another extensive field of application. The general insight of this principle also applies to weaknesses in the way people make judgments. For example, from painful experience, we may realize that we are excessively unyielding in recommending harsh solutions for others, but very nuanced and understanding in deciding what we ourselves must do in similar circumstances. If we have this self-knowledge, it means we lack courage when prescribing fixes in our own lives and are excessively severe in our recommendations to others. This means that we have to review very carefully the steps we claim are adequate to rectify a situation in our own lives as well review with greater tenderness what we deem "absolutely necessary" in the lives of others. This type of situation might be better called a near occasion of misjudgment than a near occasion of sin. Crucial to both situations, however, is self-knowledge. Using the more traditional moral language of virtues, people who want to promote the fundamental values need virtues such as temperance, courage, and prudence in order to make good judgments consistently.

Authentically moral individuals need self-knowledge, but they also need to understand human nature, that is, how people feel, act, and react. This type of knowledge goes beyond the self. It implies insight into the interior dispositions and struggles of many different kinds of people. It includes alertness to the desires, hopes, and aspirations of others that are sometimes communicated directly, but more often must be intuited and interpreted. A person who gives someone a truly apt and touching birthday present, for instance, has insight into what pleases the person and captures it in an excellent gift that charms the recipient.

Some people can be pretty savvy about other people's needs, wants, and desires, but in some cases that kind of knowledge may not be what they need to live an authentically moral life. A politician, for instance, who meets a group of potential voters may be very astute in terms of quickly determining who is politically for her and who is against her. This is important and useful knowledge for the politician. However, the same politician may have very few skills in understanding the hopes, desires, and aspirations of others outside the political context. That is, she has a genuine skill, but it may not be applied effectively in other areas of her life.

Film directors provide another case in point. Critics point out that the best film directors intuitively understand how audiences will react. Almost instinctively drawing on such knowledge, the expert director lays out the sequence of scenes and events in a film and has good insight how to block and portray individual scenes. This is a true and valuable skill for a film director pursuing, via the medium of the film, the fundamental values of playfulness, knowledge, and/or beauty. As important as this skill is, however, it may be of limited value when it comes to interpersonal relationships with family and friends or even in dealing with the actors and production staff with whom he works. A director who wants to lead an authentically moral life needs more than the ability to gauge an audience's response. He must also be sensitive to the needs, desires, hopes, and feelings of all kinds of people in a wide variety of circumstances.

Acquiring self-knowledge and knowledge of human nature is the important work of a lifetime, but it does not depend on theoretical intelligence. Very intelligent people can have little self-knowledge and only the most rudimentary knowledge of the types of hopes, fears, and aspirations which animate and motivate others.

COMMITMENT

The third moral skill we need is the ability to make and keep commitments. We cannot pursue the fundamental values to any depth unless we can make and keep commitments. This is true for the fundamental value of life (exercise and good health, as well as, geopolitically, defense of one's country), friendship (marriage and just regular friends), beauty (music, poetry, and dance require great commitment), knowledge (a sustained desire to understand requires the ability to commitment ourselves to projects), and religion (a lifelong commitment, not a temporary practice). Commitments bind us in different ways to different people. Making a commitment creates the expectation that we will deliver. The person or group to whom we make the commitment then relies on us to follow through on that commitment. Consequently, a person should not make a commitment unless she can realistically anticipate the requirements of keeping the commitment and also judge that she will be able to fulfill those requirements in the future. These are necessary conditions for making a good commitment.

The most worthwhile things in life require a sustained commitment that many adolescents find difficult to maintain. Their inability to do this is linked to at least two moral virtues discussed earlier—self-control and knowledge of self and others. Commitments require focus and the ability to control impulses so that impulses alone do not dictate actions. Teenagers struggle to control their impulses, emotions, and desires. In addition, it is difficult for teenagers to keep commitments because in most cases they do not know themselves well, are inexperienced in understanding others, and have little practice in anticipating what is needed to keep a commitment. In general, commitments require the maturity we assume of adults. Commitments produce wonderful things—deep friendship, great beauty, saints, or impressive knowledge—but keeping them requires determination and flexibility, as well as all the other moral skills.

MANAGING MEMORY AND IMAGINATION

Managing our memories and imaginations also plays a role in making and maintaining our commitments. Indeed, all three moral virtues have an impact on the ability to make and keep commitments. But this process also works in reverse: making and keeping a commitment strengthens our self-control, increases our knowledge of self and others, and helps in managing our memory and imagination. In general, the moral skills, while distinct, influence each other.

"Managing" our memories and imaginations should not imply we can manipulate our memory or imagination at will. Rather, morally attuned adults are able to nudge their thoughts and imagination in a certain direction, away from dangerous areas. Once a morally attuned adult becomes aware that certain thoughts or imaginings lead to corrosive activities rather than reasonable or exemplary ones, he develops a strategy to steer his attention away from such thoughts and images.

An example illustrates what is meant by managing memory and imagination. Suppose a man has been happily married for some years and loves his wife very much. He is generally content with his wife, their two young children, and his career, but lately he has begun to feel that, while married life has its satisfactions, it is often achingly predictable and mundane. The grand plans he shared with his young wife have given way to the monotony of daily routine. Suppose that in the midst of this restlessness, the no-longer-young husband and father begins to think about another relationship he had when he was in college. He has not seen his former lover in years, but on this day a memory of some particularly exciting moment with her in that previous relationship is ignited. What he does with that memory can make a difference for his marriage. If he lets himself linger in the mists of this romantic or erotic memory, his budding marital ennui will only deepen, and if the memory is frequently evoked in subsequent weeks and months, it will surely prove corrosive over time. One day he might even start imagining romantic possibilities with another woman with whom he has a professional relationship.

On the other hand, the husband can recognize the disruptive potential of a captivating recollection or provocative possibility. He can then act to steer his memory and imagination to a safer venue. By managing his memory or imagination in this way he can regain his perspective and strengthen his commitment to the wife and family he truly loves. This unsettled husband can draw upon a number of techniques. He could choose to remember some shared moment with his wife that regularly brings him particular joy and satisfaction. He could also say a prayer, thanking God for his wife and family and the blessings he has. He could unleash his imagination on possible ways to reinvigorate his marriage or refine the hopes and dreams that he and his wife share for their life together. He could also get busy doing something else—going for a run, playing with his children, reading a book. The point is, the husband has the power to redirect his memories and his imagination. The more skilled he is at doing so, the better able he will be to faithfully live out his commitments over time.

Not all memories are distractions from the moral life. Some memories, for example, are inspirational and have the capacity to ignite the imagination around commitments that have faded over time. Suppose, for instance, that while reading her alumnae magazine a high-powered business executive is reminded of some activities from her college days she undertook to help the poor. In recent years, the demands of her career and the needs of her aging and infirmed parents have crowded out any thoughts she might have had about those wonderful experiences. Now that she recalls them, however, what she chooses to do with those memories can make a difference in her life. She can cultivate the memories and use them as a stimulus to do something that will let her again experience the love that arises out of service. Or, she can let them fade away as she moves on to the next issue at work that demands her attention. Once again, how skilled the woman is in managing her memories matters in terms of living out her commitments.

Imagination is a wonderful asset, but it must also be controlled. Imagination involves thinking of things that might happen or might be true. In its best mode, imagination enables a person—young, middle-aged, or elderly—to pursue the fundamental values in interesting, effective ways. But imagination can also dwell on corrosive actions. Imagination is similar to curiosity. A person can legitimately be curious about many different things. However, even young people know if their curiosity always focuses, for example, on sex or on ways to get revenge or on what love relationship their favorite singer or movie star is involved in, the young people have a problem. They understand they have to put bounds on their curiosity, and if they don't, parents and other adults have to help them come to this realization. Without bonds, curiosity can stimulate or feed imagination in a vicious circle. Striving to pursue the fundamental values implies restraint on imagination and curiosity.

We need to distance ourselves from some memories and curtail our imagination and curiosity because they undermine our commitments and goals. Other memories we need to mine because they rekindle our interest in actions and activities that support our ultimate goals and strengthen our commitments. Imagination can also be linked to sympathy and love to envision the outcome of some praiseworthy endeavor. A morally accomplished person is adept at drawing positively on memory and imagination, on the one hand, and redirecting them when they lead in a potentially corrosive direction. In short, we cannot let our memory do our thinking for us. We have to manage it.

In this chapter we described four moral skills needed to live an authentically moral life: self-control, knowledge of self and others, the ability to make commitments, and the ability to manage one's memory and imagination. The question then naturally arises: What activities do people undertake in order to acquire these skills? After an account in the next chapter of one of Dave and Maria's dates, we explore the "secular" ways in which moral skills are acquired and then contrast them with the religious ways in which the same moral skills can be enhanced.

28

Blindness to Noncommitment

DAVE'S FORMER COLLEGE roommate, Frank, is living with his girlfriend, Tina. Dave sincerely hopes Frank and Tina eventually get married. Dave and some of his other college friends visited Frank and Tina in their condo on Friday night and they all had a good time.

On Saturday, Maria and Dave were invited to a birthday party for Maria's four-year-old niece. It was a fun event, with many activities for the ten young children Maria's sister-in-law had invited to the party. Of course, there were screams of delight as children played the games that had been arranged. After the party, Maria and Dave went out for an early dinner, followed by a movie. They were going to see a new movie that had premiered the week before about a man who maintains one family in Boston and another, complete with second wife, in Calcutta. Dave was not wild about seeing it, but Maria says it's funny.

Because part of the movie takes place in India, Maria says it will be fun to go to an Indian restaurant she knows. They are having a great time at the restaurant and, of course, they talk about many disparate topics as they catch up on what each was doing the previous week. As they are eating some strange dessert that was tasty but not great, Dave mentions that last night he and some friends got together with Frank and his girlfriend Tina. He said the couple has a great condo in the Downtown area. Maria knows Frank, but not well. Frank was in a wedding party with Dave, and along with Maria they all interacted at the reception. But she has only been with him three or four times.

Dave remarked that Frank and Tina seem to be getting along very well. Though not yet married, they have been living together for three years. "Both of them are friendly and intelligent," said Dave. "I'm pretty sure they will tie the knot fairly soon."

Maria had a strong reaction. "You and I have spoken about this issue before. When it was about my cousin Anthony, you thought he and Samantha should not be living together. You half convinced me. But now you think it is fine for your Frank and Tina to live together. I've never met Tina and I accept your judgment that she is very bright. But, no matter how intelligent, she's got to be a bit loopy if she thinks she and Frank are going to get married. My prediction is they don't get married. And, if they do, my back-up prediction is the marriage won't last four years, with or without children." After saying this, Maria realized that she was far too definite and negative about one of Dave's friends. So before Dave could respond, Maria backtracked a bit. "Dave, I'm sure they are good people, and, for heaven's sake, please don't tell them I ever questioned their marriage plans. I just don't understand how smart women can pass over very obvious realities."

Dave was surprised at Maria's comments, especially since she had argued the opposite side only a few months ago in their argument about Maria's cousin Anthony and his live-in girlfriend in Nebraska. But he was pleased that, for the most part, she was using his arguments! Only occasionally does Maria get upset or cross, but she was certainly getting excited. What was perplexing to Dave was that Maria doesn't even know Tina. So he decided to be candid. "Maria, you don't even know Tina. Do you think she's a witch? Why are you so negative toward her? She really is a lovely person and Frank would be crazy not to marry her."

"Hey, you just made my point and I'm going to use your good arguments from a few months ago against you!" said Maria. "If Tina is as fine a person as you say, why doesn't Frank marry her now? My inclination is to go with you, Dave. She probably is a wonderful woman and would make a great wife and mother. I accept your judgment, really. What is all wrong is that Frank does not see that." "Yeah, but Maria, that is my point. Frank does not see it yet, but give him another year or two and he may see it," said Dave.

"But, Dave, think of what you're implying in Frank's case. He's currently in a trial period with Tina. He's trying out the person who may become his wife. If she measures up to all his expectations, you presume he may finally propose to Tina. Is that right?" "Yes, that's about right," said Dave. "What girl in her right mind is going allow some guy to try her out? Is she like some new computer or a new car that Frank has to run through its paces?" said Maria. "My argument is not that they can never have sex before marriage. Though I am against sex before marriage,

I'm not arguing for that now. My point is that by living with Tina, Frank has every-thing he wants. He gets to sleep with Tina and hang out with her, and yet can walk out of the relationship any time he wants. How long is long enough before Frank makes up his mind? Three years, six years, sixteen years? Everyone, including Tina, changes over time. Maybe she will change in some important way over the next five years. You seem to be saying that, if Frank is not sure how she's going to change, he should wait until another five years or so?"

Dave was ready with his reply. "Well, yes, he should wait. Even you would agree that you should not get married unless you're really committed to your spouse. Frank is not yet committed. But it can still happen. Maybe Tina understands it is not great that she and Frank are living together. She accepts it, though, because she loves Frank and knows that Frank is slow to make commitments?" Maria responded on a conciliatory note. "Well, that is a good point," Maria said. "In our society, women often make compromises in order to get married, but I think Tina is making a foolish compromise. How is Frank going to move from 'Tina the Trial Wife' to 'Tina the Wife to Whom I Commit Myself Until Death Parts Us?'"

"Maria, I want to speak up for Tina. In my opinion, she is a lovely, lively woman with many excellent qualities. She would make a great wife and mother, certainly for Frank, and probably for many other young men. For reasons I don't under-stand, Frank does not yet see that. So, both you and Tina have to be patient. Frank can eventually come to see Tina's fine qualities. That's my opinion."

"Alright," said Maria, "I have not yet put all my cards on the table. My difficulty is the probationary period that Tina has to endure. It's not just any probationary period: Frank gets to review her performance every day. He gets to live with her, sleep with her, plan fun activities together, never worry about the possibility of children, and never feel pressure to make a decision whether to marry her. At the end of each day, he can say to himself, 'Ah, was that good enough? Will that con-tinue?' She should just throw him out of the condo. If he can't figure out how degrading this is for Tina, he's never going to make a real commitment to her. Either he has an extremely hard time making commitments in general or he has an extremely hard time making a commitment to Tina. Those are the only two possi-bilities. Tina should accept reality, throw him out, and move on."

"I think it would be very hard for Tina to throw him out," said Dave. "She is really hoping that he comes around and decides to marry her. She will be devas-tated if after all these years he decides not to marry her. But you make a reasonable point. It has been a long time. But throwing him out would cause Tina lots of pain. And I don't think she can do it."

"Being an adult means that you can accept pain and still function. I presume Tina can do that. I think the real problem for Tina is that she does not appreciate that, even if Frank were to propose to her tomorrow, Frank would probably not do so with a full, confident heart. He might be serious, but he would still be wracked with doubt, since he's doubted her for three years already! I say this not because I know Frank but because the situation he has cultivated for the past three years is all wrong. It looks like a loving relationship, but it really is more of a business proposition. It is as if Frank is an appraiser evaluating a house, but in this case it is a person, Tina. 'Is she good enough? Well, she has some faults, but she's still pretty good, structurally very solid! Will she be good enough in the future? Well, I've observed her closely now for three years and she's been stable. She probably won't change much in the future. I think I can make this commitment with a high degree of confidence.'"

Reluctantly, Dave admitted to Maria, "Something else is also in play in this relationship. Tina's not sure Frank is ready to be a husband. She knows that both in college and afterward he was deeply involved in the hook-up culture. In a sense, Tina is the one observing Frank. She wants to be sure he can be faithful." "That's even crazier," said Maria. "If she's concerned that Frank might relapse into his hook-up ways, why not put him to the real test? Let him live alone and see what happens. I say just throw him out of the condo."

Maria was now speaking a little bit too loud in the restaurant and Dave had to shush her a bit. But Maria, now reverting to her biological training, was not to be quieted. "Dave, Tina's not even conducting a decent experiment. Suppose Frank commits to Tina next week. Then she should definitely throw him out of the condo for the real hook-up test. Face it, Dave. This makes no sense either from Tina's or Frank's point of view. Frank's not committing himself to her for better or worse, richer or poorer, in sickness and in health. He's just betting that she's not going to change too much in a direction he doesn't like. In other words, the house is not going to lose too much value. And if she does change the wrong way, Frank leaves her. That's a business proposition. That's not love. In all these years, Frank has not tested Frank. He tests Tina every day, but, because he has not been willing to court her without sex and the satisfaction of living together, he has not probed himself. He does not know whether he can love her for better for worse, for richer or poorer, in sickness and health. That's the vow, but strangely he has not examined himself in a realistic way to find out whether he can realistically commit to Tina."

Dave agreed with much of what Maria was saying, even though he had not thought about it in those terms. What was puzzling for him, however, was Maria's view that, because Frank had chosen to live with Tina, he could never recover from this. It is as if Maria were saying that you choose either to live with someone and never get married or not live with someone and possibly get married. In addition, Maria seemed to allow no opportunity for the couple to consider whether their prospective spouse was the "right one." According to Maria, it seemed as if they had to agree to engagement immediately or break up.

"Maria, I understand the point you are making that Frank is always testing and making minijudgments about Tina. That is beyond the bounds of love, as you point out. But there has to be some period of testing, right? A couple does not have to decide within a month of meeting one another whether they are right for each other. That would be crazy."

"Yes, I agree, that would be crazy. Of course, there has to be some testing. I'm not really sure why I feel so strongly about this. Whatever the reason, I really resent the suggestion that the guy gets to test the woman's body and mind, how she reacts to sex, whether she feels the love deeply enough and whether he feels sufficiently satisfied. There's something abhorrent about that, something far removed from love. Sex is an important expression of love, not the test of love. But I agree there has to be testing. That's what courtship is. That's what you and I are doing. It's total fun and I am all in favor of it. Test me as much as you want, just keep going out with me!"

"Don't worry about that. It's as much fun for me as it is for you," said Dave. "So, what's the difference between the two types of probation? Is it primarily the sex? It would be strange if sex made all the difference."

"I don't really know," said Maria. "You're probably right. It's not simply sex. That's probably not the only thing that upsets me. By living together before marriage and by reflecting on the different ways Tina reacts to him and others, Frank never really says 'I love you and, however you change, I will change so that I remain committed to you.' But, honestly, Tina too seems uninterested in a lasting commitment. She knows Frank's past antics in hooking up with girls. She seems unconcerned that this behavior may return. So both Frank and Tina are testing with sex in the mix. It's unclear whether sex is ever the primary focus of a marriage, and it certainly isn't the primary focus after ten years. Neither one of them seems to care, how, absent the sex, they relate. With respect to the sex, it is far too calculating. With respect to all the other human things, it is not calculating enough. It seems a disastrous situation. And yes, I can now admit I was completely wrong about my cousin Anthony in Nebraska. He's in a mess as well."

"Well, that's gracious of you, but I also agree with your larger point," added Dave. "If Tina fears being alone, her disappointment may be even greater if she eventually marries Frank. Suppose as his wife Tina sees that Frank has not really made a commitment. He still likes her because she has not changed too much from the way she was. It's as if he's purchased a predictable robot. Eventually Tina is going to realize this is not true love, but by that time she will be stuck. And who knows what Frank will turn to then?"

Dave looked around the restaurant and noticed there were only a few couples left. He looked at his watch and realized that the movie they had intended to see had already begun. Dave was relieved. He suggested to Maria that, instead, they see some action film he had heard about. She was totally agreeable and off they went to the movie theater.

29

Moral Skills and Religious Commitment

ACCORDING TO THE natural law approach, the norms concerning sexual intimacy are certainly restrictive. They also demand a high degree of moral skill. Providentially, religious practice offers ways to enhance moral skills for those young people who take religion seriously. How exactly that happens needs some explanation. If it can be shown that practicing one's religion over a substantial period of time enhances moral skills for many people, this reality is then an instance of grace building on nature.

Every young person acquires some moral skills, whether or not they attend to religious practices. Most young people learn to avoid bad situations and strive for some good things in their lives merely through the various activities of youth and adolescence. Religious practice that enhances these skills builds on abilities acquired through the "natural process" of parents and adults helping their children reach maturity.

NORMAL ACQUISITION OF MORAL SKILLS WITHOUT RELIGIOUS PRACTICE

Figure 29.1 lists on the left a number of typical experiences children and adolescents have. In some of these activities the children learn almost by themselves how to control themselves, how to stick to their word or commitment, and how to manage their memory and imagination. A child learns many things on his own, but much of this happens by responding to pressure from other children, from his parents and teachers, from whatever religious services he attends, and also from the broader society. All these play an important role in the formation of his moral skills. Acquiring self-knowledge ultimately can only be done by oneself, but it depends on interaction or dialogue with others. The combination of dialogue and reflection is what leads to self-knowledge. Of course, parents and adults also help children acquire moral skills. They remind children how important certain skills are and they help children to think ahead to some of the tasks they will want to accomplish as teenagers or adults.

The reader should presume that the various activities listed in figure 29.1, as well as many other similar activities, coupled with direction and encouragement from parents, other adults, and institutions, help young people to reach some level of the four moral skills listed in the diagram. These are considered the normal ways in which young people acquire moral skills.

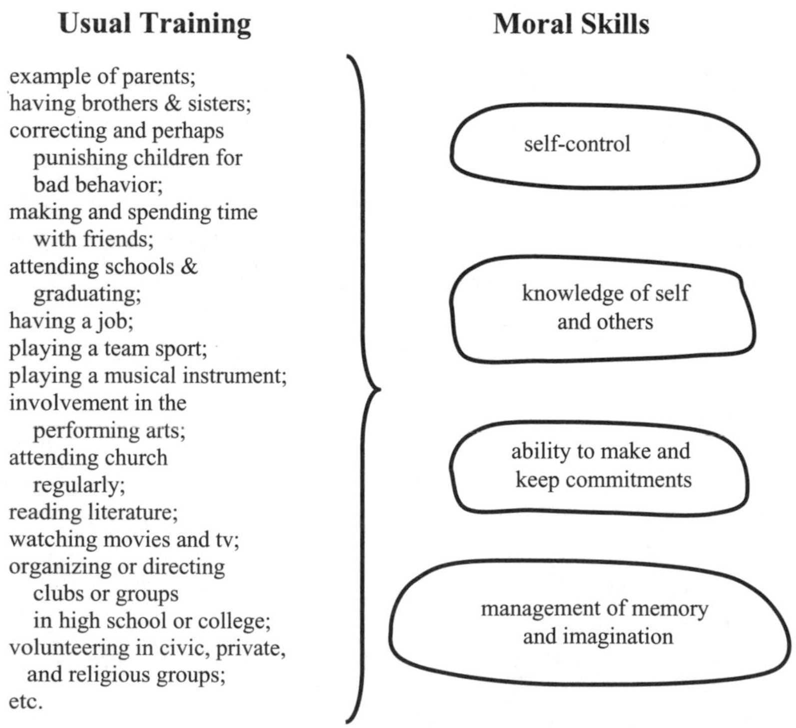

Usual Training   Moral Skills

example of parents;
having brothers & sisters;
correcting and perhaps
    punishing children for
    bad behavior;   self-control
making and spending time
    with friends;
attending schools &
    graduating;
having a job;   knowledge of self
playing a team sport;   and others
playing a musical instrument;
involvement in the
    performing arts;
attending church   ability to make and
    regularly;   keep commitments
reading literature;
watching movies and tv;
organizing or directing
    clubs or groups   management of memory
    in high school or college;   and imagination
volunteering in civic, private,
    and religious groups;
etc.

FIGURE 29.1 On the left are various activities in which children and adolescents participate. Some of these activities by themselves help develop moral skills. Others, such as playing a team sport, usually require the supervision of an adult to help children perceive what constitutes good, exciting, and fair games. On the right are the four moral skills that are necessary for adults if they are to prosper in their pursuit of the fundamental values.

THE IMPACT OF RELIGIOUS PRACTICE ON THE ACQUISITION OF MORAL SKILLS

Figure 29.2 lists some religious activities that enhance the level of moral skills young people acquire. In terms of the two figures, one should think of the activities in the left column of figure 29.2 as being added to the activities in the left column in figure 29.1. The religious activities do not replace or supplant the regular activities, which remain important for the development of moral skills. Rather, the religious activities are a supplement and often lead to a higher level of moral skills. Whether in fact they yield such results depends on the period of time and the consistency with which they are practiced. If one attends religious services once a year, one cannot expect much greater self-knowledge as a result of this activity. Similarly, if one attends such services every week but without attention to what is taking place, the impact of the activities on the enhancement of moral skills will likely be minor.

The general claim is that consistent religious practice over a long period of time enhances moral skills. The presumption in this diagram is that young adults who no longer rely on family or educational institutions for encouragement now freely undertake these religious practices. They do so because they have the gift of faith and because they are strengthened by religious practice within a faith community.

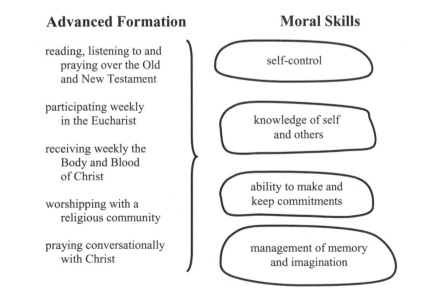

Advanced Formation **Moral Skills**

reading, listening to and praying over the Old and New Testament

participating weekly in the Eucharist

receiving weekly the Body and Blood of Christ

worshipping with a religious community

praying conversationally with Christ

self-control

knowledge of self and others

ability to make and keep commitments

management of memory and imagination

FIGURE 29.2 The religious actions listed on the left offer additional help for young adults to acquire the moral skills listed on the right.

Why is it likely that regular religious practice enhances moral skills, or through what mechanism does the enhancement occur? These are reasonable questions. In fact, people often assert that regular religious practice is associated with both a refined sense of which actions are right or wrong as well as with behavior that avoids actions that are morally wrong. There is some evidence for this, but it stems mainly from questionnaires. Being skeptical about responses to questionnaires is probably a good thing; after all, questionnaires report what people say they do, not what they actually do.

A better way to proceed is to examine the connection between religious practice and moral skills. If a person hears such an explanation, has some reasonable self-knowledge, and perceives such a connection in her own life, she will likely continue regular religious practice because it results in behavior which more definitely advances her pursuit of the fundamental values.

All five practices listed in figure 29.2 are forms of prayer. Furthermore, since the Mass includes readings from the Old and New Testaments and the reception of the Body and Blood of Christ, no separate attention will be given to the Mass. The focus will be on three religious activities: reading and praying over Scripture, receiving the Body and Blood of Christ, and worshipping regularly with a community. Since these three activities also include personal prayer, that topic is treated in the discussion of Scripture, Holy Communion, and regular worship.

Reading Scripture and Enhancing Moral Skills

Both the Old and New Testaments are the revelation of God. God chose a people, the Jews, and made a covenant with them. He not only led them out of Egypt and to the Promised Land but he also raised up leaders and prophets who, speaking and acting on his behalf, would guide his people. Because Yahweh is consistent in his words and actions as well as faithful to his promises, the Old Testament should be read not only as a record of God's saving acts with Israel but also as pointing to the remarkable revelation that comes in the New Testament, when Yahweh sends his only begotten Son to come among human beings as a man. Jesus came both to forgive our sins and to teach us how to live.

In the Sermon on the Mount (Matthew 5:1- 7: 29) Jesus sets forth ideals he wants his followers to strive for. In terms of our standard diagrams used to depict the pursuit of the fundamental values, these ideals point to the right-hand area of the diagrams, namely, the exemplary actions or practices. But Christians are also encouraged to gain control over their actions. St. Paul encourages Christians to act according to their new status: "You should put away the old self of your former way of life, corrupted through deceitful desires, and be renewed in the spirit of your minds, and put on the new self, created in God's way in righteousness and holiness of truth" (Ephesians 4:22-24; see also Ephesians 4:25- 5:33 and 1 Corinthians, chapters 9 and 11).

Jesus was attentive to both the good and bad in people. He sympathetically but candidly read the heart of the Samaritan woman at the well, in whom he perceived honesty and a desire for something more elevated than the four husbands and one nonhusband she had experienced to date (John 4:5-42). He also understood the dark motives behind the questions posed by some of the Pharisees. He clearly perceived the strengths and weaknesses of his own apostles.

Christians are expected to take Christ as their model. They too should be attentive to deeper longings, desires, and perhaps even evasions of various people in their lives. Jesus told his followers: "Behold, I am sending you like sheep in the midst of wolves; so be shrewd as serpents and simple as doves" (Matthew 10:16). Just as he searched people's hearts, he wanted his followers to do the same. He wanted them to be free of all hypocrisy (Matthew 23:13-29 and Luke 6:41-42) and also be shrewd in dealing with other people. Finally, Jesus tells his followers, "anything you ask in my name, I will do, so that the Father may be glorified in the Son" (John 14:13). All this indicates that Jesus wants us to gain knowledge of ourselves and others and that he will assist us in doing this.

With respect to memory and imagination, Jesus tells his disciples at the Last Supper that "the Advocate, the Holy Spirit that the Father will send in my name— he will teach you everything and remind you of all that I told you" (John 14:26). One who prays over Scripture passages is assured that the Holy Spirit will work to stimulate the memory to recall the words and deeds of Christ and teach a person how to put them in practice in his life.

Numerous passages in the Old and New Testaments speak about the importance of commitment. In the Torah the emphasis is on the centrality of the covenant God made with the Jews. Subsequently prophets repeatedly call the Jews to faithfulness to this covenant. Jesus also speaks of the commitment required for his followers. He tells them that they "have to take up their cross and follow him" and that the Kingdom is like the pearl of great price (Matthew 13:45-46). The Kingdom is so valuable that it is worth giving up all other wealth in order to follow Christ. Not all commitments make sense, and Jesus tells his followers (Luke 14:31-33) that, like a king considering whether to join battle with an enemy or bargain for peace, followers of Christ have to realize they have to surrender all worldly attachments in order to be part of His Kingdom. Jesus wants his followers to do the math!

Receiving the Body and Blood of Christ and Enhancing Moral Skills

From the earliest days, Christians met in houses (because Christianity was a forbidden religion in the Roman Empire, Christians were not allowed to have churches) to do in Christ's memory what he did the night before his passion and crucifixion. They gathered both in obedience to Jesus' directive to "do this in remembrance of me" (1 Corinthians 11:24 – 25) but also in order to gain strength, review the events of Christ's life, and allow the Spirit of Truth to work in them.

Receiving the Body and Blood of Christ in the Eucharist puts a believer in immediate, deep internal contact with Christ. Jesus identifies the bread and wine not only with his body and blood but also with the new covenant in his blood, poured out for all people in his passion and death. In his passion and death, Jesus yields to something he would prefer to avoid: "My Father, if it is possible, let this cup pass from me; yet, not as I will, but as you will" (Matthew 26:39). In his words and actions Jesus shows his unfailing obedience to and love of the Father. This is his moment of great strength, and it is this strength and power that Jesus shares with his followers in asking that they celebrate the Eucharist "in remembrance of me."

Receiving communion involves many activities. Receiving the Body of Christ is at once an acknowledgement of Jesus' saving act, a plea to have the same mind that was in Christ Jesus, a petition to receive from Jesus clarity about what Jesus and the Father are asking of the recipient, and a request for moral and spiritual strength emanating from Christ.

For a young person considering a lifelong commitment to a potential spouse, conversation with Christ will revolve around whether the person knows the intended spouse well enough and whether the person thinks he or she has the strength to keep a lifelong commitment. Because receiving the Body and Blood of Christ is so intimately connected with doing the will of the Father, the person receiving Communion will also pray about adhering to norms of natural law. The man may be strongly drawn to be sexually intimate with the young woman he has been going with for several weeks or months, but Communion helps the person exercise self-control and to think ahead to circumstances when he is with her to anticipate what he should say and do in order to comply with the norms of natural law.

For a young person in love, the intense prayer that should follow the reception of Communion involves the management of memory and imagination. Over many months, the young person returns each week to Christ, to seek his advice, and to incorporate the person he thinks he might love for a lifetime into a framework that fits with his Christian faith.

A person who derives strength from receiving regularly the Body and Blood of Christ will also want to know how religiously committed the girl of his dreams is. Topics like this should occasionally arise during courtship, since religious commitment plays an important role in helping the couple respect, appreciate, and love one another. A person might ask for the ability to discern between a person who is likely to keep a lifelong commitment and one who, at least at this point in his or her life, does not have the discipline or motivation to keep such a commitment.

Worshipping Regularly with a Religious Community

Consider the normal way in which young people come to maturity. They learn to do different things by interacting with people and talking with them. They don't reach maturity by just playing computer games or by watching movies or television or listening to music. They have to interact not just with their friends, but also with adults and also with children younger than they are. Only in this way do they come to learn things about themselves and others. By interacting with others of different ages, young people become more aware of things they know or can do, things they don't know, and things they aspire to. Their erroneous or controversial views are contested by others, and they learn to what extent they can persuade or motivate people to do things. Personal interaction leads to at least some self-knowledge.

Weekly participation in a religious community of worship involves some personal interaction and, therefore, the opportunity for more accurate self-knowledge. Because one is interacting with people often about religious issues, one has to confront one's past, future, and present. Over time this can result in greater clarity. But arguing in this way is akin to arguing for participating in any club that gathers regularly. As long as it's fun or relaxing spending time with club members, any participant will probably learn something more about himself.

Our claim, however, is that a person involved in regular worship learns more about herself precisely because of the worship, the topics discussed, and the types of interaction. In church one meets people who want to grow in their faith by understanding better God's activity in their lives and discerning more closely what God is calling them to do with their lives. Ideally, young adults will volunteer to give religious instruction to children preparing for First Holy Communion or Confirmation. In this way, they learn to pass on the faith to the next generation and also prepare to teach their own children how to live the faith. Furthermore, in addition to praying directly to God and reflecting on Scripture, one is called to pray especially for members of the congregation who are close to death, suffering greatly, or facing big decisions. Recommending these people to God in prayer also is an invitation to envision oneself at some future time in a similar situation and wondering what one will do.

Every person will certainly face death at some point. Whether one will have to combat sickness, joblessness, or loneliness prior to death is uncertain. However, someone considering marriage or some other long-term commitment, such as religious life, should consider whether she has the necessary fortitude to persevere in time of great difficulty. Knowing other people in these circumstances, consoling them, and promising to pray for them and keep them in one's memory—all this invites one to imagine oneself in similar circumstances. That's pretty important for a person considering whether he can commit himself to a young woman "for better, for worse, for richer, for poorer, in sickness and in health, until death do us part." It does not guarantee one will have the strength, but at the very least it means one scrutinizes oneself more closely to see whether one has the interest and desire to persevere.

That the thoughts and deliberations described above occur weekly over many years of faithful attendance at religious services means that a person cycles through a great variety of emotions as well as through periods of optimism and perhaps some depression. These cycles are part of life and certainly part of marriage. The main reasons for attending church are to praise God, hear about the revelation of God in Christ, and speak to Christ and to do that in the presence of other believers. A very tangible side benefit, however, is the invitation to envision one's own reactions to experiences of hardship and great joy.

Another side benefit of regular participation in and interaction with a worshipping community is that a person interacts with current parents. From these people of faith, the young adult hears about challenges they face in raising their children and encouraging their children in regular practice of the faith. A young adult, once married, will likely face similar challenges. The young practicing Christian who worships regularly in a community gets to know the members of the community. As the young adult gets to know and appreciate some couples, their advice about marriage or raising children is offered in a context much easier to interpret than what might encounter in a book or on television. The community is a source of wisdom for married life.

CORROSIVE ACTIONS DIMINISH MORAL SKILLS

Any corrosive action means that a person moves away from participation in a fundamental value and also undermines the value. The justification for designating the action "corrosive" is not that it damages the fundamental value but rather that it eats away or diminishes the ability of the practitioner to perceive and be attracted by the fundamental value. The person committing the corrosive action chooses either to emphasize a good intention not directly related to the action or to make believe the contemplated action falls in the category of acceptable actions.

Consider a simple example, such as a lie. For ease of analysis we use the lie to illustrate more generally that any corrosive action, especially with respect to sexual intimacy, diminishes somewhat one or more of the four moral skills we have highlighted: self-control, knowledge of self and others, ability to make and keep commitments, and management of memory and imagination.

The lie is corrosive because it undermines the movement toward knowledge. By telling a lie to another person, one intentionally tries to lead the person away from knowledge, not closer to knowledge. Even though person A tells the lie, the first intentional impact of the lie is on person B, to whom the lie is told. Whether the lie diminishes, perhaps to only a small degree, each of the four moral skills that have been highlighted depends on the motivation for the lie. We briefly consider two possible motivations for the lie and possible consequences on the moral skills.

If the lie was told to avoid embarrassing oneself or someone else, telling the lie means that the liar lacks the ability or willingness to accept the consequences of the truth. This may or may not lead to less self-control. However, if the lie is to advance one's social or economic position, it means the practitioner allows the desire for money or prestige to dictate one's action. The liar at the moment of the lie concedes, via an act of the will, priority or control to the desire for money or wealth. The direct result of the lie is to increase the power or sway of desire for wealth or prestige in the person's assortment of emotions, sentiments, and motivations. Hence, when a lie is told for the purpose of self-advancement, the lie weakens the ability of the liar to forcefully confront in the future potentially destructive personal emotions or attractions.

Whether the lie is told to avoid embarrassment or for personal gain, the liar deceives himself. He may truthfully acknowledge to himself the motive for the lie (to avoid embarrassment or for personal gain), but of necessity he uses the person to whom he tells the lie for his own benefit. But using another person for one's own benefit means one does not try to see the other person in himself or herself, as someone worthy of hearing the truth. One makes oneself the arbiter of truth. In this way, one deceives the other person, which is the primary intent of the lie, but also oneself. Hence, one diminishes one's knowledge of others and one's self-knowledge.

A lie need not diminish one's ability to keep a commitment. Indeed, the lie may reflect one's desire to keep a commitment at all costs, even at the cost of acting contrary to the fundamental value of truth. However, the normal understanding of a commitment to someone is that one will keep the promise while also adhering to the normal requirements of morality. In this case, the person does not break the formal commitment, but he or she does wander into corrosive territory. This action makes it a little more likely that in the future, when faced with embarrassment of the prospect of personal gain, one will keep the commitment at the cost of undermining one of the fundamental values. However, being faithful to a commitment while acting unethically involves self-deception, since this is not what abiding by one's word or commitment means.

Finally, a lie demonstrates an ability to mismanage one's memory and imagination. The liar thinks how he can fit the lie into past experience. After telling the lie, he has to figure out how to keep the lie consistent with future events. Due to memory and imagination, one lie, if it is not to be uncovered, necessarily begets many lies. So a lie diminishes a person's ability to correctly manage memory and imagination.

Whether the lie adversely impacts all four moral skills depends on the motivation behind the lie. However, it is clear that several of the moral skills are adversely impacted. We can generalize somewhat and conclude that corrosive actions broadly diminish some important moral skills. Whether each corrosive action diminishes each of the highlighted moral skills depends in part on the motivation for the corrosive action.

EXPECTED RESULTS

As a general rule, one can say that the less time one gives to prayer and Eucharist, the smaller the impact these activities will have on enhancing moral skills. Prayer and Eucharist aim at developing a relationship with God through his only begotten Son. Like any relationship, it requires time, imagination, and some maturity. Just as a couple "matures" in their relationship with each other, so the same happens in prayer.

Through Scripture, liturgy, and grace, God calls us to imitate Christ. For a young person thinking about marriage, conversing with Christ will entail sharing one's deepest hopes and concerns. So, it will be natural that a young man or woman speaks to Christ of the person they love. One constant refrain will be to wonder whether this young man, for example, is the "man of my dreams." In answering this question, the young woman will be asking for help in coming to know herself and her dreams. Eventually, she will wonder whether her dreams correspond with what Jesus is asking of her.

Even an imperfect follower of Christ who over many years strives for self-knowledge should arrive at some honest assessments. The power of the relationship with Christ is that he is our example, both in the moral skills and in pursuing the fundamental values. In his preaching and actions, Christ calls us to realize exemplary actions among the fundamental values. But also, through prayer, we become confident that Christ will give us the strength we need to do the exemplary things we hope to do.

Of course there can be serious faults or lapses in a relationship. The couple may have been intimate sexually and regret it. They regret it not because they do not look forward to sexual intimacy but because they are convinced that sexual intimacy should be the expression of their lifelong commitment, not a means toward producing that commitment. In situations like this, one or both of the partners may seek help from Jesus and the Holy Spirit in redirecting his their lives and Catholics should be reconciled to the Christian community via confession.

We are all sinners. A young man contemplating a big step in life may be aware of many terrible decisions he has made. He may even be fearful that some of these mistakes will be repeated. By searching through his memory with the Gospel stories in mind, he places a marker or two, indicating where he has erred in the past and alerting him to dangerous situations in the future. His prayer rearranges the context for the future in a positive way. That is, he re-imagines how he will interact with this young woman he hopes to marry. Whatever may have been the circumstances in his past life that led to weakness in this area, the young man now takes responsibility for it all in the presence of Christ. Reconciliation purifies the memory. An important outcome of confession and prayer is a renewed commitment to be part of a community of believers and regularly participate in those activities which celebrate the saving presence of Christ in the person's life and in the life of the community.

The reflections above suggest that people of faith should find strength and support in regular religious practice. Data indicate that married couples who attend religious services weekly are much less likely to get a divorce. Religious practice is not a guarantee there will be no divorce, but the data and our personal experience suggest that religious people often have enhanced moral skills.

30

Temptation and Religious Commitment

AS THEY WALKED away from Saint Elizabeth's, Maria told Dave she was happy he came to Mass with her this Sunday, since it was the anniversary of her grand-mother's death. Grandma had died ten years ago and when Maria attended the funeral Mass in Iowa, hundreds of "Grandma memories" returned to her. They brought her both great happiness as well as unnerving sorrow in the following weeks.

Maria was a bit nervous because she realized she had to say something to Dave that might prove difficult. She repeated how happy she was that Dave came to Mass with her. "But," she said, "I don't want you going to Mass just because of me. I know you want to please me, and I appreciate that. But when it comes to Mass, it is not just about me. Also, I don't want to think you go regularly, only to find out that you will easily drop the practice years from now."

Dave acknowledged to Maria something she already knew. He was an occasional Catholic who attended Mass just a few times a year—at least until recently. Dave admitted to Maria he started going to Mass regularly about two months ago with one of his college friends. "Honestly," he said, "it was because of you, but not for the reasons you think. It was less to gain favor with you than to overcome some of the difficulties I have when I am with you."

Maria knew that she could come on strong and that she could easily dismiss opinions she disagreed with. But because she liked Dave so much, she always tried to control these impulses when she was with him. When she went to Mass, she would pray to Jesus after Communion and ask Him for the strength to hold her tongue and think before she spoke, especially with David, as she liked to call him. Jesus and the Holy Spirit were certainly helping her because she thought she had been fairly successful. The only downside was a few slightly awkward silences in their conversations. In these little lapses, Maria was thinking furiously about a kind way of saying what she wanted to say.

"Am I allowed to know what those difficulties are?" "Oh you know," Dave said, "the usual guy stuff. Whenever we get together, I start thinking about sex." Maria smiled and blushed and said, "Well, I'm happy that's the difficulty."

Dave pointed out that it's fine for her to be relieved, but it wasn't so great for him. Dave knew it wasn't just the sexual attraction to her, but he did not know how to express his difficulties. Maria said, "Well, it's not as if we have never kissed and we do get pretty physical and intimate sometimes." "I know," Dave said, "but I am always thinking of doing much more with you and I know that's a problem."

Maria was going to say something smart, but thought better of it. Instead she said, "Now, just a minute. It's fine that you like my body—even the Catholic Church says there's nothing wrong with that. Remember Genesis 1: both you and I are made in the image and likeness of God. But Genesis points out that we were also created to become one in marriage. It's okay that we are attracted to each other, we just have to be careful how we handle it."

"Maybe I'm thinking too much about one thing," Dave said. "We'd both be better off if I had a more well-rounded approach!"

Maria said suddenly: "This is ridiculous. We should not even be talking about these things, at least not after just having been to church. I know I was the one who asked you, but it just seems to me we should change the topic." "Fine with me," said Dave with exasperation.

Later Maria thought about it and realized she was wading into difficult territory without much information. She wanted to talk with someone about what she was feeling and what she should do. But she expected most of her friends would think she was being ridiculous. They'd just tell her to let nature take its course. Finally, she decided to talk to her mom. It might be a little awkward, but her mother would know what to say and would take her seriously. After Maria was clearer about what she should do, she would bring the topic up with David one more time. After all, she had to tell David that it was an important topic and they both had to act responsibly.

The next time Maria spoke with her mother she broached the subject. Her mother had met David and she knew how much Maria liked him. She also knew they were getting pretty serious about each other. Maria described the conversation she and David had had after Mass at Saint Elizabeth's. Her mother listened carefully. Maria explained this was only the third or fourth time she and Dave had talked about having sex. The first time Maria made it clear she was not interested in casual sex or friends with benefits. Sex would be an option only if she was ready to commit to Dave. The conversation they had after Mass at St. Elizabeth's was less direct. Maria thought it was a good sign that Dave was wrestling with the issue. Also, Maria admitted to her mother that she wasn't a total prude. Between Dave and her there was certainly more going on than handshakes and good-night kisses. But Maria also admitted that the more she and Dave talked about these things, the weirder it seemed. It was making Maria uncomfortable, and that's why she decided to cut the last conversation short. Later, though, she thought she had been wrong to stop things so abruptly. After all, she had encouraged David to bring it up in the first place.

Her mother then said, "Maria dear, just tell me one more thing. What do you mean when you say there's more going on than good-night kisses?" Maria explained that it was practically nothing, "just some touching and fondling my breasts. You know what I mean! I certainly want him to know I really care about him." Maria also made clear that she didn't let things get out of hand. "After a few minutes, I kind of push him away," she told her mother, "and he always accepts that."

Her mother said, "Yes, it does sound as if you are trying to be careful and yet still encouraging to this young man. But I don't think you understand how confusing this probably is for poor Dave. He clearly wants to do what you want, but he also wants to be more intimate with you. You are sending mixed messages. I think you have to spend some time thinking and praying about this."

Maria's mother then explained, "On the one hand, you are saying that intimate touching is all right. And on the other hand, you are adamant that there's a time limit. Sex is not a by-the-clock activity, you know. Young men are not made that way, and frankly, you are not made that way either. Once that activity starts, it is hard to stop. It may be easy for you now, but you are basically telling Dave you want him to do this. This is the normal activity that leads to sex. Yes, I know you have told him that, as much as you like him, sex at this point is out of the question. But still, your actions are saying something else."

Maria and her mother talked a little while longer, but it was becoming clear to Maria what she would have to do. Maria was thanking her mom for her advice and getting ready to end the conversation, but before she could hang up the phone her mother said, "Maria, I know you will figure out what to do and I trust you and Dave will do the right thing. Whatever you do, Dave will appreciate it if only you and he know about this, not me. So don't think I expect you to share it with me."

By the end of the conversation, Maria could already see a little plan that would give Dave clarity and also be more realistic about their relationship. But first she would do what her mother said. She would stop by Saint Elizabeth's on Saturday morning and pray about it, to make sure she was doing what God wanted. She went in, knelt down, and then spoke to Jesus. In her mind, she slowly went through her plan. Then she started talking quietly with Jesus. "Jesus, topics like this must have come up in some form or another in your life on earth. I am sure, Jesus, you gave good advice to young women and men in Nazareth. You were great with the Samaritan woman at the well. The Holy Spirit is the one who recalls to us what you said and did. Let your Holy Spirit be with me that I can do the right thing with dear David." Then she went over to the Blessed Mother's altar to say a prayer for David, that the Blessed Virgin Mary help him understand what Maria is doing and that he accept it with grace. She especially prayed that grace would be abundant for both of them during the upcoming conversation she planned.

About a month after the anniversary of her grandmother's death, Maria invited Dave to join her for Sunday Mass and then brunch. Once they got to the restaurant after Mass that next Sunday, Maria asked if they could sit on the patio instead of inside. It was a cool fall day and no one else was eating outside, but Dave knew how much Maria enjoyed every minute she could spend outside. What he did not know, however, was that it was privacy more than the environs that prompted Maria's request.

After making sure phones were off, some chitchat, and then ordering their food, Maria got right to the point. "David, I have been thinking about that conversation we had a few weeks ago about your difficulties with me. I know I was the one who prompted the conversation and then abruptly cut it off. I want to apologize for what happened. You were honest, which I wanted you to be. But I was uncomfortable about where the conversation was headed, so I ended it."

Maria then explained that she had been thinking and praying about what happened ever since. What she realized was that she did not really know what she wanted from Dave. She knew she liked being with him. She liked it when Dave got all snuggly with her, but she also liked lots of other things about their relationship. Dave liked surprising her and he was so good at figuring out the very things she would most enjoy. He also challenged her to try new things she would otherwise avoid. As a result of Dave's encouragement Maria had gone to an opera, eaten sushi, and learned to sail.

Dave was also an enthusiastic participant in events and experiences Maria initiated. He enjoyed her family and invited her to join him with his own family, encouraging her to be part of their extended discussions. And she also admitted how much she enjoyed the physical closeness they shared. "David, you treat me like royalty and I love it," Maria said. "Perhaps one day I will want to be treated as a wife, but for now royalty will do. So, when you think about pleasing me, think of all those things, all the things you are now doing. As for the snuggly stuff, let's keep that to hugs and kisses for now—at least until we know where we are going in this relationship." Dave smiled and leaned across the table to offer one of those sanctioned kisses. He knew how hard it had been for Maria to set her boundaries and he wanted her to know that even if he hoped for more, he understood.

Before they finished brunch, Maria returned again to the topic. "One last thing, David," she interjected. "I realize it may be difficult for you just to be satisfied with just hugs and kisses. But this is what I want. And also, I prayed for you at Our Lady's altar at Saint Elizabeth's this morning. I am sure she is going to help you. We both can get strength to focus on the most important things if we pray regularly for help."

CONTEXT

Not everything in a relationship has to be crystal clear, but each partner being clear about expectations helps enormously. As human beings we communicate our expectations by what we say and what we do. In talking with her mother, Maria realized her communication was confusing at best; the words were not in sync with the actions. By being a bit too clever, Maria was leading Dave to expect greater intimacy. Dave was certainly thinking about sex, but he also thought Maria might be interested too and he was ready to accommodate her. Maria understood she had to clarify in her own mind what she wanted. She prayed and reflected on this, allowed it to settle in her mind, and then spoke to David with admirable clarity. For Maria, clarity came both through the conversation with her mother and through her own reflection and prayers. Keeping to the game plan requires ongoing vigilance and continuing reflection and prayer.

31

Courtship and Sexual Deferment

A PLAUSIBLE OBJECTION to the claim that sexual intimacy should reflect a lasting public commitment and not occur prior to such a commitment is that it's too stringent a norm. The awakening of sexual desire occurs in the teenage years, yet since many young people now get married in their late 20s or early 30s, some claim that waiting so long for sexual fulfillment is too long. Because the drive for sexual fulfillment is strong and life is fleeting, most young people will inevitably and justifiably (so goes the claim) indulge in premarital sex.

The issue of premarital sex has already been addressed from a number of theoretical and personal perspectives, and we are not walking back the results of previous chapter. Nonetheless, the issue of being social while remaining chaste over many years of increased levels of hormone activity is a significant one. This chapter outlines four general practices that are helpful in maintaining and developing close personal, but chaste, relationships. Before doing so, let us briefly review one general argument that has been made in earlier chapters.

SEXUAL INTIMACY BLOCKS DEEP PERSONAL KNOWLEDGE

Sexual intimacy prior to marriage is not a good path to self-knowledge or knowledge of the other person. At first, it might seem that performing such an intimate act with another person would lead to significant knowledge about the other person and perhaps oneself. One undoubtedly learns something. However, in previous chapters we have pointed out that, for the most part, what is learned is not particularly germane to the issue whether this person is "the one" and, for the type of knowledge that does emerge, it is not the only source.

Of course, it is possible to learn something significant through the sexual act. For example, a young woman might learn that her companion gets violent or abusive when having sex. This is significant data, but the brutality or abusive behavior could also have been learned via a normal, nonintimate relationship. It may have required a few months for this to emerge, but it certainly would become apparent in the normal give and take of a relationship. So even if there is an exception to the general rule that extramarital sex is not a path to self-knowledge, a safer, more human way to get the pertinent relationship is to go out with the person over a period of months.

Why does sexual intimacy block significant insight rather than lead to it? The reason is the pleasure of the sexual act realized with a particular young man or woman leads one to look forward to the next physical encounter. It does not lead one to look more deeply and consider whether the young woman, for example, with whom one is having this physical relationship is actually a spousal candidate. If one is committed to avoiding sex until marriage, one may succumb in a moment of weakness and yet still get back on track. However, if one's *modus operandi* is to have sex with anyone making an implied commitment, one is blocking personal development as well as insight into oneself and one's partner. Yes, a fair amount of physical satisfaction is also being accumulated. But the desire for the physical satisfaction undermines deeper thinking about the other person's qualities and also impedes the development of one's own moral skills in relation to whatever young woman with whom one happens to be having a "significant relationship."

Consider a modified defense of sex prior to marriage: moderate sexual contact. This approach claims that as long as sexual intimacy is occasional, things will work out well. How realistic is this proposed course of action? Is it possible for a non-married couple to have sex occasionally and, because it is only occasional, not preclude reaching important insights about each other? The challenge in this approach is to restrict the sexual act to occasional encounters. In moral terms, however, permitting sex is a green light to allow it to happen anytime both partners are willing. "A little sex" prior to marriage is not a viable strategy, even if it were permitted morally.

The challenge then is for young people to feel carefree in meeting others and getting to know them better, but keeping sexual intimacy at bay. In order for this to work, both the young man and woman have to be committed to developing their relationship without sexual intimacy prior to marriage. Since the sexual urge is so strong, couples have to take some measures to make sure that even if on some occasions they are overcome by the emotion of the moment, sexual intimacy does not take place due to other factors.

Finding a life partner is an important undertaking for a young adult. However, a young Christian adult also has other plans he would like to implement. In particular, Christians are called to respond to and promote the Kingdom of God. Requirements for the Kingdom of God are articulated by Jesus in the beatitudes, which are part of the Sermon on the Mount (Matthew 5:1-10). For Jesus, the beatitudes constitute a type of "religious platform," that is, his basic message to those who would be his followers. The beatitudes tell of the joy of the pursuit, not the misery of sexual abstinence. And it was the joy that attracted his listeners.

A young Christian adult should be happy if she is poor in spirit, but rich in reflecting on and enjoying God's gifts. Being free to mourn with others entails responsiveness to the situation of others. Being clean of heart in a relationship with a young man or woman may be a struggle, but the young person knows that in this way he is doing justice to his partner, even if she does not turn out to be a life partner. Sex should not loom too large at a point when the fruit of sex—a baby—cannot be welcomed wholeheartedly. The message of Jesus is that implementing the beatitudes brings lasting satisfaction. Young people have to focus on lasting contentment, not ephemeral pleasures.

FOUR ADDITIONAL PRACTICES

Despite the previous debunking of purported benefits of sex before marriage, young people committed to sexual abstinence before marriage are not left with nothing. On the contrary, they can launch a thrilling, romantic, satisfying, but chaste courtship. But it means they need a realistic plan. Because romance is often unexpected, one cannot force it to happen. However, one should have a plan to make sure whatever romance occurs is a chaste romance.

In this section, four additional practices are proposed to help young adults remain open to courtship and romance, on the one hand, while overcoming the desire to take the sexual plunge prior to marriage. Young people are often excited about new relationships, but they should also be realistic in their relationships with members of the opposite sex.

All four practices relate to dating, an activity that seems to be making a comeback among young people in college and beyond. Finding the correct man or woman to be your spouse is not easy and no surefire formula is offered here. Rather, the four general practices proposed help keep the relationship on an exciting, satisfying track while allowing for, but not presuming, the emergence of a possible long-term commitment.

Before presenting the four additional general practices, it is helpful to recall two of the practices already recommended in chapter 26. Practice 1 urges young men who want to lead an authentically moral life to signal to any new female acquaintance what they are not expecting. That is, the young man should tactfully communicate to the young woman that he is not expecting sexual intimacy anywhere near the beginning of this relationship. The second practice from chapter 26 is not to let a relationship develop too deeply if one is not yet ready to make a major commitment. Much soul-searching is required before making a lifelong commitment. For a great variety of cultural reasons, any young adult possibly interested in marrying some young man or woman should enjoy the relationship for several years, but at least for a year or two. During this time, the young person should do a moral inventory to make sure he has the moral skills that will enable him to keep a lifelong commitment. So, signaling early on that one is not expecting sexual favors and proceeding slowly until the one's ability to keep a lifelong commitment has been properly tested are the shorthand expression of these practices.

To summarize, the first two practices taken from chapter 26 are the following:

Practice 1:   Early on in a relationship a young man should signal to the young woman that he is not expecting sexual intimacy as a condition for the relationship to develop nicely.

Practice 2:   A young man or woman should "slow down" a relationship, especially as the couple gets emotionally closer to one another, until each person is fairly sure that both parties are capable of making and keeping a lifelong commitment.

In addition to these two practices, the following four practices help young adults develop healthy relationships. A brief description and example of each additional practice is given, and then the fuller meaning and justification for each practice is explored.

Practice 3:   When a couple is on a date or more generally doing things together, the couple should always plan ahead to be with one another either in public places or in private situations where other adults are present. They should avoid being alone as a couple in completely private places.

Practice 4:   Once a couple has been out on a number of dates together, the man or woman should use good imagination in the ensuing months and years in proposing different events that the couple would be open to sharing in. Their activities don't have to be the couple's favorite activities; however, they should explore the full range of their general interests.

Practice 5:   Before a formal proposal or even an informal commitment is made, the couple should spend a fair amount of time in potentially stressful situations, including lengthier interactions with the family of one's future spouse. This interaction ideally would include a vacation with the family or some other concentrated time where the family is living together in close quarters and interacting with each other for several days.

Practice 6:   The man and woman on their own should regularly engage in prayer. In addition, at least occasionally they should attend religious services together.

A person acquires moral skills by particular practices. Also, a person is morally good or bad because of the actions he or she performs. One does not become a good person by merely thinking about what constitutes a good person. Having clear thoughts is more important to some people than others. But just because thoughts are clear does not mean they will lead to good and helpful practices.

Human experience teaches that developing a lasting relationship between a man and woman is tricky. A good relationship requires a sensitive and alert disposition at the beginning, middle, and end of the relationship. Practices 3 through 6 are guidelines that help a young person develop a solid relationship in the early years.

Practice 3 encourages couples to develop their relationship in public places or places where other adults mill around or pass by. Traditionally cultures have implicitly established this norm for young men and women. The reason for the norm is obvious. As a couple gets emotionally closer to one another and shares more intimate thoughts, feelings, and aspirations, the desire to be intimate sexually with one another becomes very strong. Experience teaches that resisting such feelings when the couple is completely alone is challenging, and in some cases almost impossible. As we pointed out much earlier, the couple being alone in a bedroom at 3 A.M. is a near occasion of sin, precisely because resistance to being intimate is almost impossible.

The norm of developing one's relationship in public or adult spaces imposes a constraint, but the constraint makes sense and is clear. The point is to make sure that, even in circumstances when the couple may wish to be intimate, the fact that others are around constrains their actions. This is a good check. A couple that dates in public or are always around other adults are less tempted to be very intimate, and yet they can still have enormous amounts of fun and find true satisfaction.

The purpose of practice 4 is to help individuals explore the great variety of interests they might have. Young people know some of their interests, but certainly not all of them, mainly because their experiences are still limited. What activities they consider "interesting" or "promising" depends on the couple and their backgrounds. Activities such as the following can be fun: going to the opera, seeing a play, taking a nature hike, going to see a professional baseball or basketball game, visiting vineyards or orchards, climbing a mountain, rowing on a lake, taking young nieces and nephews to special events, volunteering to help the poor and otherwise disadvantaged, offering to host a program for the young or elderly in a local parish, and many others.

In addition to regular activities such as going to the movies, concerts, and interesting restaurants, both the woman and the man should suggest regular activities, such as the ones listed above, as well as nonstandard activities they can do together. The goal is to discover more about the world, but, more importantly, understand better each other's likes and dislikes. For example, they may choose to go to the top of a mountain or a tall building, and then decide once was enough. That's fine. They probably enjoyed the one time, since at least they were together, and next time they'll do something else. These activities expand or simply verify their current horizons. Such activities help each one gain self-knowledge and knowledge of their partner.

Much earlier it was noted that young people were asked in an interview to describe their most romantic experience. In one particular study, it turned out that all, with one exception, referred to some event where sex did not enter into the picture. The young romantics most often described an evening where they were with a young man or woman; it was a beautiful, though perhaps simple setting, and they just talked and shared for hours. Some romantic moments can be planned, but many happen because things fall into place that evening. One advantage of varying the types of dates one has is that it increases the likelihood of serendipitous romantic evenings.

In medicine and the financial sectors, stress tests have become popular. Stress tests naturally occur in building a relationship, and they can be very important in understanding oneself and one's partner. If a young man is privileged to go on a vacation with the family of the young woman he has been seeing for some months, he will learn a lot about her and also about himself. In many cases, these are delightful experiences, though in some cases they can be trying. Even difficult experiences teach a person much about how he or she has to relate to the family if the family will eventually become part of his or her extended family. Young people today grow up in locally distinct cultures. Much depends on the music one listens to, the movies and television shows one sees, the schools one attended, and the type of employment one has. Prior to marriage, it is helpful for a partner to become at least somewhat familiar with the culture into which he or she is marrying.

Any couple getting serious with one another should pray for themselves and their partner. Speaking with Christ is like going up the mountain. By rising higher, the perspective gets broader and more embracing. By addressing Christ in a personal way as one develops feelings for one's partner, a young man is asking for strength to be flexible and insightful enough to remain committed for a lifetime to the young woman he hopes to marry. Attending church services together enables the couple to grow together in supernatural love. It also offers lots of opportunities at brunch to reflect on what was said in church and what role religious practices plays in the life of each partner.

"I'LL TAKE ANY RELATIONSHIP!" AND "WHY BOTHER?"

Many a modern young person would find the practices proposed in the previous section not wrong but irrelevant. In desperation for any date, they might scream: "I'll take any relationship!" Indeed, it is very difficult for young people in the United States to meet young people with similar interests and on a terrain that does not slope toward almost immediate sexual gratification. This is a genuine challenge. Permissive sex has made it more difficult, not easier, for young people interested in a lifelong relationship to meet and find a partner suitable for them. The practices advocated in this chapter at least identify a terrain on which young people with similar hopes and expectations can meet and develop relationships which might prove fruitful.

The practices proposed here make sense only if one is trying to remain chaste. Even then, skeptical thoughts about how realistic such practices are will occur even to very committed natural law advocates. Why even bother pursuing this approach? Can it really be so wrong to engage in sex before marriage if so many others are doing it? "It's not as if the man of my dreams is going to turn me down because I already had sex with someone," says the young woman reluctant to close off avenues or access. Alternatively, a young man might consider lack of sexual experience a disadvantage because it suggests to the young woman that he is too conservative or is unwilling to take some risks. And finally, what's the benefit of not being sexually experienced prior to marriage? It's not as if the abstinence approach is going to bring health, wealth, or happiness. It's just a requirement of the natural law, and a fairly burdensome one.

Some of these skeptical claims are superficially plausible, but by no means compelling. A guy who avoids sex before marriage may be avoiding risks, but it's got to be a strange type of woman who wants her husband-to-be to have had sex with another woman in order to prepare him better for marriage with her. If a woman really thought this (or, in a similar way, the guy thought this about the woman), she would lack basic self-confidence, in a way almost fatal to a lasting relationship. Any woman should be confident she can please (or quickly learn to please) her husband in bed.

Yes, in our age, a young woman or man is unlikely to turn down a potential partner for life just because he or she has had prior sexual liaisons. But the issue should be not whether you get turned down, but whether you have developed the skills needed for a marriage to last a lifetime.

The advantage of postponing sex to marriage is that the couple focuses on lots of other important things during the run-up to marriage. A young woman, for example, should be able to think clearly and accurately about her prospects in marrying a young man. The following self-reflection identifies areas about which she should be able to make confident judgments. "Yes, I know him pretty well. On some things, he's rock solid. On most of these issues, I agree with him, and the areas of disagreement I just have to accept. He is flexible on many things, but what I like is that he does not change his mind about education, neatness, beauty, children, and respect to parents. Yes, it's a drawback that he is not more prayerful and religious. Also, a few of his political views are distasteful to me, but I can live with that. After all, he has to live with my political views. I wish he liked dogs, but maybe the pleadings of, God willing, our children will change that. He and I both hope for happiness in marriage, but we have also talked about 'for better, for worse, in sickness and health.' The most important 'for better' we have discussed: having healthy, loving children. The most difficult 'for worse' would be if a child of ours were seriously sick. The few times that came up in conversation, it was difficult for me to focus. I was superstitious. I thought that if we talked about it, it would make it more likely it would occur. But I know that's wrong. And what he said is comforting: 'I'm marrying you. You're the one I'm committed to. Especially if you get seriously sick, I want you know I will still be with you and loving you.'

Once we got engaged, we said we would address big issues on a date once every two or three weeks. This was to make sure we are prepared. I think I am."

Postponing sexual intimacy to marriage does not bring health, wealth, and happiness. However, the policy of postponement helps the partners focus thoughts and skills that will help secure their marriage until death parts the couple. Surely that counts for a lot.

32

Unwanted Changes

BOTH DAVE AND Maria had separate family commitments on Sunday, so they decided to go to Mass on Saturday evening in Maria's parish, after which they would go out for a simple dinner. Part of their Lenten activity was to make sure they go to church each week, volunteer once a week at a local soup kitchen, and avoid movies, desserts, or alcohol during Lent.

The Saturday evening Mass at Maria's parish was not very lively and the church was only half full. After Mass, Maria told Dave she was disappointed at the turnout, even though it was about the same number of people who usually attend that Mass during the year. "I thought that as we got closer to Holy Week and Easter, the casual Catholics would want to get ready for these big events by coming to Mass more regularly," explained Maria. They had been invited to an informal early dinner by Dave's sister, Ann. Ann was married with three younger children and this was their normal Saturday night dinner. Ann thought it would be nice for the children to have dinner with Dave and Maria, and Maria and Dave were happy to interact with the children and spend some time with Ann and her husband.

After dinner and much playing with Ann's children, Dave and Maria said their good-byes and headed off to a coffee shop they liked. As they were ordering their favorite blends, Dave mentioned he had seen some interesting statistical information this past week. Someone gave him an article providing a summary of studies that explored the relationship between religious practice and divorce. He was amazed to learn that couples who went to church, synagogue, or mosque

263

regularly were less prone to get divorced by a factor of approximately four to one. And, he said, this had nothing to do with which religion one practiced. Those who didn't practice had divorce rates close to 50 percent, while those who practiced regularly had divorce rates a bit more than 10 percent.

Maria had heard similar data once before, but she did not realize the divorce rates were so starkly lower for those who practice their religion regularly. So she said, "Well, Dave, what's the conclusion you draw? Doesn't it mean that you should be going to church on your own more regularly, and not just with me?" Dave admitted he was trying to go to church every week. "But, Maria, someone's only going to go to church if he believes the religion is true. I do believe. Or better, until I met you, I thought I believed. You convinced me that belief without practice is a very thin type of belief and so I am trying to connect the dots from belief to practice."

"That's a good response," said Maria. "Going to church to prevent divorce, but not believing in what you practice in church is crazy. So I agree: the data are interesting, but they don't point to a definite plan."

"Maria, you and I both know some divorced couples, a few who are fairly young, and others who are older. What do you think leads to divorce? Do you think infrequent church attendance is the key?" "Well, I guess the religious practice does make a big difference. But, frankly, I have never really focused on the regularity of church attendance. I guess I should think a bit more deeply about this. Dave, what do you think leads to divorce?"

"I think going to church regularly does make a difference, but it is not what leaps to mind when I think about divorced couples I know. Of course, I don't know that many, but I know what makes me cringe when I am with some couples. It really bothers me when a married couple can fight in public and say really harsh things to one another in earshot of other people. I can only imagine what things they say to one another privately if they are willing to be so frontal and cruel to one another in public."

Maria nodded assent. "I agree it's embarrassing and I find it very uncomfortable even being privy to the conversation. But, depending on the couple, those types of arguments may not mean that much. It may be just one of their normal ways of interacting, not happening every day perhaps, but occasionally. The couple then forgets about the exchange and they are back on track. That type of feuding need not lead to divorce. Nonetheless, I agree with you that for many people it is dangerous territory, certainly for you and me."

"Do you think the territory is dangerous because you and I are more sensitive to the harshness of the arguments?" asked Dave. When Maria hesitated and did not respond right away, Dave said, "Aha, a sensitive topic!" "No," Maria replied, "as I said before, my thoughts are not clear, or at least not very fixed on this issue, though I really do believe it is an important topic. Here's what I'm thinking. You and I get along swimmingly. We are cordial and courteous. Occasionally we have some little arguments, but nothing big. All this happens because we both want to please one another. What is so disconcerting about those spats or fights between married couples is that it often appears as if love does not enter into the picture at all. Maybe there is some underlying love, but it's pretty well hidden during these fights. Here's the big point for me. How does a couple go from being completely lovey-dovey, as you and I are now, to no longer wanting to please the other person? It disturbs me that this can happen. I'm being honest; it bothers me that it could happen to me or to you. I don't see any evidence for it, but could we wind up actually not wanting to please one another? That seems impossible to me, but I know couples do fight and get divorced."

Dave was ready to make a distinction, even though he was not yet prepared to address Maria's underlying concern. "The couple who are fighting with one another may actually want to please the other person in general, but not in this case. For example, he may think that what she wants to do will hurt the family long-term, even though it may seem good at the time. He may be wrong, but he really is trying to please her in the long-term. So, they may both have excellent motives and fine mutual goodwill, but they just disagree with the right strategy."

Maria agreed, but not completely. "Again, what you say is reasonable," said Maria. "But what worries me is the long-term. Not the long-term strategy, but rather the long-term attitude. Dave, I love you very much and I want to please you. I no longer worry about not pleasing you sexually because I trust we have worked this out and one day the sexual relationship will be real. The issue is what happens over time to our feelings, our dispositions to please. God willing, we will have the joy of raising children and then grow old together, loving in different ways. That's the ideal, that's noble love. But, will I wake up one day twenty years from now and think to myself, 'Amazing. I never thought this would happen. But it has. I no longer want to please this guy.' I certainly don't want this to happen, but this is what worries me. It may happen, and then what do I do? Also, what do you do, since it could just as easily happen to you?"

Dave was not going to get negative either on Maria or himself. He understood Maria was troubled by these possibilities, but deep down she was a scientist. She was always looking for a practical way to prevent bad things from happening and to make it more likely that good things would come to pass. "Maria, you are just worrying about your feelings. You're a very rational person. You don't let yourself be led by your feelings. So, don't worry about them. And if these things bother you, isn't church a good place to resolve them? Maybe that's why the statistics on nondivorce are so favorable to those who practice their faith weekly."

"Dave, yes I think I am pretty rational. But in marriage, I hope to be able to let myself go a bit. I don't mean that I would be wild and crazy with kids around, but part of the fun of marriage is that the couple is secure in their love. They don't have to worry about being 'unloved,' because they are committed to one another. That's a good thing that comes with commitment. That I like. But suppose I get pretty used to being committed, and despite this, feelings come upon me. After some months or years, don't the feelings start to determine the outcome? And what if the feelings are, 'I don't want to please you anymore'? Those are really bad feelings, scary ones too, especially if they last for not just months but for years."

"But, Maria," Dave said, "in marriage you may yield more to your feelings, but it is not as if I fall out of the picture while you tend to your feelings. I don't always find it easy to follow your various thoughts and ups and downs in our conversations. That doesn't annoy me. It's a wonderful challenge. It may be easier for you to understand me, but I presume that the time you spend devising plans for me or wondering what's going on inside my head and heart is time well spent. Also, you regularly call upon Christ for help. If twenty years from now, you wake up with some terrible thoughts, you know what you will do. You will ask Christ and the Virgin Mary for help. Their lives and example are a great stimulus to your imagination."

"Dave, you do know me well. If we get married, of course we are going to do it in church. There we receive the sacrament of matrimony. This means God blesses us and helps us to love one another and others as Christ loves us and the church of his believers. That makes a big difference. But I also like what you say about being confused and turning to Christ for help. There are many things I find confusing about you. Don't worry. It's not that you annoy me. It simply takes sorting through things to figure out where you are. The Gospels say that the Virgin Mary stored things up in her heart, that she had to ponder what things were happening with Jesus, her son and the Son of God. If Mary had to ponder things about Jesus, certainly I have to do that for you! You are already in my prayers. How could it be otherwise? At this point, you and Christ are the most important people in my life. I hope you do the same for me. Do you pray for me?"

"C'mon, Maria, I'm trying to get better at these religious things. When I'm in church at Mass, of course I pray for you. But I pray for me too. I get confused about whether I have the strength to be committed for a lifetime. It's not that I doubt you, but I doubt myself. We can't know the future. On the other hand, the marriage vow is that, whatever the future, I will remain committed to you. I need strength to be able to say and do that."

"Fine," said Maria. "How about we pray together specifically for this?"

"Hey, I am still not great on praying, and praying together is scary, especially with you," said Dave. "Don't worry," said Maria. "You don't have to say anything out loud. Well, maybe only a few prayers out loud which you already know. Here's a little plan. We can't do anything tomorrow because we both have to be with our families. How about Monday night after work? St. Michael's is a lovely church near where you work and they keep it open until about 8 P.M. Since I get out of work a little earlier than you, I will drive over to St. Michael's and meet you in the church around 6:15. We'll just go up to the front of the church and kneel for a few minutes in front of Our Lady's altar. We just kneel there, silent together for five minutes. Neither one of us says anything out loud. But we agree now to pray during that time that we always be committed to one another. I pray for personal strength, and I also pray for equal strength for you. You do the same for me. No words out loud, but you have to be saying things to Jesus and the Virgin Mary. Then at the end, we say together, out loud, an Our Father, Hail Mary, and Glory Be to the Father. Even if someone is in the church, it won't make a difference that we say something aloud. After that we go to Mario's for our simple Lenten dining. How's that?"

"Wow," said Dave, "a total prayer date!"

33

Changing One's Moral Practices

MORALITY IS ABOUT action. In fact, this book is all about striving for important human values by performing various practices. The most basic claim is that some activities lead to deep participation in the fundamental human values, other activities are okay but not outstanding, and a smaller number of activities are prohibited because by their very nature they impair our ability to reach or even see clearly the human values we strive to attain. Now that we have reached the final chapter, what should one expect as the primary take-away?

After urging the reader to reconceive or reimagine the way he thinks of something, one can expect a reader to reflect on the arguments advanced and then decide how to proceed. The moral life is a bit different, however. In most circumstances, one does not change practices as a result of information and arguments alone. Rather, if one is a young adult and fairly experienced in the world, information accompanied by good arguments is usually insufficient to bring about change. One can change only if one has already had experiences that more or less conform to the way of thinking being proposed as the new model. For this reason, even if the moral thoughts or goals depicted in this book are somewhat attractive to a reader, in most instances thinking alone is not enough to change a person's behavior.

In limited situations, information alone can be powerful. Consider two instances in the moral realm where information (along with implicit or formal arguments) might work. If a heavy drinker and drug user understands that he is killing himself but also damaging his family, he might change and decide to participate in an AA program. But even this would require a type of breakthrough insight about how in his current condition he can no longer provide for his family. Furthermore, in most situations like this the alcoholic will not change on his own because he knows he does not have the strength to give up drink. Another instance in which information alone might work is when the information is intensely embarrassing. Consider a person (call her Debra) who regularly lies about her age, making herself out to be four years younger than she is. If Debra finds out that her former class-mate from high school, Jane, has moved back in town and always states her correct age, Debra might start worrying about how she is perceived. The sheer embarrass-ment of being caught in a lie will likely be enough to get Debra to stop lying about her age. Nonetheless, this information may have a very limited effect, since Debra may continue lying about a host of other things.

Both examples of information alone likely yielding change rely on the person experiencing something new that is both awkward and seemingly nonsustainable. That is, the experience makes the information more immediate and forceful to the person. In most cases the person already possesses the relevant information without, however, undertaking any fundamental changes. Indeed, the person may have had all the relevant data for years, but the data have no impact. Even if a young man knew how insulting it is to a young woman to try to sleep with her the first date he is on with her, he is unlikely to change his behavior if someone points out to him how he demeans the young woman. He's not going to change, because he doesn't really care what she thinks. In addition, he probably already knows he is being rude and brutish with her. He's not concerned about that; he might even think his boorish behavior impresses his male friends. More basically, he will likely claim he just wants to have some fun and get some pleasure with the young woman. As long as she says yes, even if she sees very little short-term benefit in the liaison, he's content to have fun. The hurt and disappointment she experiences is beyond his ken. Sadly, seeing clearly her pain and embarrassment is unlikely to change his behavior.

Suppose a person has a strong inclination to change one's life, but says he needs more time. He might say he is looking for a bit more information to enable him to make the decision. But information alone is unlikely to produce change; personal behavior is guided by previous experiences, patterns, and decisions. Most people continue on the same trajectory with their behavior. Reflecting on behavior is a good thing, but not enough to change behavior in a significant way. Oddly, one first has to decide to change the behavior and then reflect on the new experience. Only by acting in a new way that at least approximates what one may want to become does one experience the good, satisfying, but possibly painful feelings associated with the new way of acting.

Deciding to change is difficult. If one feels an inclination toward change for the better, a spiritual person should pray to God for strength in bringing about the change. A person who wants to change should also try to keep company with people who act in a similar way to what he aspires. This is what athletes do; they hang out with other good athletes. And not only athletes, but also musicians, dancers, actors, scientists, businesspeople, and many others. A person who wants to change should spend time with people who act in the way he wants to act. Unless he does this, he is likely to follow whatever his previous behavioral patterns were.

The first part of the book, based on careful, nonreligious reasoning, offered theoretical arguments for doing what most people do naturally but imperfectly, namely, pursue the fundamental values through particular actions. In our treatment, avoiding corrosive actions makes sense since corrosive practices undermine our pursuit of the fundamental values, and only the fundamental values lead to genuine human flourishing. Part II explored types of friendships that sometimes lead to sexual intimacy. Here we noticed a social inclination to accept sex before marriage, even though we showed why it is an activity that corrodes lasting, intimate friendship. In part III we examined the process by which moral skills are acquired and strengthened. Just as regular religious activities strengthen moral skills, it turns out that corrosive actions generally diminish self-control, cloud one's understanding, undermine one's ability to keep a commitment, and introduce bad examples into the memory bank.

As was said many times in reference to the fundamental values, before one knows reflectively that they are fundamental to the human situation, one has already pursued them in hundreds of ways. In the pursuit of the fundamental values, action precedes reflection. Activities in pursuit of the fundamental values provide evidence for the satisfaction one experiences in their pursuit.

Similarly in personal relationships, correct practice is a great help to experience the satisfaction and sense of human fulfillment that accompanies good and exemplary actions in the pursuit of friendship. Parents who emphasize proper behavior to their children understand this well. This satisfaction enables us to appreciate the arguments that justify our behavior as reasonable, good, or even exemplary. In effect, this means that before anyone can take seriously the arguments of this book, he or she has to have at least one chaste, holy relationship with a young man or woman of interest. Many readers of this book already have had many such relationships, or at least pretty good approximations of such relationships. But all of us need to improve the love and respect we have for other people.

Following this line of thought, in order to be a change agent in how one seeks a deep, intimate relationship, one has to decide to live an authentic moral relationship first, and then afterward reflect on it further. In the context of personal relationships, for many people behavioral changes very often precede full appreciation of the arguments for change. If one is inclined to change how one relates to other women or men, one should not look first for airtight theoretical arguments. Provided one experiences an attraction to this new type of living, one should try it out. One should commit to living wholesome, nonexploitative relationships for two or three years and then reflect on the experience. Of course, in order to accomplish this, one needs reasonable moral skills. Regular religious practice often leads to a significant enhancement of moral skills. Realistically, therefore, a person has to decide to live in conformity with the natural law and accompany this decision with regular religious practice. This approach greatly increases the likelihood of carrying out the experiment faithfully for two or three years. After a period of living a chaste relationship, one is in a position to appreciate the force of natural law arguments.

A young person might object that he does not want to waste two or three years of his life trying out something he may never choose definitively. At this point, however, he has no basis on which to decide it will be a "waste." Also, if the account of moral insight given here is correct, he has to at least entertain the possibility he has already "wasted" several years in behavior that cannot possibly lead to either lasting love and intimacy or genuine human satisfaction.

A valid reason to engage in a period of virtuous experimentation is that the person feels drawn to an alternative that promises greater human fulfillment. In order for change to make sense, a man (or woman) has to at least feel a tug on his emotions, desires, sentiment, or intellect to experiment with a more promising way to relate to women (or men). More precisely, he wants to change the way he relates to women to whom he feels attracted so that he respects and honors them. By regularly respecting and honoring all women, he suspects he will increase the likelihood he will respect his whole life long the one woman to whom he commits and with whom he chooses to be intimate. At this point, the "honor and respect" method may only be a hunch. If so, it will need verification by virtuous experience.

In his letter to the Romans, St. Paul writes how the attitudes of Christians to their bodies should be transformed by their commitment to Christ. "I urge you therefore, brothers and sisters, by the mercies of God, to offer your bodies as a living sacrifice, holy and pleasing to God, your spiritual worship. Do not conform yourselves to this age but be transformed by the renewal of your mind, that you may discern what is the will of God, what is good and pleasing and perfect" (Romans 12:1-2). Paul says that we should use our bodies to praise God by offering God fitting sacrifice. He also notes that Christians in his time should not form their ideals in terms of the norms of the secular society. Rather, Christians should act in ways conforming to faith in a loving God who gives good gifts, even the gift of a loving and joyful spouse. In this way, Christians allow themselves to be trans-formed by their faith to seek what is pleasing and perfect.

St. Paul's encouragement is helpful for young people in our modern age. To the extent that St. Paul's admonition applies well to the age in which young people are coming to maturity in their relationships, his encouragement provides a succinct summary of this final part of the book. Religious people draw some norms from the prevailing practices of secular society. Secular practices, however, should be subject to a thorough critique, and that is what has been offered in this book. The norms generated by natural law are rooted in human nature and apply to all people and cultures. Since the norms with respect to sexual intimacy challenge the pre-vailing secular norms, after considering the arguments presented here a reason-able person at the very least must acknowledge that secular norms lack any serious moral foundation. Furthermore, if one is a Christian or adheres to another reli-gion that endorses the natural law, a person wants to make sure her actions are compatible with the norms articulated in the Old and New Testaments. Being steeped in the Old and New Testaments allows us to achieve the "renewal of mind" of which St. Paul speaks.

As Jesus reminds the disciples at the Last Supper, they were chosen from the world to be with Christ and share in his life with the Father (John 15:19). Followers of Christ are of this world certainly in the sense that they share the basic human longings that animate people around the world. As children of the natural law, human beings, whether religious, merely spiritual, or nonreligious, have in common a full human nature. This body-soul-in-society human nature enables us to perceive excellences, pursue them, and avoid actions that undermine the very excellences we seek. This puts us squarely in the world. However, through baptism, Christians have also died to those secular practices that seek satisfaction and fulfillment primarily in this world, in the things of "below." Disciples of Christ find fulfillment in him. United with Christians throughout the ages, modern Christians are part of the Church of Christ and they aspire to love as perfectly as they can. Perfect love requires sacrifice, both before and during marriage. Christians who get married willingly offer this sacrifice because in this way they not only follow in the footsteps of Christ but also aim for the higher things, including participation in divine love.

The Jews praised God for his laws and decrees (Psalm 119) and reflected on how appealing and fair-minded were the laws they received from God through Moses. Moses himself spoke to the people and said: "What great nation has statutes and decrees that are as just as this whole law which I am setting before you today?" (Deuteronomy 4:8) Natural law is more fundamental than the Mosaic law. Not only is it written on all human hearts, but it is also confirmed by the teachings of many Jewish groups and Christian churches and by the practices of Jewish and Christian communities for thousands of years.

Through various religious practices, Christians are encouraged to allow their faith to inform and permeate all significant sectors of their lives. Their religious commitment urges them on to seek what is pleasing and perfect by following Christ and his teachings. This is an undertaking with implications for body and soul. Sexual intimacy is a wonderful capacity involving the human body and mind. In accordance with St. Paul, this book encourages young adults to see how this powerful and tender activity finds its proper expression in marriage.

The basic recipe presented in this book is: add some religious practice to natural law reasoning and one will have a deeply fulfilling love, though not usually without pain or suffering. A much more classic expression of this approach is given by Jesus himself. According to John's gospel, at the Last Supper he tells his disciples that his "New Law" is straightforward: "This is my commandment: love one another as I love you" (John 15: 12). New and challenging in this commandment is to love as Jesus loved and continues to love us.

In gospel accounts of his interactions with others, we see how Jesus himself shows his firm possession of the four moral skills we have highlighted in his loving interactions with others. His love showed good knowledge of others and their motivations. His love acknowledged faults and weaknesses in his disciples, but using this same love Jesus also challenged some people, such as Simon the Pharisee, even in his own home (Luke 7:37-50) to rethink his commitment to love of neighbor. The ordinary love of Jesus was brave since it was not deterred by negative gossip. People complained when Jesus ate with Matthew and his tax collector friends (Matthew 9:9-13), but Jesus pointed out that doctors are most often around those who are sick. As another example, he invited himself to the house of Zacchaeus, who was criticized in the community for being tight with his great wealth (Luke 19:1-10). Even more striking and brave was the extraordinary commitment of Jesus in the passion to show that love is more powerful than death. This love, even to death on a cross, did not yield to threats, pain, or failure in the eyes of the world.

Jesus did not lose himself in his love for others, nor was he overly concerned about the reaction of people to his words. He desire to "stay on message" is evidenced by the many times he sought to be alone in prayer with his Father. Still, both for his Father and for others he could be passionate. When he arrived at Bethany after the death of Lazarus, he was moved by deep emotions when he spoke with Martha about Lazarus and yet he used the death of Lazarus to remind Martha that he is the resurrection and the life (John 11:20-36).

Good imagination characterized Jesus' loving words and deeds. He expressed his love in vivid parables such as the Good Samaritan (Luke 10:25-37) and the Prodigal Son (Luke 15:11-32). With praise and a miracle, Jesus responded to the witty but trusting Cannanite woman (Matthew 15:21-28) who was eager to profit from whatever scraps Jesus was willing to throw to the dogs, among which she included herself. In a potentially embarrassing situation for Jesus, a sinful but repentant woman washed his feet with her tears, dried them with her hair, and then anointed his feet with ointment. Jesus did not distance himself from her actions but stood up for her in his comments to Simon the Pharisee (Luke 7:37-50) by interpreting her actions as signs of great love by someone whose great debts have been forgiven. For a believer, the greatest demonstration of Jesus' love for all people is evident in his passion and death; despite pain, suffering, and ignominy, he persevered in his love for the Father and for all of us, that we may flourish here in his Kingdom which begins on earth in the Church and continues in heaven.

As was pointed out in chapter 29, regular religious practice in community tends to strengthen moral skills. Regular religious practice is one path to salubrious change. Someone who attends religious services weekly can reasonably be expected to enhance one's moral skills. One likely result is that the person comes to accept the norms of natural law.

A Christian husband or wife who abides by the norms of natural law can expect deep human satisfaction. The basis for this satisfaction is that in matters of intimacy the practices conform to the way God wants them to love. At the basis of the natural law is the reality that certain acts (by the object of the act) tend by their nature either to help participate in the fundamental values or corrode the pursuit of one or more of the values.

This final chapter makes the case for a noble experiment in love and life. If one's heart is moved by the arguments and illustrations of this book, one now has to switch over to action. One has to live for a while the new way of life outlined here. One must attempt to pursue the fundamental values in exalted ways, at the same time one avoids corrosive actions. Only then will one have a sufficient basis in experience for reflection. Without actions, theoretical reflection on practical morality produces only virtual results!

SOURCES AND COMMENTS

CHAPTER ONE

Sex and the Soul: Juggling Sexuality, Spirituality, Romance, and Religion on America's College Campuses (New York: Oxford University Press, 2008) by Donna Freitas presents an excellent description of the practices, hopes, disappointments, and aspirations of college students. The data come from personal interviews with about 100 students and also from survey questionnaires filled out by about 600 students.

CHAPTER TWO

Figure 2.1 portrays in a graphic way that most moral worlds, including the one presented in this book, emphasize that activities are the path by which people flourish or not flourish. That is, human beings aim for goals that correspond to their inclinations and convictions as human beings. In striving to achieve certain goals via specific activities, humans achieve fulfillment, and thereby happiness. Every moral world is characterized by three types of activities: those deemed acceptable or helpful, those judged to be exemplary, and some limited activities that should be avoided by any person of good will. In most moral worlds, the group of forbidden actions is relatively small relative to the group of reasonable and exemplary actions.

The reason for esmphasizing the role of institutions is that they influence the way in which we perceive what is reasonable, exemplary, and forbidden. Institutions are groupings of people or practices; the institutions have their own culture, but they exist within a larger civic culture. Along with families, clubs, religious groups, schools, and other associations, they constitute the ambience in which young people undertake various activities they find satisfying. They also influence what young people eventually come to think as normal, natural, and good.

CHAPTER FOUR

Using the standard diagram, the chapter shows how moral worlds differ and also how individuals within any moral world differ with respect to the actions they choose to realize in their lives. This basic diagram conforms to a Thomistic account of actions that are morally good, neutral, or bad. See *Aquinas's Ethics: Metaphysical Foundations, Moral Theory, and Theological Context* by Rebecca Konyndyk DeYoung, Colleen McCluskey, and Christina Van Dyke (Notre Dame: University of Notre Dame Press, 2009), chapters 4 and 5.

In subsequent chapters in part I and in all chapters of part II I set aside Christian revelation in order to focus on the natural law approach. One necessary claim for any natural law approach is that its formulation be such that it can be affirmed by most human beings. MacIntyre expresses it as follows: "Every account of natural law, no matter how minimal, makes at least two claims: first, that our human nature is such that, as rational beings, we cannot but recognize that obedience to some particular set of precepts is required, if we are to achieve our good or goods, a recognition that is primarily expressed in our practice and only secondarily in our explicit formulation of precepts; and, second, that it is at least one central function of any system of law to spell out those precepts and to make them mandatory by providing for their enforcement." See Alasdair MacIntyre, "Theories of Natural Law in the Culture of Advanced Modernity," in *Common Truths: New Perspectives on Natural Law*, edited by Edward B. McLean (Wilmington, DE: ISI Books, 2000), pp. 94–95.

CHAPTER SIX

Formulating the basic human drives as the natural pursuit of the fundamental values stems from the work of John Finnis. With a few important modifications I rely on his *Natural Law and Natural Rights* (Oxford: Clarendon, 1980). One important difference from Finnis in my approach, which employs the seven fundamental goods of Finnis, is that striving for these goods corresponds to human nature. That is, human beings existing in community find partial fulfillment in striving for these goods. By taking this approach, I align my position with that of Alasdair MacIntyre. His criticism of the approach taken by Finnis and others is articulated in "Theories of Natural Law in the Culture of Advanced Modernity," which is chapter 5 (pp. 91–115) in *Common Truths: New Perspectives on Natural Law*, edited by Edward B. McLean (Wilmington, DE: ISI Books, 2000).

The material on DNA and the emergence of modern man is based on John F. Haught's *Christianity and Science: Toward a Theology of Nature* (New York: Orbis, 2007). See especially pp. xi–xv and 82–107.

Janet Smith also emphasizes that the "plain person" understands that certain things in life are good and that others must be avoided. The "plain person" does not need philosophy, theology, or advanced learning to grasp the compelling nature of natural law. See Janet E. Smith, "Natural Law and Sexual Ethics," which is chapter 9 (pp. 193–215) in *Common Truths: New Perspectives on Natural Law*, edited by Edward B. McLean (Wilmington, DE: ISI Books, 2000).

CHAPTER EIGHT

For the distinction between object of the act, intention of the act, and circumstances of the act, see *Catechism of the Catholic Church*, 433-35. This three-fold distinction stems from Thomas Aquinas. Ralph McInerny offers a clear, careful treatment in *Ethica Thomistica* (Washington, DC: Catholic University of America, 1997), pp. 60–89, as does John Finnis in *Aquinas* (Oxford, 1998), pp. 79-93 and 138–54.

Sin occurs because the human will chooses to disregard the information from the intellect. It deliberately construes the sinful action as acceptable because it promotes some human good. The will focuses on the benefits of the sinful act and overlooks the deleterious effects. This is the standard Thomistic approach to personal sin. Alasdair MacIntyre provides a clear account of the relationship between will and intellect according to Thomas Aquinas. See his *God, Philosophy, and Universities: A Selective History of the Catholic Philosophical Tradition* (New York: Sheed & Ward, 2009), pp. 89–92. See also chapter 5 of *Aquinas's Ethics* by Konyndyk DeYoung, McCluskey, and Van Dyke (University of Notre Dame Press, 2009).

CHAPTER TEN

Much of the material in this chapter stems from an earlier study by the author. See John Piderit, S.J., *The Ethical Foundations of Economics* (Washington, DC: Georgetown University Press, 1993), pp. 42–111. Particularly important is the role played by the hierarchy of actions leading to a particular fundamental value. This hierarchy enables one to identify actions which are in a narrow sense contrary to a fundamental value, but nonetheless permitted. They are allowed because, although the action is against the fundamental value at one level, it actually enables participation in the fundamental value at a higher level. Actions "contrary to a fundamental value" are to be distinguished from actions "directly contrary to a fundamental value." These latter actions are impermissible, or corrosive, because they are directly contrary to the fundamental value itself. That is, the action goes against the value without resulting in any higher realization of the same value. Killing a chicken for food is "contrary to" but not "directly contrary to" the value of life. While the life of the chicken is taken, it enables life at a higher level—human life—to be supported. Killing another human person, however, is directly contrary to life, unless the act is in reaction to unjust aggression, actual or threatened, and is likely to result in more human lives being saved. This latter example is fully developed in the Catholic intellectual tradition in the theory of just war.

CHAPTER TWELVE

In this chapter I also follow John Finnis in *Natural Law and Natural Rights* (Oxford: Clarendon, 1980). His account of the fundamental values is presented with two important modifications. The first is, as mentioned earlier, the pursuit of these fundamental values corresponds to the way we are constituted as human beings. That is, the pursuit of them wells up within us from our human nature. Human pursuit of fundamental values result from inclinations that are part of our genetic make-up and which can never be totally suppressed by sin or culture. The second modification is that in some fundamental values one can distinguish a hierarchy. That is, there are various levels at which the fundamental value is realized.

In this chapter, the significance of the hierarchy is muted since, where a hierarchy can be rationally established, I only use examples of practices that lead to the realization of the fundamental values at their highest levels. That is, under the fundamental value of life, I look at human life, and in the area of knowledge, I look at truth, which is the most important quality of knowledge. As was pointed out in chapter 10, establishing a reasonable hierarchy of practices for any fundamental value is a challenging undertaking and far beyond the scope of this book.

A summary of the natural law approach has recently been issued by the International Theological Commission of the Vatican. Entitled "The Search for Universal Ethics: A New Look at Natural Law," it appeared on the Vatican Web site in May 2009 and is available at http://www.vatican.va/roman_curia/congregations/cfaith/cti_index.htm. Without relying on the work of Finnis or referring to the basic goals in life as fundamental values, this account of natural law treats five of the fundamental values: life, knowledge, friendship, conscience (what is termed "religion" in this book), and practical reasonableness. See paragraphs 48–52 in "The Search for Universal Ethics." "Practical reasonableness" is not named as such, but the whole essay is an exercise explores how people make good decisions about how to act. Beauty and playfulness can be included as part of friendship, because they are particular ways to pursue and promote friendship.

CHAPTER FOURTEEN

The verisimilitude of the situations presented in this chapter is supported by Donna Freitas's *Sex and the Soul* (Oxford, 2008). The chapter addresses two natural law principles: solidarity and subsidiarity. Most treatments of the principles of subsidiarity and solidarity are on the macro level in society. Such analyses explore, for example, the responsibilities of municipalities compared with the duties of states or nations, or they more generally compare the benefits of private corporations providing a particular service with the same service that might be provided by a government entity. However, the principles have equal validity on the micro level and in this chapter they are applied to groups of friends and families. This application extends treatment of these issues by the author in *Ethical Foundations of Economics*, pp. 118–128.

CHAPTER FIFTEEN

This chapter follows the natural law approach that emphasizes that the sexual act is a physical, generative act as well as a symbol of lasting commitment. It allows for the fact that it may have taken thousands of years for the symbolic component to materialize clearly. If so, this only means that human beings were not immediately aware of all the facets of their environment when they first gained consciousness. There is an alternative explanation why the symbolic component did not appear quickly in the development of human society. The inclination to include a symbolic component may have been present in the genetic makeup of early humans. However, it certainly took some trial and error to perceive genuine ways (activities which do not undermine the pursuit of the values) in which human sexuality can be used in the deepest forms of friendship. Eventually by trial and error or some other process, human beings came to appreciate the importance for children and harmony in marriage to restrict sexual intercourse to marriage.

CHAPTER SIXTEEN

Although posed as a question, the claim is made (134) that commitment to sexual fidelity between a married man and woman [is] universal." In Western society it is almost universal, at least as an ideal. However, if one considers a great range of societies, a few do not hold up sexual fidelity in marriage as an ideal. In *Purity and Danger: An Analysis of the Concept of Pollution* (New York: Routledge, 2002 [1966]), Mary Douglas shows how the concept of pollution (conceived to embrace personal and social, physical and relational dimensions) is related to the underlying structure in society. She describes a few societies that allow marital infidelity. However, even in this case the unfaithful husband has to care for his new conquest and include her among his wives. Doing this also means he has to have the ability or financial resources to ward off attacks by the other husband of the woman with whom he has sexual relations.

CHAPTER TWENTY

The data on single mothers are for 2007 and they are presented and analyzed in "Changing Patterns of Nonmarital Childbearing in the United States," No. 18 (May), Center for Disease Control and Prevention: Atlanta, 2009.

CHAPTER TWENTY-FOUR

Culture can partially block the ability of people to see the corrosive effect of various actions. For this reason, actions that are objectively bad according to natural law may appear to be reasonable or good in a society that does not generally adhere to the tenets of natural law. Alasdair MacIntyre makes this case on a broad scale in *Three Rival Versions of Moral Inquiry: Encyclopaedia, Genealogy, and Tradition* (Notre Dame: University of Notre Dame Press, 1990) and in "Theories of Natural Law in the Culture of Advanced Modernity," which appears as chapter 5 (pp. 91-115) in

Common Truths: New Perspectives on Natural Law, edited by Edward B. McLean (Wilmington, DE: ISI Books, 2000).

In his recent book *God, Philosophy, and Universities* (New York: Sheed & Ward, 2009), 89–92, MacIntyre identifies the conditions of possibility for two different societies to come to agreement about activities in conformity or inconformity with the natural law. He imagines the two cultures having an extended discussion about their distinctly different ways of doing things. It turns out that in order to engage in genuine deliberation about the relative merits of ethical systems, during the actual discussion one has to be seeking knowledge and truth, respecting life, beauty, friendship, and playfulness, and be committed to practical reason. That is, the normal requirements for peaceful discussion and an honest search for the truth involve an implicit commitment to the fundamental values. If a society fails to enter into a genuine discussion, it will also fail in its pursuit of at least one of the fundamental values. In this case, the society may not perceive the cogency of some requirements of the natural law.

Charles Taylor speaks of the nova effect in *A Secular Age* (Cambridge: Belknap Press of Harvard University Press, 2007), pp. 299–313.

CHAPTER TWENTY-FIVE

The Catechism of the Catholic Church, 446-51, has a helpful discussion of the supernatural virtues of faith, hope, and charity.

CHAPTER TWENTY-SEVEN

A very important component of the natural law tradition is an emphasis on virtue. Following the approach of Aristotle in the Nichomachean Ethics and St. Thomas Aquinas in the Summa Theologica, contemporary virtue ethics receives much attention in ethics and moral theology. Rev. Richard M. Gula, S.S., nicely outlines the place of virtue ethics in two of his works. A straightforward, brief, but illuminating overview, good for young adults, is his "The Shifting Landscape of Moral Theology," which appears in *Church* (Spring 2009), pp 44-53. In his book *Reason Informed by Faith: Foundations of Catholic Morality* (New York: Paulist, 1997) he provides a more extensive analysis of virtue ethics. For young adults, virtue ethics certainly offers many helpful insights. Since it takes a positive and practical approach, one can wonder why this author opted for the natural law approach. The main reason is that only by the use of right reason in the natural law approach can one distinguish with confidence between actions which are at least acceptable and those which are corrosive. For this reason, it can be said that virtue ethics is a very good derivative of natural law, since it follows upon natural law.

Virtue ethics emphasizes the acquisition of good habits, that is, repeated ways of acting. The focus in virtue ethics is how to pursue the good reliably by consistently performing acts that lead to human flourishing. Such an approach also addresses interesting questions of responsibility and merit because it attends to moral culpability depending on where one is in a sequence of actions. Consider, for example, a particular good action involving how one honors one's father or mother. Then think of 100 of these actions performed over a period of a few years. Among other things, virtue ethics considers the moral characteristics of actions at the beginning, middle, and end of this sequence. This analysis leads to good and helpful insights about the type of person one becomes as a result of similar actions over a period of time.

For modern young adults living in an "anything goes" society, however, it is also necessary to examine carefully within the natural law tradition why some actions are approved and others are prohibited. Understanding why a particular action is good is important. And young people should similarly understand and appreciate clearly which actions are corrosive and why. The fundamental values approach offers intuitive arguments and clarity about particular types of actions.

The focus in the latter third of this book is on developing moral skills. Since moral skills reflect to the ability to act in certain ways, they are certainly akin to virtues, which are habitual ways of acting. Virtues come after the moral skills are honed. Modern young adults must first focus on acquiring good moral skills; such skills are necessary prerequisites for the pursuit of virtues. An emphasis on skills also enables a good balance between striving for exemplary actions and avoiding sin, or corrosive actions.

The importance of self-knowledge in practical reason is highlighted in two essays in *Intractable Disputes About the Natural Law: Alasdair MacIntyre and His Critics*, Lawrence S. Cunningham, ed. (Notre Dame: University of Notre Dame Press, 2009). The issue is first treated by Thomas Hibbs in his essay "The Fearful Thoughts of Morals: Aquinas on Conflict, Self-Knowledge, and the Virtues of Practical Reasoning," pp. 273–312, and then integrated into a broader reflection in MacIntryre's final essay, "From Answers to Questions: A Response to the Responses," pp. 312–51.

BIBLIOGRAPHY

Douglas, Mary. *Purity and Danger: An Analysis of the Concept of Pollution*. New York: Routledge, 2002 [1966].

Finnis, John. *Aquinas: Moral, Political, and Legal Theory*. New York: Oxford University Press, 1998.

Finnis, John. *Natural Law and Natural Rights*. Oxford: Clarendon, 1980.

Freitas, Donna. *Sex and the Soul: Juggling Sexuality, Spirituality, Romance and Religion on America's College Campuses*. New York: Oxford University Press, 2008.

Gula, Richard M., S.S. "The Shifting Landscape of Moral Theology." *Church* (Spring 2009): 44–53.

Gula, Richard M., S.S. *Reason Informed by Faith: Foundations of Catholic Morality*. New York: Paulist, 1997.

Haught, John F. *Christianity and Science: Toward a Theology of Nature*. New York: Orbis, 2007.

Hibbs, Thomas. "The Fearful Thoughts of Morals: Aquinas on Conflict, Self-Knowledge, and the Virtues of Practical Reasoning." In *Intractable Disputes About the Natural Law: Alasdair MacIntyre and His Critics*, ed. Lawrence S. Cunningham, 273–311. Notre Dame: University of Notre Dame Press, 2009.

International Theological Commission of the Vatican. "The Search for Universal Ethics: A New Look at Natural Law." http://www.vatican.va/roman_curia/congregations/cfaith/cti_index.htm, 2009.

Konyndyk DeYoung, Rebecca, Colleen McCluskey, and Christina Van Dyke. *Aquinas's Ethics: Metaphysical Foundations, Moral Theory, and Theological Context*. University of Notre Dame Press: Notre Dame, 2009.

MacIntyre, Alasdair. "Theories of Natural Law in the Culture of Advanced Modernity." In *Common Truths: New Perspectives on Natural Law*, ed. Edward B. McLean, 91-115. Wilmington, DE: ISI Books, 2000.

MacIntyre, Alasdair. *God, Philosophy, and Universities: A Selective History of the Catholic Philosophical Tradition*. New York: Sheed & Ward, 2009.

MacIntryre, Alasdair. "From Answers to Questions: A Response to the Responses." in *Intractable Disputes About the Natural Law: Alasdair MacIntyre and His Critics*, ed. Lawrence S. Cunningham, 312–51. Notre Dame: University of Notre Dame Press, Indiana, 2009.

MacIntyre, Alasdair. *Three Rival Versions of Moral Inquiry: Encyclopaedia, Genealogy, and Tradition*. Notre Dame: University of Notre Dame Press, 1990.

McInerny, Ralph. *Ethica Thomistica: The Moral Philosophy of Thomas Aquinas*. Washington, DC: Catholic University of America, 1997.

Piderit, John. *The Ethical Foundations of Economics*. Washington, DC: Georgetown University Press, 1993.

Smith, Janet E. "Natural Law and Sexual Ethics." In *Common Truths: New Perspectives on Natural Law*, ed. Edward B. McLean, 193–215. Wilmington, DE: ISI Books, 2000.

Taylor, Charles. *A Secular Age*. Cambridge: Belknap Press of Harvard University Press, 2007.

The Vatican. *The Catechism of the Catholic Church*, 2nd. ed. Libreria Editrice Vaticana: Rome, Italy, 1997.

INDEX